P9-AZW-785

Essential

American

Idioms

About the Author and Editor

Richard A. Spears, Ph.D. is Adjunct Associate Professor of Linguistics, Northwestern University, and specialist in lexicography, English Language structure, phonetics, English as a Second Language, and American culture. He is also the Director of the Dictionary Department at National Textbook Company.

Linda Schinke-Llano, Ph.D. is Associate Professor of English and Hardy Distinguished Professor of English, Millikin University. She is a specialist in English as a second language, bilingual education, and second language acquisition.

Essential American Idioms

Richard A. Spears

Printed on recyclable paper

National Textbook Company
NTC a division of *NTC Publishing Group* • Lincolnwood, Illinois USA

Also Available in This Series

NTC's American Idioms Dictionary
NTC's Dictionary of American Slang and Colloquial Expressions
NTC's Dictionary of Phrasal Verbs and Other Idiomatic Verbal Phrases
NTC's Dictionary of Grammatical Terminology
NTC's English Idioms Dictionary
Forbidden American English
Essential American Idioms
Contemporary American Slang
Common American Phrases

1994 Printing

Published by National Textbook Company, a division of NTC Publishing Group.
© 1990 by NTC Publishing Group, 4255 West Touhy Avenue,
Lincolnwood (Chicago), Illinois 60646-1975 U.S.A.
All rights reserved. No part of this book may be reproduced, stored
in a retrieval system, or transmitted in any form or by any means,
electronic, mechanical, photocopying, recording or otherwise, without
the prior permission of NTC Publishing Group.
Library of Congress Catalog Card Number 90-60251
Manufactured in the United States of America.

4 5 6 7 8 9 VP 9 8 7 6 5

TO THE USER

Every language has phrases that cannot be understood literally. Even if you know the meanings of all the words in such a phrase and you understand the grammar completely, the total meaning of the phrase may still be confusing. English has many thousands of such idiomatic expressions. This dictionary is a selection of the most frequently encountered idiomatic expressions found in everyday American English. The collection is small enough to serve as a useful study guide for learners, and large enough to serve as a reference for daily use.

The phrases in the dictionary come from many sources. Many have been collected from newspapers and magazines. Others have come from existing dictionaries and reference books. Students studying English as a second or foreign language at Northwestern University have also provided many of the entries, and their lists and questions have helped in selecting the particular idiomatic expressions that appear in this book.

Essential American Idioms should prove useful for people who are learning how to understand idiomatic English, the hearing impaired, and for all speakers of English who want to know more about the language.

How to Use This Dictionary

1. Expressions are entered in an alphabetical order that ignores hyphens, spaces, and other punctuation. Each expression is entered in its normal form and word order. Entries that begin with short function words such as *a, an, as, at, be, by, do, for, from, have, in, off, on, out, under,* and *up* appear both in normal word order and in inverted word order, cross-referenced to the normal entry; for example, at the entry **active duty, on** the reader is referred to the entry **on active duty.**

2. A main entry may have one or more alternate forms. The main entry and its alternate forms are printed in **boldface type,** and the alternate forms are preceded by "AND." Two or more alternate forms are separated by a semicolon. Words enclosed in parentheses in any entry form are optional. For example: **break (out) into tears** stands for **break out into tears** and **break into tears.** When entry phrases are referred to in the dictionary, they are printed in *slanted type.*

3. Some of the entry phrases have more than one major sense. These meanings are numbered with boldface numerals. Numbered senses may also have additional forms that are shown in boldface type after the numeral. See, for example, **get something sewed up.**

4. Some entries have additional related forms within the entry. These forms are introduced by "ALSO," and cross-referencing leads the user to each of these embedded entries. See, for example, **get a black eye.**

5. Alternate forms of the definitions are separated by semicolons, and some definitions are followed by comments or explanations in parentheses. See, for example, **add fuel to the fire.**

6. In some cases where the entry phrase refers to either people or things—as expressed by **"someone or something"**—the numbered senses can be used with people only or things only. In such cases the numbered sense begins with "[with *someone*]" or "[with *something*]." See, for example, **cut someone or something to the bone.**

7. Each entry or sense has at least two examples printed in *italics.*

TERMS AND SYMBOLS

☐ (a box) marks the beginning of an example.

ALSO: introduces an additional variant form within an entry, which is related to the main entry, but has a slightly different meaning or form. See point four in "How to Use This Dictionary."

AND   indicates that an entry phrase has variant forms that are the same or almost the same in meaning as the entry phrase. One or more variant forms are preceded by AND. See point two in "How to Use This Dictionary."

cliché   describes an expression that is used too frequently and too casually.

Compare to   means to consult the entry indicated and examine its form or meaning in relation to the entry phrase containing the "Compare to" instruction.

informal   describes a very casual expression that is most likely to be spoken and not written.

proverb   describes a frequently quoted fixed saying that gives advice or makes a philosophical observation.

rude   describes an expression that is insulting or harsh.

See   means to turn to the entry indicated.

See also means to consult the entry indicated for additional information or to find expressions similar in form or meaning to the entry phrase containing the "See also" instruction.

See under means to turn to the entry phrase indicated and look for the phrase you are seeking within the entry indicated.

slang describes an expression that is recognized as casual or playful. Such terms are not considered appropriate for formal writing.

A

A bird in the hand is worth two in the bush. a proverb meaning that something you already have is better than something you might get. □ *Bill has offered to buy my car for $3,000. Someone else might pay more, but Bill made a good offer, and a bird in the hand is worth two in the bush.* □ *I might be able to find a better offer, but a bird in the hand is worth two in the bush.*

according to Hoyle according to the rules; in keeping with the way it is normally done. (Refers to the rules for playing games. Edmond Hoyle wrote a book about games. This expression is usually used for something other than games.) □ *That's wrong. According to Hoyle, this is the way to do it.* □ *The carpenter said, "This is the way to drive a nail, according to Hoyle."*

a chip off the old block a person (usually a male) who behaves in the same way as his father or resembles his father. (The father is the "old block.") □ *John looks like his father—a real chip off the old block.* □ *Bill Jones, Jr., is a chip off the old block. He's a banker just like his father.*

act high-and-mighty to act proud and powerful; to act haughty. □ *Why does the doctor always have to act so high-and-mighty?* □ *If Sally wouldn't act so high-and-mighty, she'd have more friends.*

Actions speak louder than words. a proverb meaning that it is better to do something about a problem than just talk about it. □ *Mary kept promising to get a job. John finally looked her in the eye and said, "Actions speak louder than words!"* □ *After* *listening to the senator promising to cut federal spending, Ann wrote a simple note saying, "Actions speak louder than words."*

active duty, on   See *on active duty.*

act of God   an occurrence (usually an accident) for which no human is responsible; an act of nature such as a storm, an earthquake, or a windstorm. □ *My insurance company wouldn't pay for the damage because it was an act of God.* □ *The thief tried to convince the judge that the diamonds were in his pocket due to an act of God.*

act one's age   to behave more maturely; to act as grown-up as one really is. (This is frequently said to a child or a teenager.) □ *Come on, John, act your age. Stop throwing rocks.* □ *Mary! Stop picking on your little brother. Act your age!*

add fuel to the fire AND **add fuel to the flame**   to make a problem worse; to say or do something that makes a bad situation worse; to make an angry person get even more angry. □ *To spank a crying child just adds fuel to the fire.* □ *Bill was shouting angrily, and Bob tried to get him to stop by laughing at him. Of course, that was just adding fuel to the flame.*

add fuel to the flame   See the previous entry.

add insult to injury   to make a bad situation worse; to hurt the feelings of a person who has already been hurt. (A cliché.) □ *First, the basement flooded, and then, to add insult to injury, a pipe burst in the kitchen.* □ *My car barely started this morning, and to add insult to injury, I got a flat tire in the driveway.*

A fool and his money are soon parted.   a proverb meaning that a person who acts unwisely with money soon loses it. (Often said about a person who has just lost a sum of money because of poor judgment.) □ *When Bill lost a $400 bet on a horse race, Mary said, "A fool and his money are soon parted."* □ *When John bought a cheap used car that fell apart the next day, he said, "Oh, well, a fool and his money are soon parted."*

afraid of one's own shadow   easily frightened; always frightened, timid, or suspicious. (Never used literally.) □ *After Tom was robbed, he was even afraid of his own shadow.* □ *Jane has always been a shy child. She has been afraid of her own shadow since she was three.*

A friend in need is a friend indeed.   a proverb meaning that a true friend is a person who will help you when you really need some help. □ *When Bill helped me with geometry, I really learned the meaning of "A friend in need is a friend indeed."* □ *"A friend in need is a friend indeed" sounds silly until you need someone very badly.*

against the clock   in a race with time; in a great hurry to get something done before a particular time. □ *Bill set a new track record, running against the clock. He lost the actual race, however.* □ *In a race against the clock, they rushed the special medicine to the hospital.*

air, in the   See *in the air.*

air, off the   See *off the air.*

air, on the   See *on the air.*

air someone's dirty linen in public   to discuss private or embarrassing matters in public, especially when quarreling. (This *linen* refers to problems as if they were sheets and tablecloths or other soiled cloth.) □ *John's mother had asked him repeatedly not to air the family's dirty linen in public.* □ *Mr. and Mrs. Johnson are arguing again. Why do they always have to air their dirty linen in public?*

air, up in the   See *up in the air.*

a little bird told me   learned from a mysterious or secret source. (Often given as an evasive answer to someone who asks how you learned something. Rude in some circumstances.) □ *"All right," said Mary, "where did you get that information?" John replied,*

"A little bird told me." □ *A little bird told me I'd probably find you here.*

A little knowledge is a dangerous thing. a proverb meaning that incomplete knowledge can embarrass or harm someone or something. □ *The doctor said, "Just because you've had a course in first aid, you shouldn't have treated your own illness. A little knowledge is a dangerous thing."* □ *John thought he knew how to take care of the garden, but he killed all the flowers. A little knowledge is a dangerous thing.*

all fours, on See *on all fours.*

all in a day's work part of what is expected; typical or normal. □ *I don't particularly like to cook, but it's all in a day's work.* □ *Putting up with rude customers isn't pleasant, but it's all in a day's work.* □ *Cleaning up after other people is all in a day's work for a chambermaid.*

all over but the shouting decided and concluded; finished except for a celebration. (An elaboration of *all over,* which means "finished.") □ *The last goal was made just as the final whistle sounded. Tom said, "Well, it's all over but the shouting."* □ *Tom worked hard in college and graduated last month. When he got his diploma, he said, "It's all over but the shouting."*

All roads lead to Rome. a proverb meaning that there are many different routes to the same goal. □ *Mary was criticizing the way Jane was planting the flowers. John said, "Never mind, Mary, all roads lead to Rome."* □ *Some people learn by doing. Others have to be taught. In the long run, all roads lead to Rome.*

all skin and bones See under *nothing but skin and bones.*

All's well that ends well. a proverb meaning that an event that has a good ending is good even if some things went wrong along the way. (This is the name of a play by Shakespeare. It is now used as a cliché.) □ *I'm glad you finally got here, even though your car had a flat tire on the way. Oh, well. All's well that ends* *well.* □ *The groom was late for the wedding, but everything worked out all right. All's well that ends well.*

All that glitters is not gold. a proverb meaning that many attractive and alluring things have no value. □ *The used car looked fine but didn't run well at all. "Ah, yes," thought Bill, "all that glitters is not gold." * □ *When Mary was disappointed about losing Tom, Jane reminded her, "All that glitters is not gold."*

all thumbs very awkward and clumsy, especially with one's hands. (It really means that one's hands have only thumbs.) □ *Poor Bob can't play the piano at all. He's all thumbs.* □ *Mary is all thumbs when it comes to gardening.*

all walks of life all social, economic, and ethnic groups. (A fixed phrase. Does not occur in the singular or without *all*.) □ *We saw people there from all walks of life.* □ *The people who came to the art exhibit represented all walks of life.*

All work and no play makes Jack a dull boy. a proverb meaning that one should have recreation as well as work. (*Jack* does not refer to anyone in particular, and the phrase can be used for persons of either sex.) □ *Stop reading that book and go out and play! All work and no play makes Jack a dull boy.* □ *The doctor told Mr. Jones to stop working on weekends and start playing golf, because all work and no play makes Jack a dull boy.*

An eye for an eye, a tooth for a tooth. a biblical theme indicating that punishment should equal the offense. (Now used as a proverb. Not literal.) □ *Little John pulled Jane's hair, so the teacher pulled John's hair as punishment, saying, "An eye for an eye, a tooth for a tooth." * □ *He kicked me in the leg, so I kicked him in the leg. After all, an eye for an eye, a tooth for a tooth.*

An ounce of prevention is worth a pound of cure. a proverb meaning that it is easier and better to prevent something bad than to deal with the results. □ *When you ride in a car, buckle your seat belt. An ounce of prevention is worth a pound of cure.* □ *Every child should be vaccinated against polio. An ounce of prevention is worth a pound of cure.*

5

A penny saved is a penny earned. a proverb meaning that money saved through thrift is the same as money earned by employment. (Sometimes used to explain stinginess.) □ *"I didn't want to pay that much for the book," said Mary. "After all, a penny saved is a penny earned."* □ *Bob put his money in a new bank that pays more interest than his old bank, saying, "A penny saved is a penny earned."*

apple of someone's eye someone's favorite person or thing; a boyfriend or a girlfriend; a person or a thing that someone wants. (A person or a thing that has caught someone's eye or attracted someone's attention.) □ *Tom is the apple of Mary's eye. She thinks he's great.* □ *John's new stereo is the apple of his eye.*

armed to the teeth heavily armed with deadly weapons. (As if all types of armaments were used, up to and including the teeth.) □ *The bank robber was armed to the teeth when he was caught.* □ *There are too many guns around. The entire country is armed to the teeth.*

arm in arm of persons linked or hooked together by the arms. □ *The two lovers walked arm in arm down the street.* □ *Arm in arm, the line of dancers kicked high, and the audience roared its approval.*

arms, up in See *up in arms.*

A rolling stone gathers no moss. a proverb that describes a person who keeps changing jobs or residences and, therefore, accumulates no possessions or responsibilities. (Usually meant as a criticism.) □ *"John just can't seem to stay in one place," said Sally. "Oh, well, a rolling stone gathers no moss."* □ *Bill has no furniture to bother with because he keeps on the move. He keeps saying that a rolling stone gathers no moss.*

as a duck takes to water easily and naturally. (Refers to baby ducks, who seem to be able to swim the first time they enter the water.) □ *She took to singing, just as a duck takes to water.* □ *The baby adapted to bottle-feeding as a duck takes to water.*

as an aside as a comment; as a comment that is not supposed to be heard by everyone. □ *At the wedding, Tom said as an aside, "The bride doesn't look well."* □ *At the ballet, Billy said as an aside to his mother, "I hope the dancers fall off the stage!"*

as bad as all that as bad as reported; as bad as it seems. (Usually expressed in the negative.) □ *Come on! Nothing could be as bad as all that.* □ *Stop crying. It can't be as bad as all that.*

as blind as a bat with imperfect sight; blind. (The first *as* can be omitted. Typically, bats are not blind, however. Survives because of the alliteration.) □ *My grandmother is as blind as a bat.* □ *I'm getting blind as a bat. I can hardly read this page.*

as busy as a beaver AND **as busy as a bee** very busy. (The first *as* can be omitted. Survives because of the alliteration.) □ *I don't have time to talk to you. I'm as busy as a beaver.* □ *You don't look busy as a beaver to me.* □ *Whenever there is a holiday, we are all as busy as bees.*

as busy as a bee See the previous entry.

as busy as Grand Central Station very busy; crowded with customers or other people. (The first *as* can be omitted. This refers to Grand Central Station in New York City.) □ *This house is as busy as Grand Central Station.* □ *When the tourist season starts, this store is busy as Grand Central Station.*

as clear as mud not understandable. (Informal or joking. The first *as* can be omitted.) □ *Your explanation is as clear as mud.* □ *This doesn't make sense. It's clear as mud.*

as comfortable as an old shoe very comfortable; very comforting and familiar. (The first *as* can be omitted. Refers to a shoe that has been worn a while and is comfortable.) □ *This old house is fine. It's as comfortable as an old shoe.* □ *That's a great tradition—comfortable as an old shoe.*

as cool as a cucumber calm and not agitated; with one's wits about one. (The first *as* can be omitted. Cucumbers are not necessarily cool, however. Survives because of the alliteration.) □ *The captain remained as cool as a cucumber as the passengers boarded the lifeboats.* □ *During the fire the homeowner was cool as a cucumber.*

as crazy as a loon   very silly; completely insane. (The first *as* can be omitted. A loon is a waterfowl whose call sounds like a silly laugh.) □ *If you think you can get away with that, you're as crazy as a loon.* □ *Poor old John is crazy as a loon.*

as dead as a dodo   dead; no longer in existence. (The first *as* can be omitted. The dodo—an ancient bird of Mauritius—is extinct. The phrase survives because of the alliteration.) □ *Yes, Adolf Hitler is really dead—as dead as a dodo.* □ *That silly old idea is dead as a dodo.*

as dead as a doornail   dead. (The first *as* can be omitted. Of course, doornails were never alive. Survives because of the alliteration.) □ *This fish is as dead as a doornail.* □ *John kept twisting the chicken's neck even though it was dead as a doornail.*

as different as night and day   completely different. (The first *as* can be omitted.) □ *Although Bobby and Billy are twins, they are as different as night and day.* □ *Birds and bats appears to be similar, but they are different as night and day.*

as easy as (apple) pie   very easy. (The first *as* can be omitted. Making pies is assumed to be easy.) □ *Mountain climbing is as easy as pie.* □ *Making a simple dress out of cotton cloth is easy as pie.*

as easy as duck soup   very easy; requiring no effort. (When a duck is cooked, it releases a lot of fat and juices, making a "soup" without effort. The first *as* can be omitted.) □ *Finding your way to the shopping center is easy as duck soup.* □ *Getting Bob to eat fried chicken is as easy as duck soup.*

as far as it goes   as much as something does, covers, or accomplishes. (Usually said of something that is inadequate.) □ *Your plan is fine as far as it goes. It doesn't seem to take care of every-*

thing, though. □ *As far as it goes, this law is a good one. It should require stiffer penalties, however.*

as fit as a fiddle   healthy and physically fit. (The first *as* can be omitted. Makes no sense. Survives because of the alliteration.) □ *Mary is as fit as a fiddle.* □ *Tom used to be fit as a fiddle. Look at him now!*

as flat as a pancake   very flat. (The first *as* can be omitted.) □ *The punctured tire was as flat as a pancake.* □ *Bobby squashed the ant flat as a pancake.*

as free as a bird   carefree; completely free. (The first *as* can be omitted.) □ *Jane is always happy and free as a bird.* □ *The convict escaped from jail and was as free as a bird for two days.* □ *In the summer I feel free as a bird.*

as full as a tick AND **as tight as a tick**   very full of food or drink. (Refers to a tick that has filled itself full of blood. The first *as* can be omitted.) □ *Little Billy ate and ate until he was as full as a tick.* □ *Our cat drank the cream until he became full as a tick.*

as funny as a crutch   not funny at all. (The first *as* can be omitted.) □ *Your trick is about as funny as a crutch. Nobody thought it was funny.* □ *The well-dressed lady slipped and fell in the gutter, which was funny as a crutch.*

as good as done   the same as being done; almost done. (Many different past participles can replace *done* in this phrase: *cooked, dead, finished, painted, typed,* etc.) □ *This job is as good as done. It'll just take another second.* □ *Yes, sir, if you hire me to paint your house, it's as good as painted.* □ *When I hand my secretary a letter to be typed, I know that it's as good as typed right then and there.*

as good as gold   genuine; authentic. (A cliché. The first *as* can be omitted. Survives because of the alliteration.) □ *Mary's promise is as good as gold.* □ *Yes, this diamond is genuine—good as gold.*

9

as happy as a clam happy and content. (The first *as* can be omitted. Note the variations in the examples. Clams are not necessarily happy or sad.) □ *Tom sat there smiling, as happy as a clam.* □ *There they all sat, eating corn on the cob and looking happy as clams.*

as happy as a lark visibly happy and cheerful. (The first *as* can be omitted. Note the variations in the examples.) □ *Sally walked along whistling, as happy as a lark.* □ *The children danced and sang, happy as larks.*

as hard as nails very hard; cold and cruel. (Refers to the nails that are used with a hammer. The first *as* can be omitted.) □ *The old loaf of bread was dried out and became as hard as nails.* □ *Ann was unpleasant and hard as nails.*

as high as a kite AND **as high as the sky** (The first *as* can be omitted.) **1.** very high. □ *The tree grew as high as a kite.* □ *Our pet bird got outside and flew up high as the sky.* **2.** drunk or drugged. □ *Bill drank beer until he got as high as a kite.* □ *The thieves were high as the sky on drugs.*

as high as the sky See the previous entry.

as hungry as a bear very hungry. (The first *as* can be omitted.) □ *I'm as hungry as a bear. I could eat anything!* □ *Whenever I jog, I get hungry as a bear.*

aside, as an See *as an aside*.

as innocent as a lamb guiltless; naive. (A cliché. The first *as* can be omitted.) □ *"Hey! You can't throw me in jail," cried the robber. "I'm innocent as a lamb."* □ *Look at the baby, as innocent as a lamb.*

as it were as one might say. (Sometimes used to qualify an assertion that may not sound reasonable.) □ *He carefully constructed, as it were, a huge sandwich.* □ *The Franklins live in a small, as it were, exquisite house.*

ask for the moon   to ask for too much; to make great demands; to ask for something that is difficult or impossible to obtain. (Not literal.) □ *When you're trying to get a job, it's unwise to ask for the moon.* □ *Please lend me the money. I'm not asking for the moon!*

ask for trouble   to do or say something that will cause trouble. □ *Stop talking to me that way, John. You're just asking for trouble.* □ *Anybody who threatens a police officer is asking for trouble.*

asleep at the switch   not attending to one's job; failing to do one's duty at the proper time. (Need not have anything to do with a real switch.) □ *The guard was asleep at the switch when the robber broke in.* □ *If I hadn't been asleep at the switch, I'd have seen the stolen car.*

as light as a feather   of little weight. (The first *as* can be omitted.) □ *Sally dieted until she was as light as a feather.* □ *Of course I can lift the box. It's light as a feather.*

as likely as not   probably; with an even chance either way. (The first *as* can be omitted. A fixed phrase; there are no other forms.) □ *He will as likely as not arrive without warning.* □ *Likely as not, the game will be canceled.*

as luck would have it   by good or bad luck; as it turned out; by chance. (A fixed phrase; there are no other forms.) □ *As luck would have it, we had a flat tire.* □ *As luck would have it, the check came in the mail today.*

as mad as a hatter   **1.** crazy. (From the character called the Mad Hatter in Lewis Carroll's *Alice's Adventures in Wonderland.* The first *as* can be omitted.) □ *Poor old John is as mad as a hatter.* □ *All these screaming children are driving me mad as a hatter.* **2.** angry. (This is a misunderstanding of *mad* in the first sense. The first *as* can be omitted.) □ *You make me so angry! I'm as mad as a hatter.* □ *John can't control his temper. He's always mad as a hatter.*

as mad as a hornet angry. (The first *as* can be omitted. Hornets are known to have terrible tempers.) □ *You make me so angry. I'm as mad as a hornet.* □ *Jane can get mad as a hornet when somebody criticizes her.*

as mad as a March hare crazy. (From the name of a character in Lewis Carroll's *Alice's Adventures in Wonderland.* The first *as* can be omitted.) □ *Sally is getting as mad as a March hare.* □ *My Uncle Bill is mad as a March hare.*

as mad as a wet hen angry. (The first *as* can be omitted. One can assume that a fussy hen would become angry if wet.) □ *Bob was screaming and shouting—as mad as a wet hen.* □ *What you said made Mary mad as a wet hen.*

as one as if a group were one person. (Especially with *act, move,* or *speak.*) □ *All the dancers moved as one.* □ *The chorus spoke as one.*

as plain as day (The first *as* can be omitted.) **1.** very plain and simple. □ *Although his face was as plain as day, his smile made him look interesting and friendly.* □ *Our house is plain as day, but it's comfortable.* **2.** clear and understandable. (As transparent as daylight.) □ *The lecture was as plain as day. No one had to ask questions.* □ *His statement was plain as day.*

as plain as the nose on one's face obvious; clearly evident. (The first *as* can be omitted.) □ *What do you mean you don't understand? It's as plain as the nose on your face.* □ *Your guilt is plain as the nose on your face.*

as poor as a church mouse very poor. (A cliché. The first *as* can be omitted. Assuming that those associated with churches are impoverished, the lowly mouse would be the poorest creature in a church.) □ *My aunt is as poor as a church mouse.* □ *The Browns are poor as church mice.*

as pretty as a picture very pretty. (A cliché. The first *as* can be omitted. Survives because of the alliteration.) □ *Sweet little*

Mary is as pretty as a picture. □ *Their new house is pretty as a picture.*

as proud as a peacock   very proud; haughty. (A cliché. The first *as* can be omitted. Refers to the beautiful tail feathers that the peacock displays. Survives because of the alliteration.) □ *John is so arrogant. He's as proud as a peacock.* □ *The new father was proud as a peacock.*

as quick as a wink   very quickly. (A cliché. The first *as* can be omitted. Refers to the wink of an eye.) □ *As quick as a wink, the thief took the lady's purse.* □ *I'll finish this work quick as a wink.*

as quiet as a mouse   very quiet; shy and silent. (Often used with children. The first *as* can be omitted.) □ *Don't yell; whisper. Be as quiet as a mouse.* □ *Mary hardly ever says anything. She's quiet as a mouse.*

as regular as clockwork   dependably regular. (The first *as* can be omitted.) □ *She comes into this store every day, as regular as clockwork.* □ *Our tulips come up every year, regular as clockwork.*

as scarce as hens' teeth AND **scarcer than hens' teeth**   very scarce or nonexistent. (A cliché. Chickens don't have teeth. The first *as* can be omitted.) □ *I've never seen one of those. They're as scarce as hens' teeth.* □ *I was told that the part needed for my car is scarcer than hens' teeth, and it would take a long time to find one.*

as sick as a dog   very sick; sick and vomiting. (The first *as* can be omitted. Refers to the agonized retching of a dog.) □ *We've never been so ill. The whole family was sick as dogs.* □ *Sally was as sick as a dog and couldn't go to the party.*

as slippery as an eel   devious; undependable. (Also used literally. The first *as* can be omitted.) □ *Tom can't be trusted. He's as slippery as an eel.* □ *It's hard to catch Joe in his office because he's slippery as an eel.*

as smart as a fox   smart and clever. (The first *as* can be omitted.) □ *My nephew is as smart as a fox.* □ *You have to be smart as a fox to outwit me.*

as snug as a bug in a rug   cozy and snug. (The kind of thing said when putting a child to bed. The first *as* can be omitted. Survives because of the rhyme.) □ *Let's pull up the covers. There you are, Bobby, as snug as a bug in a rug.* □ *What a lovely little house! I know I'll be snug as a bug in a rug.*

as sober as a judge   (A cliché. The first *as* can be omitted.) **1.** very formal, somber, or stuffy. □ *You certainly look gloomy, Bill. You're sober as a judge.* □ *Tom's as sober as a judge. I think he's angry.* **2.** not drunk; alert and completely sober. (This is a misunderstanding of the first sense.) □ *John's drunk? No, he's as sober as a judge.* □ *You should be sober as a judge when you drive a car.*

as soft as a baby's bottom   very soft and smooth to the touch. (The first *as* can be omitted.) □ *This cloth is as soft as a baby's bottom.* □ *No, Bob doesn't shave yet. His cheeks are soft as a baby's bottom.*

as soon as possible   at the earliest time. □ *I'm leaving now. I'll be there as soon as possible.* □ *Please pay me as soon as possible.*

as strong as an ox   very strong. (The first *as* can be omitted.) □ *Tom lifts weights and is as strong as an ox.* □ *Now that Ann has recovered from her illness, she's strong as an ox.*

as stubborn as a mule   very stubborn. (The first *as* can be omitted.) □ *My husband is as stubborn as a mule.* □ *Our cat is stubborn as a mule.*

as the crow flies   straight across the land, as opposed to distances measured on a road, river, etc. (This assumes that crows fly in a straight line.) □ *It's twenty miles to town on the highway, but only ten miles as the crow flies.* □ *Our house is only a few miles from the lake as the crow flies.*

as thick as pea soup very thick. (Usually used in reference to fog. The first *as* can be omitted.) □ *This fog is as thick as pea soup.* □ *Wow, this coffee is strong! It's thick as pea soup.*

as thick as thieves very close-knit; friendly; allied. (A cliché. The first *as* can be omitted. Survives because of the alliteration.) □ *Mary, Tom, and Sally are as thick as thieves. They go everywhere together.* □ *Those two families are thick as thieves.*

as tight as a tick See under *as full as a tick.*

as tight as Dick's hatband very tight. (The first *as* can be omitted. Very old.) □ *I've got to lose some weight. My belt is as tight as Dick's hatband.* □ *This window is stuck tight as Dick's hatband.*

a stone's throw away a short distance; a relatively short distance. (May refer to distances in feet or miles.) □ *John saw Mary across the street, just a stone's throw away.* □ *Philadelphia is just a stone's throw away from New York City.*

as weak as a kitten weak; weak and sickly. (The first *as* can be omitted. Refers to a newborn kitten.) □ *John is as weak as a kitten because he doesn't eat well.* □ *Oh! Suddenly I feel weak as a kitten.*

as white as the driven snow very white. (A cliché. The first *as* can be omitted.) □ *I like my bed sheets to be as white as the driven snow.* □ *We have a new kitten whose fur is white as the driven snow.*

as wise as an owl very wise. (The first *as* can be omitted.) □ *My grandfather is as wise as an owl.* □ *My goal is to be wise as an owl.*

at a premium at a high price; priced high because of something special. □ *Sally bought the shoes at a premium because they were of very high quality.* □ *This model of car is selling at a premium because so many people want to buy it.*

at a snail's pace very slowly. □ *When you watch a clock, time seems to move at a snail's pace.* □ *You always eat at a snail's pace. I'm tired of waiting for you.*

at death's door near death. (Euphemistic and literary.) □ *I was so ill that I was at death's door.* □ *The family dog was at death's door for three days, and then it finally died.*

at half-mast halfway up or down. (Primarily referring to flags. Can be used for things other than flags as a joke.) □ *The flag was flying at half-mast because the general had died.* □ *Americans fly flags at half-mast on Memorial Day.* □ *The little boy ran out of the house with his pants at half-mast.*

at loggerheads in opposition; at an impasse; in a quarrel. □ *Mr. and Mrs. Franklin have been at loggerheads for years.* □ *The two political parties were at loggerheads during the entire legislative session.*

at loose ends restless and unsettled; unemployed. □ *Just before school starts, all the children are at loose ends.* □ *When Tom is home on the weekends, he's always at loose ends.* □ *Jane has been at loose ends ever since she lost her job.*

at one fell swoop AND **in one fell swoop** in a single incident; as a single event. (This phrase preserves the old word *fell*, meaning "terrible" or "deadly." Now a cliché, sometimes with humorous overtones.) □ *The party guests ate up all the snacks at one fell swoop.* □ *When the stock market crashed, many large fortunes were wiped out in one fell swoop.*

at one's wit's end at the limits of one's mental resources. □ *I'm at my wit's end with this problem. I cannot figure it out.* □ *Tom could do no more. He was at his wit's end.*

at sea (about something) confused; lost and bewildered. (As if one were lost at sea.) □ *Mary is all at sea about getting married.* □ *When it comes to higher math, John is totally at sea.*

at sixes and sevens disorderly; lost and bewildered. (Borrowed from gambling with dice.) □ *Mrs. Smith is at sixes and sevens since the death of her husband.* □ *Bill is always at sixes and sevens when he's home by himself.*

at someone's doorstep AND **on someone's doorstep** in someone's care; as someone's responsibility. (Not literal.) □ *Why do you always have to lay your problems at my doorstep?* □ *I shall put this issue on someone else's doorstep.* □ *I don't want it on my doorstep.*

at the bottom of the ladder at the lowest level of pay and status. □ *Most people start work at the bottom of the ladder.* □ *When Ann got fired, she had to start all over again at the bottom of the ladder.*

at the drop of a hat immediately and without urging. □ *John was always ready to go fishing at the drop of a hat.* □ *If you need help, just call on me. I can come at the drop of a hat.*

at the eleventh hour at the last possible moment. □ *She always turned her term papers in at the eleventh hour.* □ *We don't worry about death until the eleventh hour.*

at the end of one's rope AND **at the end of one's tether** at the limits of one's endurance. □ *I'm at the end of my rope! I just can't go on this way!* □ *These kids are driving me out of my mind. I'm at the end of my tether.*

at the end of one's tether See the previous entry.

at the last minute at the last possible chance. □ *Please don't make reservations at the last minute.* □ *Why do you ask all your questions at the last minute?*

at the outside at the very most. □ *The car repairs will cost $300 at the outside.* □ *I'll be there in three weeks at the outside.*

at the top of one's lungs See the following entry.

at the top of one's voice AND **at the top of one's lungs**   with a very loud voice; as loudly as is possible to speak or yell. □ *Bill called to Mary at the top of his voice.* □ *How can I work when you're all talking at the top of your lungs?*

at this stage (of the game)   at the current point in some event; currently. □ *We'll have to wait and see. There isn't much we can do at this stage of the game.* □ *At this stage, we are better off not calling the doctor.*

average, on the   See *on the average.*

A watched pot never boils.   a proverb meaning that concentration on a problem will not help solve it. (Refers to the seemingly long time it takes water to boil when you are waiting for it. Said about a problem that a person is watching very closely.) □ *John was looking out the window, waiting eagerly for the mail to be delivered. Ann said, "Be patient. A watched pot never boils."* □ *Billy weighed himself four times a day while he was trying to lose weight. His mother said, "Relax. A watched pot never boils."*

away from one's desk   not available for a telephone conversation; not available to be seen. (Sometimes said by the person who answers a telephone in an office. It means that the person whom the caller wants is not immediately available due to personal or business reasons. Typically, the person has gone to the restroom.) □ *I'm sorry, but Ann is away from her desk just now. Can you come back later?* □ *Tom is away from his desk, but if you leave your number, he will call you right back.*

ax to grind, have an   See *have an ax to grind.*

B

babe in the woods   a naive or innocent person; an inexperienced person. □ *Bill is a babe in the woods when it comes to dealing with plumbers.* □ *As a painter, Mary is fine, but she's a babe in the woods as a musician.*

back in circulation   1. [for something to be] available to the public again. (Said especially of things that are said to circulate, such as money, library books, and magazines.) □ *I've heard that gold coins are back in circulation in Europe.* □ *I would like to read* War and Peace. *Is it back in circulation, or is it still checked out?* 2. [for a person to be] socially active again; dating again after a divorce or breakup with one's lover. □ *Now that Bill is a free man, he's back in circulation.* □ *Tom was in the hospital for a month, but now he's back in circulation.*

back-to-back   1. adjacent and touching backs. □ *They started the duel by standing back-to-back.* □ *Two people who stand back-to-back can manage to see in all directions.* 2. following immediately. (Said of things or events. In this case, the events are figuratively back-to-front.) □ *The doctor had appointments set up back-to-back all day long.* □ *I have three lecture courses back-to-back every day of the week.*

back to the drawing board   time to start over again; it is time to plan something over again. (Note the variations in the examples. Refers to the drafting board, where buildings or machines are designed.) □ *It didn't work. Back to the drawing board.* □ *I flunked English this semester. Well, back to the old drawing board.*

back to the salt mines time to return to work, school, or something else that might be unpleasant. (The phrase implies that the speaker is a slave who works in the salt mines.) □ *It's eight o'clock. Time to go to work! Back to the salt mines.* □ *School starts again in the fall, and then it's back to the salt mines again.*

back to the wall, have one's See *have one's back to the wall.*

bad as all that, as See *as bad as all that.*

bad faith, in See *in bad faith.*

bad sorts, in See *in bad sorts.*

bad taste, in See *in bad taste.*

bag and baggage AND **part and parcel** with one's luggage; with all one's possessions. (A fixed phrase.) □ *Sally showed up at our door bag and baggage one Sunday morning.* □ *All right, if you won't pay the rent, out with you, bag and baggage!* □ *Get all your stuff—part and parcel—out of here!*

bag of tricks a collection of special techniques or methods. □ *What have you got in your bag of tricks that could help me with this problem?* □ *Here comes Mother with her bag of tricks. I'm sure she can help us.*

bang, go over with a See *go over with a bang.*

bang one's head against a brick wall See under *beat one's head against the wall.*

bank on something to count on something; to rely on something. (To trust in something the way one might trust in a bank.) □ *The weather service said it wouldn't rain, but I wouldn't bank on it.* □ *My word is to be trusted. You can bank on it.*

bargain, in the See *in the bargain.*

bark up the wrong tree   to make the wrong choice; to ask the wrong person; to follow the wrong course. (Refers to a hunting dog that has chased a creature up a tree, but stands barking or howling at the wrong tree.) □ *If you think I'm the guilty person, you're barking up the wrong tree.* □ *The baseball players blamed their bad record on the pitcher, but they were barking up the wrong tree.*

base, off   See *off base.*

bat for someone, go to   See *go to bat for someone.*

bat out of hell, like a   See *like a bat out of hell.*

bats in one's belfry, have   See *have bats in one's belfry.*

batting an eye, without   See *without batting an eye.*

be a copycat   to be a person who copies or mimics what someone else does. (Usually juvenile.) □ *Sally wore a pink dress just like Mary's. Mary called Sally a copycat.* □ *Bill is such a copycat. He bought a coat just like mine.*

be a fan of someone   to be a follower of someone; to idolize someone. (This word *fan* is from *fanatic* [follower].) □ *My mother is still a fan of the Beatles.* □ *I'm a great fan of the mayor of the town.*

beard the lion in his den   to face an adversary on the adversary's home ground. (To tease or threaten—as if grabbing the beard of —something frightening, such as a lion.) □ *I went to the tax collector's office to beard the lion in his den.* □ *He said he hadn't wanted to come to my home, but it was better to beard the lion in his den.*

bear one's cross AND **carry one's cross**   to carry or bear one's burden; to endure one's difficulties. (This is a biblical theme. It is always used figuratively except in the biblical context.) □ *It's a very bad disease, but I'll bear my cross.* □ *I can't help you with it. You'll just have to carry your cross.*

bear someone or something in mind   See under *keep someone or something in mind.*

bear the brunt (of something)   to withstand or endure the worst part or the strongest part of something, such as an attack. □ *I had to bear the brunt of her screaming and yelling.* □ *Why don't you talk with her the next time? I'm tired of bearing the brunt.*

bear watching   to need watching; to deserve observation or monitoring. (This is the verb *to bear.*) □ *This problem will bear watching.* □ *This is a very serious disease, and it will bear watching for further developments.*

beat about the bush   See under *beat around the bush.*

beat a dead horse   to continue fighting a battle that has been won; to continue to argue a point that is settled. (A phrase meaning that a dead horse will not run no matter how hard it is beaten.) □ *Stop arguing! You have won your point. You are just beating a dead horse.* □ *Oh, be quiet. Stop beating a dead horse.*

beat a path to someone's door   [for people] to come to someone in great numbers. (A phrase meaning that so many people will wish to come and see you that they will wear down a pathway to your door.) □ *I have a product so good that everyone is beating a path to my door.* □ *If you really become famous, people will beat a path to your door.*

beat around the bush AND **beat about the bush**   to avoid answering a question; to stall; to waste time. □ *Stop beating around the bush and answer my question.* □ *Let's stop beating about the bush and discuss this matter.*

be a thorn in someone's side   to be a constant bother or annoyance to someone. □ *This problem is a thorn in my side. I wish I had a solution to it.* □ *John was a thorn in my side for years before I finally got rid of him.*

beat one's head against the wall AND **bang one's head against a brick wall**   to waste one's time trying to accomplish something that is completely hopeless. (Not literal.) □ *You're wasting your time trying to fix up this house. You're just beating your head against the wall.* □ *You're banging your head against a brick wall trying to get that dog to behave properly.*

beat the gun to manage to do something before the ending signal. (Originally from sports, referring to making a goal in the last seconds of a game.) □ *The ball beat the gun and dropped through the hoop just in time.* □ *Tom tried to beat the gun, but he was one second too slow.*

Beauty is only skin deep. a proverb meaning that looks are only superficial. (Often implying that a beautiful person may be very cruel inside.) □ BOB: *Isn't Jane lovely?* TOM: *Yes, but beauty is only skin deep.* □ *I know that she looks like a million dollars, but beauty is only skin deep.*

be down on one's luck to be temporarily unlucky; to be short of money because of bad luck. □ *He was down on his luck and needed some money.* □ *I try to help people when they are down on their luck.*

bee in one's bonnet, have a See *have a bee in one's bonnet.*

been through the mill been badly treated; exhausted. (Like grain that has been pulverized in a mill.) □ *This has been a rough day. I've really been through the mill.* □ *This old car is banged up, and it hardly runs. It's been through the mill.*

before you can say Jack Robinson almost immediately. (Often found in children's stories.) □ *And before you could say Jack Robinson, the bird flew away.* □ *I'll catch a plane and be there before you can say Jack Robinson.*

be from Missouri to require proof; to have to be shown (something). (From the nickname of the state of Missouri, the Show Me State.) □ *You'll have to prove it to me. I'm from Missouri.* □ *She's from Missouri and has to be shown.*

Beggars can't be choosers. a proverb meaning that one should not criticize something one gets for free; if one asks or begs for something, one does not get a choice of things. □ *I don't like the old hat that you gave me, but beggars can't be choosers.* □ *It doesn't matter whether people like the free food or not. Beggars can't be choosers.*

begin to see daylight to begin to see the end of a long task. (As if facing dawn at the end of a long night of work.) □ *I've been working on my thesis for two years, and at last I'm beginning to see daylight.* □ *I've been so busy. Only in the last week have I begun to see daylight.*

begin to see the light to begin to understand (something). □ *My algebra class is hard for me, but I'm beginning to see the light.* □ *I was totally confused, but I began to see the light after your explanation.*

be halfhearted (about someone or something) to be unenthusiastic about someone or something. □ *Ann was halfhearted about the choice of Sally for president.* □ *She didn't look halfhearted to me. She looked angry.*

believe it or not to choose to believe something or not. □ *Believe it or not, I just got home from work.* □ *I'm over fifty years old, believe it or not.*

bench, on the See *on the bench.*

bend, go (a)round the See *go (a)round the bend.*

bend someone's ear to talk to someone, perhaps annoyingly. (Not literal. The person's ear is not touched.) □ *Tom is over there, bending Jane's ear about something.* □ *I'm sorry. I didn't mean to bend your ear for an hour.*

be old hat to be old-fashioned; to be outmoded. (Refers to anything—except a hat—that is like a hat that is out of style.) □ *That's a silly idea. It's old hat.* □ *Nobody does that anymore. That's just old hat.*

be poles apart to be very different; to be far from coming to an agreement. (Refers to the North and South poles of the earth, which are thought to be as far apart as any two points on earth.) □ *Mr. and Mrs. Jones don't get along well. They are poles apart.* □ *They'll never sign the contract because they are poles apart.*

be the spit and image of someone AND **be the spitting image of someone** to look very much like someone; to resemble someone very closely. □ *John is the spit and image of his father.* □ *I'm not the spit and image of anyone.* □ *At first, I thought you were saying spitting image.*

be the spitting image of someone See the previous entry.

be the teacher's pet to be the teacher's favorite student. (To be treated like a pet, such as a cat or a dog.) □ *Sally is the teacher's pet. She always gets special treatment.* □ *The other students don't like the teacher's pet.*

between a rock and a hard place AND **between the devil and the deep blue sea** in a very difficult position; facing a hard decision. □ *I couldn't make up my mind. I was caught between a rock and a hard place.* □ *He had a dilemma on his hands. He was clearly between the devil and the deep blue sea.*

between the devil and the deep blue sea See the previous entry.

beyond one's depth **1.** in water that is too deep. (Literal.) □ *Sally swam out until she was beyond her depth.* □ *Jane swam out to get her even though it was beyond her depth, too.* **2.** beyond one's understanding or capabilities. □ *I'm beyond my depth in algebra class.* □ *Poor John was involved in a problem that was really beyond his depth.*

beyond one's means more than one can afford. □ *I'm sorry, but this house is beyond our means. Please show us a cheaper one.* □ *Mr. and Mrs. Brown are living beyond their means.*

beyond the pale unacceptable; outlawed. □ *Your behavior is simply beyond the pale.* □ *Because of Tom's rudeness, he's considered beyond the pale and is never asked to parties anymore.*

big frog in a small pond to be an important person in the midst of less important people. □ *I'd rather be a big frog in a small pond than the opposite.* □ *The trouble with Tom is that he's a big frog in a small pond. He needs more competition.*

big mouth, have a See *have a big mouth.*

bird in the hand is worth two in the bush, A. See *A bird in the hand is worth two in the bush.*

birds and the bees human reproduction. (A euphemistic way of referring to human sex and reproduction.) □ *My father tried to teach me about the birds and the bees.* □ *He's twenty years old and doesn't understand about the birds and the bees.*

Birds of a feather flock together. a proverb meaning that people of the same type seem to gather together. □ *Bob and Tom are just alike. They like each other's company because birds of a feather flock together.* □ *When Mary joined a club for red-headed people, she said, "Birds of a feather flock together."*

birthday suit, in one's See *in one's birthday suit.*

bite off more than one can chew to take (on) more than one can deal with; to be overconfident. (This is used literally for food and figuratively for other things, especially difficult projects.) □ *Billy, stop biting off more than you can chew. You're going to choke on your food someday.* □ *Ann is exhausted again. She's always biting off more than she can chew.*

bite one's nails to be nervous or anxious; to bite one's nails from nervousness or anxiety. (Used both literally and figuratively.) □ *I spent all afternoon biting my nails, worrying about you.* □ *We've all been biting our nails from worry.*

bite one's tongue   to struggle not to say something that you really want to say. (Used literally only to refer to an accidental biting of one's tongue.) □ *I had to bite my tongue to keep from telling her what I really thought.* □ *I sat through that whole conversation biting my tongue.*

bite the dust   to fall to defeat; to die. (Typically heard in movies about the U.S. western frontier.) □ *A bullet hit the sheriff in the chest, and he bit the dust.* □ *Poor old Bill bit the dust while mowing the lawn. They buried him yesterday.*

bite the hand that feeds one   to do harm to someone who does good things for you. (Not literal. Refers to the act of a thankless dog.) □ *I'm your mother! How can you bite the hand that feeds you?* □ *She can hardly expect much when she bites the hand that feeds her.*

black and white, in   See *in black and white.*

black, in the   See *in the black.*

black sheep of the family   the worst member of the family. (A black sheep is an unwanted offspring in a herd of otherwise white sheep.) □ *Mary is the black sheep of the family. She's always in trouble with the police.* □ *He keeps making a nuisance of himself. What do you expect from the black sheep of the family?*

blind alley, up a   See *up a blind alley.*

blind as a bat, as   See *as blind as a bat.*

blind leading the blind   having to do with a situation where people who don't know how to do something try to explain it to other people. □ *Tom doesn't know anything about cars, but he's trying to teach Sally how to change the oil. It's a case of the blind leading the blind.* □ *When I tried to show Mary how to use a computer, it was the blind leading the blind.*

block, on the   See *on the block.*

blood, in the   See *in the blood.*

blow off steam   See under *let off steam.*

blow one's own horn   See under *toot one's own horn.*

blow someone's cover   to reveal someone's true identity or purpose. (Informal or slang.) □ *The spy was very careful not to blow her cover.* □ *I tried to disguise myself, but my dog recognized me and blew my cover.*

blow something out of all proportion   See under *out of all proportion.*

blow the whistle (on someone)   to report someone's wrongdoing to someone (such as the police) who can stop the wrongdoing. (As if one were blowing a police whistle.) □ *The citizens' group blew the whistle on the street gangs by calling the police.* □ *The gangs were getting very bad. It was definitely time to blow the whistle.*

blue, out of the   See *out of the blue.*

boggle someone's mind   to overwhelm someone; to mix up someone's thinking; to astound someone. □ *The size of the house boggles my mind.* □ *She said that his arrogance boggled her mind.*

bolt out of the blue, like a   See *like a bolt out of the blue.*

bone of contention   the subject or point of an argument; an unsettled point of disagreement. (Like a bone that dogs fight over.) □ *We've fought for so long that we've forgotten what the bone of contention is.* □ *The question of a fence between the houses has become quite a bone of contention.*

bone to pick (with someone), have a   See *have a bone to pick (with someone).*

born with a silver spoon in one's mouth   born with many advantages; born to a wealthy family; already showing the signs of great wealth at birth. □ *Sally was born with a silver spoon in her mouth.* □ *I'm glad I was not born with a silver spoon in my mouth.*

born yesterday, not   See *not born yesterday.*

both hands tied behind one's back, with   See *with both hands tied behind one's back.*

bottom of one's heart, from the   See *from the bottom of one's heart.*

bottom of the ladder, at the   See *at the bottom of the ladder.*

bound hand and foot   with hands and feet tied up. □ *The robbers left us bound hand and foot.* □ *We remained bound hand and foot until the maid found us and untied us.*

bow and scrape   to be very humble and subservient. (To bow low and touch the ground. Not usually literal.) □ *Please don't bow and scrape. We are all equal here.* □ *The salesclerk came in, bowing and scraping, and asked if he could help us.*

bread and butter   someone's livelihood or income. (The source of money that puts bread and butter, or other food, on the table.) □ *Selling cars is a lot of hard work, but it's my bread and butter.* □ *It was hard to give up my bread and butter, but I felt it was time to retire.*

break camp   to close down a campsite; to pack up and move on. □ *Early this morning we broke camp and moved on northward.* □ *Okay, everyone. It's time to break camp. Take those tents down and fold them neatly.*

break new ground   to begin to do something that no one else has done; to pioneer (in an enterprise). □ *Dr. Anderson was breaking new ground in cancer research.* □ *They were breaking new ground in consumer electronics.*

break one's back (to do something)   See the following entry.

break one's neck (to do something) AND **break one's back (to do something)**   to work very hard to do something. (Never used in its literal sense.) □ *I broke my neck to get here on time.* □ *That's the last time I'll break my neck to help you.* □ *There is no point in breaking your back. Take your time.*

break out in a cold sweat   to perspire from fever, fear, or anxiety; to begin to sweat profusely, suddenly. □ *I was so frightened I broke out in a cold sweat.* □ *The patient broke out in a cold sweat.*

break (out) into tears AND **break out in tears**   to start crying suddenly. □ *I was so sad that I broke out into tears.* □ *I always break into tears at a funeral.* □ *It's hard not to break out in tears under those circumstances.*

break someone's fall   to cushion a falling person; to lessen the impact of a falling person. □ *When the little boy fell out of the window, the bushes broke his fall.* □ *The old lady slipped on the ice, but a snowbank broke her fall.*

break someone's heart   to cause someone emotional pain. (Not literal.) □ *It just broke my heart when Tom ran away from home.* □ *Sally broke John's heart when she refused to marry him.*

break the ice   to initiate social interchanges and conversation; to get something started. (The *ice* sometimes refers to social coldness. Also used literally.) □ *Tom is so outgoing. He's always the first one to break the ice at parties.* □ *It's hard to break the ice at formal events.* □ *Sally broke the ice by bidding $20,000 for the painting.*

break the news (to someone)   to tell someone some important news, usually bad news. □ *The doctor had to break the news to Jane about her husband's cancer.* □ *I hope that the doctor broke the news gently.*

breathe down someone's neck   **1.** to keep close watch on someone; to watch someone's activities. (Refers to standing very close behind a person. Can be used literally.) □ *I can't work with you breathing down my neck all the time. Go away.* □ *I will get through my life without your help. Stop breathing down my neck.* **2.** to try to hurry someone along; to make someone get something done on time. (The subject does not have to be a person. See the second example.) □ *I have to finish my taxes today. The tax collector is breathing down my neck.* □ *I have a deadline breathing down my neck.*

breathe one's last   to die; to breathe one's last breath. □ *Mrs. Smith breathed her last this morning.* □ *I'll keep running every day until I breathe my last.*

bring something to light   to make something known; to discover something. (As if someone were bringing some hidden thing out into the light of day.) □ *The scientists brought their findings to light.* □ *We must bring this new evidence to light.*

bring the house down AND **bring down the house**   to excite a theatrical audience to laughter or applause or both. (Not literal.) □ *This is a great joke. The last time I told it, it brought the house down.* □ *It didn't bring down the house; it emptied it.*

bring up the rear   to move along behind everyone else; to be at the end of the line. (Originally referred to marching soldiers.) □ *Here comes John, bringing up the rear.* □ *Hurry up, Tom! Why are you always bringing up the rear?*

broad daylight, in   See *in broad daylight.*

brush with something, have a   See *have a brush with something.*

build castles in Spain   See the following entry.

build castles in the air AND **build castles in Spain**   to daydream; to make plans that can never come true. (Neither phrase is used literally.) □ *Ann spends most of her time building castles in*

Spain. □ *I really like to sit on the porch in the evening, just building castles in the air.*

bull in a china shop a very clumsy person around breakable things; a thoughtless or tactless person. (China is fine crockery.) □ *Look at Bill, as awkward as a bull in a china shop.* □ *Get that big dog out of my garden. It's like a bull in a china shop.* □ *Bob is so rude, a regular bull in a china shop.*

bullpen, in the See *in the bullpen.*

bump on a log, like a See *like a bump on a log.*

burn one's bridges (behind one) **1.** to make decisions that cannot be changed in the future. □ *If you drop out of school now, you'll be burning your bridges behind you.* □ *You're too young to burn your bridges that way.* **2.** to be unpleasant in a situation that you are leaving, ensuring that you'll never be welcome to return. □ *If you get mad and quit your job, you'll be burning your bridges behind you.* □ *No sense burning your bridges. Be polite and leave quietly.* **3.** to cut off the way back to where you came from, making it impossible to retreat. □ *The army, which had burned its bridges behind it, couldn't go back.* □ *By blowing up the road, the spies had burned their bridges behind them.*

burn someone at the stake **1.** to set fire to a person tied to a post (as a form of execution). □ *They used to burn witches at the stake.* □ *Look, officer, I only ran a stop sign. What are you going to do, burn me at the stake?* **2.** to chastise or denounce someone severely, but without violence. □ *Stop yelling. I made a simple mistake, and you're burning me at the stake for it.* □ *Sally only spilled her milk. There is no need to shout. Don't burn her at the stake for it.*

burn someone or something to a crisp to burn someone or something totally or very badly. □ *The flames burned him to a crisp.* □ *The cook burned the meat to a crisp.*

burn the candle at both ends to work very hard and stay up very late at night. (A way of getting the most out of a candle or, figuratively, of oneself.) □ *No wonder Mary is ill. She has been burning the candle at both ends for a long time.* □ *You can't keep on burning the candle at both ends.*

burn the midnight oil to stay up working, especially studying, late at night. (Refers to working by the light of an oil lamp at an earlier time.) □ *I have to go home and burn the midnight oil to-night.* □ *If you burn the midnight oil night after night, you'll probably become ill.*

burn with a low blue flame to be very angry. (Refers to the imaginary heat caused by extreme anger. A low blue flame is very hot despite its smallness and calmness.) □ *By the time she showed up three hours late, I was burning with a low blue flame.* □ *Whenever Ann gets mad, she just presses her lips together and burns with a low blue flame.*

burst at the seams 1. [for someone] to explode (figuratively) with pride or laughter. □ *Tom nearly burst at the seams with pride.* □ *We laughed so hard we just about burst at the seams.* 2. to explode from fullness. □ *The room was so crowded that it almost burst at the seams.* □ *I ate so much I almost burst at the seams.*

burst with joy to be full to the bursting point with happiness. □ *When I got my grades, I could have burst with joy.* □ *Joe was not exactly bursting with joy when he got the news.*

bury one's head in the sand AND **hide one's head in the sand** to ignore or hide from obvious signs of danger. (Refers to an ostrich, which we picture with its head stuck into the sand or the ground.) □ *Stop burying your head in the sand. Look at the statistics on smoking and cancer.* □ *And stop hiding your head in the sand. All of us will die somehow, whether we smoke or not.*

bury the hatchet to stop fighting or arguing; to end old resentments. (Burying a hatchet is symbolic of ending a war or a battle.) □ *All right, you two. Calm down and bury the hatchet.* □ *I wish Mr. and Mrs. Franklin would bury the hatchet. They argue all the time.*

business, go about one's   See *go about one's business.*

busy as a beaver, as   See *as busy as a beaver.*

busy as a bee, as   See *as busy as a bee.*

busy as Grand Central Station, as   See *as busy as Grand Central Station.*

button one's lip   to get quiet and stay quiet. (Often used with children.) □ *All right now, let's button our lips and listen to the story.* □ *Button your lip, Tom! I'll tell you when you can talk.*

button, on the   See *on the button.*

buy a pig in a poke   to purchase or accept something without having seen or examined it. (*Poke* means "bag" or "sack.") □ *Buying a car without test-driving it is like buying a pig in a poke.* □ *He bought a pig in a poke when he ordered a diamond ring by mail.*

buy something   to believe someone; to accept something to be a fact. (Also used literally.) □ *It may be true, but I don't buy it.* □ *I just don't buy the idea that you can swim that far.*

buy something for a song   to buy something cheaply. □ *No one else wanted it, so I bought it for a song.* □ *I could buy this house for a song, because it's so ugly.*

buy something sight unseen   to buy something without seeing it first. □ *I bought this land sight unseen. I didn't know it was so rocky.* □ *It isn't usually safe to buy something sight unseen.*

by a hair's breadth AND **by a whisker**   just barely; by a very small distance. □ *I just missed getting on the plane by a hair's breadth.* □ *The arrow missed the deer by a whisker.*

by a whisker   See the previous entry.

by leaps and bounds rapidly; by large movements forward. (Not often used literally, but it could be.) □ *Our garden is growing by leaps and bounds.* □ *The profits of my company are increasing by leaps and bounds.*

by return mail by a subsequent mailing (back to the sender). (A phrase indicating that an answer is expected soon, by mail.) □ *Since this bill is overdue, would you kindly send us your check by return mail?* □ *I answered your request by return mail over a year ago. Please check your records.*

by the nape of the neck by the back of the neck. (Mostly found in real or mock threats. Grabbing in the way that one picks up a puppy.) □ *He grabbed me by the nape of the neck and told me not to turn around if I valued my life. I stood very still.* □ *If you do that again, I'll pick you up by the nape of the neck and throw you out the door.*

by the same token in the same way; reciprocally. □ *Tom must be good when he comes here, and, by the same token, I expect you to behave properly when you go to his house.* □ *The mayor votes for his friend's causes. By the same token, the friend votes for the mayor's causes.*

by the seat of one's pants by sheer luck and very little skill; just barely. (Especially with *to fly.*) □ *I got through school by the seat of my pants.* □ *The jungle pilot spent most of his days flying by the seat of his pants.*

by the skin of one's teeth just barely; by an amount equal to the thickness of the (imaginary) skin on one's teeth. □ *I got through that class by the skin of my teeth.* □ *I got to the airport late and missed the plane by the skin of my teeth.*

by the sweat of one's brow by one's efforts; by one's hard work. □ *Tom raised these vegetables by the sweat of his brow.* □ *Sally polished the car by the sweat of her brow.*

by virtue of something because of something; due to something. □ *She's permitted to vote by virtue of her age.* □ *They are members of the club by virtue of their great wealth.*

by word of mouth by speaking rather than writing. (A fixed phrase.) □ *I learned about it by word of mouth.* □ *I need it in writing. I don't trust things I hear about by word of mouth.*

C

cake and eat it too, have one's   See *have one's cake and eat it too.*

call a spade a spade   to call something by its right name; to speak frankly about something, even if it is unpleasant. □ *Well, I believe it's time to call a spade a spade. We are just avoiding the issue.* □ *Let's call a spade a spade. The man is a liar.*

call it a day   to quit work and go home; to say that a day's work has been completed. □ *I'm tired. Let's call it a day.* □ *The boss was mad because Tom called it a day at noon and went home.*

call it quits   to quit; to resign from something; to announce that one is quitting. □ *Okay! I've had enough! I'm calling it quits.* □ *Time to go home, John. Let's call it quits.*

call someone on the carpet   to reprimand a person. (The phrase presents images of a person called into the boss's carpeted office for a reprimand.) □ *One more error like that and the boss will call you on the carpet.* □ *I'm sorry it went wrong. I really hope he doesn't call me on the carpet again.*

call the dogs off AND **call off the dogs**   to stop threatening, chasing, or hounding (a person); (literally) to order dogs away from the chase. (Note the variations in the examples.) □ *All right, I surrender. You can call your dogs off.* □ *Tell the sheriff to call off the dogs. We caught the robber.* □ *Please call off your dogs!*

can't carry a tune unable to sing a simple melody; lacking musical ability. (Almost always negative. Also with *cannot.*) □ *I wish that Tom wouldn't try to sing. He can't carry a tune.* □ *Listen to poor old John. He really cannot carry a tune.*

can't hold a candle to someone not equal to someone; not worthy to associate with someone; unable to measure up to someone. (Also with *cannot.* Refers to not being worthy enough even to hold a candle to light someone's way.) □ *Mary can't hold a candle to Ann when it comes to auto racing.* □ *As for singing, John can't hold a candle to Jane.*

can't make heads or tails (out) of someone or something unable to understand someone or something; unable to tell one end of someone or something from the other. (Because the thing or person is obscured or confusing. Also with *cannot.*) □ *John is so strange. I can't make heads or tails of him.* □ *Do this report again. I can't make heads or tails out of it.*

can't see beyond the end of one's nose unaware of the things that might happen in the future; not farsighted; self-centered. (Also with *cannot.*) □ *John is a very poor planner. He can't see beyond the end of his nose.* □ *Ann can't see beyond the end of her nose. She is very self-centered.*

can't see one's hand in front of one's face unable to see very far, usually due to darkness or fog. (Also with *cannot.*) □ *It was so dark that I couldn't see my hand in front of my face.* □ *Bob said that the fog was so thick he couldn't see his hand in front of his face.*

cards, in the See *in the cards.*

carry a torch (for someone) AND **carry the torch** to be in love with someone who is not in love with you; to brood over a hopeless love affair. □ *John is carrying a torch for Jane.* □ *Is John still carrying a torch?* □ *Yes, he'll carry the torch for months.*

carry coals to Newcastle to do something unnecessary; to do something that is redundant or duplicative. (An old proverb from

England. Newcastle was a town from which coal was shipped to other parts of England. It would be senseless to bring coal into this town.) □ *Taking food to a farmer is like carrying coals to Newcastle.* □ *Mr. Smith is so rich he doesn't need any more money. To give him money is like carrying coals to Newcastle.*

carry one's cross   See under *bear one's cross.*

carry the ball   **1.** to be the player holding the ball, especially in football when a goal is made. □ *It was the fullback carrying the ball.* □ *Yes, Tom always carries the ball.* **2.** to be in charge; to make sure that a job gets done. □ *We need someone who knows how to get the job done. Hey, Sally! Why don't you carry the ball for us?* □ *John can't carry the ball. He isn't organized enough.*

carry the torch   to uphold a set of goals; to lead or participate in a (figurative) crusade. □ *The battle was over, but John continued to carry the torch.* □ *If Jane hadn't carried the torch, no one would have followed, and the whole thing would have failed.*

carry the weight of the world on one's shoulders   to appear to be burdened by all the problems in the whole world. □ *Look at Tom. He appears to be carrying the weight of the world on his shoulders.* □ *Cheer up, Tom! You don't need to carry the weight of the world on your shoulders.*

carry weight (with someone)   [for someone] to have influence with someone; [for something] to have significance for someone. (Often in the negative.) □ *Everything Mary says carries weight with me.* □ *Don't pay any attention to John. What he says carries no weight around here.* □ *Your proposal is quite good, but since you're not a member of the club, it carries no weight.*

case in point   an example of what one is talking about. □ *Now, as a case in point, let's look at nineteenth-century England.* □ *Fireworks can be dangerous. For a case in point, look what happened to Bob Smith last week.*

cash-and-carry   having to do with a sale of goods or a way of selling that requires payment at the time of sale and requires that you take the goods with you. □ *I'm sorry. We don't deliver. It's strictly cash-and-carry.* □ *You cannot get credit at that drugstore. They only sell cash-and-carry.*

cash in (on something) to earn a lot of money at something; to make a profit at something. □ *This is a good year for farming, and you can cash in on it if you're smart.* □ *It's too late to cash in on that particular clothing fad.*

cast (one's) pearls before swine to waste something good on someone who doesn't care about it. (From a biblical quotation. As if throwing something of great value under the feet of pigs. It is considered insulting to refer to people as swine.) □ *To sing for them is to cast pearls before swine.* □ *To serve them French cuisine is like casting one's pearls before swine.*

cast the first stone to make the first criticism; to be the first to attack. (From a biblical quotation.) □ *Well, I don't want to be the one to cast the first stone, but she sang horribly.* □ *John always casts the first stone. Does he think he's perfect?*

catch cold AND **take cold** to contract a cold (the disease). □ *Please close the window, or we'll all catch cold.* □ *I take cold every year at this time.*

catch one's death (of cold) AND **take one's death of cold** to contract a cold; to catch a serious cold. □ *If I go out in this weather, I'll catch my death of cold.* □ *Dress up warm or you'll take your death of cold.* □ *Put on your raincoat or you'll catch your death.*

catch someone off-balance to catch a person who is not prepared; to surprise someone. (Also used literally.) □ *Sorry I acted so flustered. You caught me off-balance.* □ *The robbers caught Ann off-balance and stole her purse.*

catch someone's eye AND **get someone's eye** to establish eye contact with someone; to attract someone's attention. (Also with *have,* as in the examples.) □ *The shiny red car caught Mary's eye.*

□ *Tom got Mary's eye and waved to her.* □ *When Tom had her eye, he smiled at her.*

caught in the cross fire caught between two fighting people or groups. (As if one were stranded between two opposing armies who are firing bullets at each other.) □ *In western movies, innocent people are always getting caught in the cross fire.* □ *In the war, Corporal Smith was killed when he got caught in the cross fire.*

caught short to be without something you need, especially money. □ *I needed eggs for my cake, but I was caught short.* □ *Bob had to borrow money from John to pay for the meal. Bob is caught short quite often.*

cause (some) eyebrows to raise to shock people; to surprise and dismay people. □ *John caused eyebrows to raise when he married a poor girl from Toledo.* □ *If you want to cause some eyebrows to raise, just start singing as you walk down the street.*

cause (some) tongues to wag to cause people to gossip; to give people something to gossip about. □ *The way John was looking at Mary will surely cause some tongues to wag.* □ *The way Mary was dressed will also cause tongues to wag.*

champ at the bit to be ready and anxious to do something. (Originally said about horses.) □ *The kids were champing at the bit to get into the swimming pool.* □ *The dogs were champing at the bit to begin the hunt.*

change horses in midstream to make major changes in an activity that has already begun; to choose someone or something else after it is too late. (Usually regarded as a bad idea.) □ *I'm already baking a cherry pie. I can't bake an apple pie. It's too late to change horses in midstream.* □ *The house is half-built. It's too late to hire a different architect. You can't change horses in midstream.*

channels, go through See *go through channels*.

Charity begins at home.   a proverb meaning that one should be kind to one's own family, friends, or fellow citizens before trying to help others. □ *"Mother, may I please have some pie?" asked Mary. "Remember, charity begins at home."* □ *At church, the minister reminded us that charity begins at home, but we must remember others also.*

chip off the old block, a   See *a chip off the old block.*

chip on one's shoulder, have a   See *have a chip on one's shoulder.*

circulation, back in   See *back in circulation.*

circulation, out of   See *out of circulation.*

clean hands, have   See *have clean hands.*

clear as mud, as   See *as clear as mud.*

clear blue sky, out of a   See *out of a clear blue sky.*

clear the table   to remove the dishes and other eating utensils from the table after a meal. □ *Will you please help clear the table?* □ *After you clear the table, we'll play cards.*

climb on the bandwagon   to join others in supporting someone or something. □ *Come join us! Climb on the bandwagon and support Senator Smith!* □ *Look at all those people climbing on the bandwagon! They don't know what they are getting into!*

clip someone's wings   to restrain someone; to reduce or put an end to a teenager's privileges. (As with birds or fowl whose wings are clipped to keep them at home.) □ *You had better learn to get home on time, or I will clip your wings.* □ *My mother clipped my wings. I can't go out tonight.*

clock, against the   See *against the clock.*

clockwork, go like   See *go like clockwork.*

close at hand   within reach; handy. □ *I'm sorry, but your letter isn't close at hand. Please remind me what you said in it.* □ *When you're cooking, you should keep all the ingredients close at hand.*

close call, have a   See *have a close call.*

close ranks   **1.** to move closer together in a military formation. □ *The soldiers closed ranks and marched on the enemy.* □ *All right! Stop that talking and close ranks.* **2.** to join (with someone). □ *We can fight this menace only if we close ranks.* □ *Let's all close ranks behind Ann and get her elected.*

close shave, have a   See *have a close shave.*

cloud nine, on   See *on cloud nine.*

cloud (of suspicion), under a   See *under a cloud (of suspicion).*

coast is clear, The.   See *The coast is clear.*

coast-to-coast   from the Atlantic to the Pacific Ocean (in the U.S.A.); all the land between the Atlantic and Pacific oceans. □ *My voice was once heard on a coast-to-coast radio broadcast.* □ *Our car made the coast-to-coast trip in eighty hours.*

cock-and-bull story   a silly, made-up story; a story that is a lie. □ *Don't give me that cock-and-bull story.* □ *I asked for an explanation, and all I got was your ridiculous cock-and-bull story!*

cold, out   See *out cold.*

color, off   See *off-color.*

come a cropper   to have a misfortune; to fail. (Literally, to fall off one's horse.) □ *Bob invested all his money in the stock market just before it fell. Boy, did he come a cropper.* □ *Jane was out all night before she took her tests. She really came a cropper.*

come apart at the seams   to lose one's emotional self-control suddenly. (From the literal sense, referring to a garment falling apart.) □ *Bill was so upset that he almost came apart at the seams.* □ *I couldn't take anymore. I just came apart at the seams.*

come away empty-handed   to return without anything. □ *All right, go gambling. Don't come away empty-handed, though.* □ *Go to the bank and ask for the loan again. This time don't come away empty-handed.*

come by something   **1.** to travel by a specific carrier, such as a plane, a boat, or a car. (The literal sense.) □ *We came by train. It's more relaxing.* □ *Next time, we'll come by plane. It's faster.* **2.** to find or get something. □ *How did you come by that haircut?* □ *Where did you come by that new shirt?*

come down in the world   to lose one's social position or financial standing. □ *Mr. Jones has really come down in the world since he lost his job.* □ *If I were unemployed, I'm sure I'd come down in the world, too.*

come home (to roost)   to return to cause trouble (for someone). (As chickens or other birds return home to roost.) □ *As I feared, all my problems came home to roost.* □ *Yes, problems all come home eventually.*

come in out of the rain   to become alert and sensible. (Also used literally.) □ *Pay attention, Sally! Come in out of the rain!* □ *Bill will fail if he doesn't come in out of the rain and study.*

come into one's or its own   **1.** [for one] to achieve one's proper recognition. □ *Sally finally came into her own.* □ *After years of trying, she finally came into her own.* **2.** [for something] to achieve its proper recognition. □ *The idea of an electric car finally came into its own.* □ *Film as an art medium finally came into its own.*

come of age   to reach an age when one is old enough to own property, get married, and sign legal contracts. □ *When Jane* *comes of age, she will buy her own car.* □ *Sally, who came of age last month, entered into an agreement to purchase a house.*

come off second-best to win second place or worse; to lose out to someone else. □ *John came off second-best in the race.* □ *Why do I always come off second-best in an argument with you?*

come out ahead to end up with a profit; to improve one's situation. □ *I hope you come out ahead with your investments.* □ *It took a lot of money to buy the house, but I think I'll come out ahead.*

come out in the wash to work out all right. (This means that problems or difficulties will go away as dirt goes away in the process of washing.) □ *Don't worry about that problem. It'll all come out in the wash.* □ *This trouble will go away. It'll come out in the wash.*

come out of the closet **1.** to reveal one's secret interests. □ *Tom Brown came out of the closet and admitted that he likes to knit.* □ *It's time that all of you lovers of chamber music came out of the closet and attended our concerts.* **2.** to reveal that one is a homosexual. □ *Tom surprised his parents when he came out of the closet.* □ *It was difficult for him to come out of the closet.*

come to a bad end to have a disaster, perhaps one that is deserved or expected; to die an unfortunate death. □ *My old car came to a bad end. Its engine burned up.* □ *The evil merchant came to a bad end.*

come to a dead end to come to an absolute stopping point. □ *The building project came to a dead end.* □ *The street came to a dead end.* □ *We were driving along and came to a dead end.*

come to a head to come to a crucial point; to come to a point when a problem must be solved. □ *Remember my problem with my neighbors? Well, last night the whole thing came to a head.* □ *The battle between the two factions of the city council came to a head yesterday.*

come to an end to stop; to finish. □ *The party came to an end at midnight.* □ *Her life came to an end late yesterday.*

come to an untimely end to come to an early death. □ *Poor Mr. Jones came to an untimely end in a car accident.* □ *Cancer caused Mrs. Smith to come to an untimely end.*

come to a standstill to stop, temporarily or permanently. □ *The building project came to a standstill because the workers went on strike.* □ *The party came to a standstill until the lights were turned on again.*

come to grief to fail; to have trouble or grief. □ *The artist wept when her canvas came to grief.* □ *The wedding party came to grief when the bride passed out.*

come to grips with something to face something; to comprehend something. □ *He found it difficult to come to grips with his grandmother's death.* □ *Many students have a hard time coming to grips with algebra.*

come to light to become known. □ *Some interesting facts about your past have just come to light.* □ *If too many bad things come to light, you may lose your job.*

come to one's senses to wake up; to become conscious; to start thinking clearly. □ *John, come to your senses. You're being quite stupid.* □ *In the morning I don't come to my senses until I have had two cups of coffee.*

come to pass to happen. (Literary.) □ *When did all of this come to pass?* □ *When will this event come to pass?*

come to the point AND **get to the point** to get to the important part (of something). □ *He has been talking a long time. I wish he would come to the point.* □ *Quit wasting time! Get to the point!* □ *We are talking about money, Bob! Come on, get to the point.*

come to think of it I just remembered . . . ; now that I think of it . . . □ *Come to think of it, I know someone who can help.* □ *I have a screwdriver in the trunk of my car, come to think of it.*

come true to become real; [for a dream or a wish] actually to happen. □ *When I got married, all my dreams came true.* □ *Coming to the big city was like having my wish come true.*

come up in the world to improve one's status or situation in life. □ *Since Mary got her new job, she has really come up in the world.* □ *A good education helped my brother come up in the world.*

come what may no matter what might happen. □ *I'll be home for the holidays, come what may.* □ *Come what may, the mail will get delivered.*

comfortable as an old shoe, as See *as comfortable as an old shoe.*

commission, out of See *out of commission.*

conspicuous by one's absence to have one's absence (from an event) noticed. □ *We missed you last night. You were conspicuous by your absence.* □ *How could the bride's father miss the wedding party? He was certainly conspicuous by his absence.*

construction, under See *under construction.*

contrary, on the See *on the contrary.*

control the purse strings to be in charge of the money in a business or a household. □ *I control the purse strings at our house.* □ *Mr. Williams is the treasurer. He controls the purse strings.*

cook someone's goose to damage or ruin someone. (To do something that cannot be undone.) □ *I cooked my own goose by not showing up on time.* □ *Sally cooked Bob's goose for treating her the way he did.*

cook the accounts to cheat in bookkeeping; to make the accounts appear to balance when they do not. □ *Jane was sent to jail for cooking the accounts of her mother's store.* □ *It's hard to tell whether she really cooked the accounts or just didn't know how to add.*

cool as a cucumber, as See *as cool as a cucumber.*

cool one's heels to wait (for someone). □ *I spent all afternoon cooling my heels in the waiting room while the doctor talked on the telephone.* □ *All right. If you can't behave properly, just sit down here and cool your heels until I call you.*

copycat, be a See *be a copycat.*

corner of one's eye, out of the See *out of the corner of one's eye.*

cost an arm and a leg See under *pay an arm and a leg (for something).*

cost a pretty penny to cost a lot of money. □ *I'll bet that diamond cost a pretty penny.* □ *You can be sure that house cost a pretty penny. It has seven bathrooms.*

counter, under the See *under the counter.*

count noses AND **count heads** to count people. (Because there is only one of these per person.) □ *I'll tell you how many people are here after I count noses.* □ *Everyone is here. Let's count noses so we can order hamburgers.*

count one's chickens before they hatch to plan how to utilize good results of something before those results have occurred. (Frequently used in the negative.) □ *You're way ahead of yourself. Don't count your chickens before they hatch.* □ *You may be disappointed if you count your chickens before they hatch.*

cover a lot of ground 1. to travel over a great distance; to investigate a wide expanse of land. □ *The prospectors covered a lot of* *ground, looking for gold.* □ *My car can cover a lot of ground in one day.* **2.** to deal with much information and many facts. □ *The history lecture covered a lot of ground today.* □ *Mr. and Mrs. Franklin always cover a lot of ground when they argue.*

cover for someone **1.** to make excuses for someone; to conceal someone's errors. □ *If I miss class, please cover for me.* □ *If you're late, I'll cover for you.* **2.** to handle someone else's work. □ *Dr. Johnson's partner agreed to cover for him during his vacation.* □ *I'm on duty this afternoon. Will you please cover for me? I have a doctor's appointment.*

crack a joke to tell a joke. □ *She's never serious. She's always cracking jokes.* □ *As long as she's cracking jokes, she's okay.*

crack a smile to smile a little, perhaps reluctantly. □ *She cracked a smile, so I knew she was kidding.* □ *The soldier cracked a smile at the wrong time and had to march for an hour as punishment.*

cramp someone's style to limit someone in some way. □ *I hope this doesn't cramp your style, but could you please not hum while you work?* □ *To ask him to keep regular hours would really be cramping his style.*

crazy as a loon, as See *as crazy as a loon.*

cream of the crop the best of all. (A cliché.) □ *This particular car is the cream of the crop.* □ *The kids are very bright. They are the cream of the crop.*

creation, in See *in creation.*

Crime doesn't pay. a proverb meaning that crime will not benefit a person. □ *At the end of the radio program, a voice said, "Remember, crime doesn't pay."* □ *No matter how tempting it may appear, crime doesn't pay.*

cross a bridge before one comes to it to worry excessively about something before it happens. (Note the variations in the examples.) □ *There is no sense in crossing that bridge before you* *come to it.* □ *She's always crossing bridges before coming to them. She needs to learn to relax.*

cross a bridge when one comes to it to deal with a problem only when one is faced with the problem. (Note the variations in the examples.) □ *Please wait and cross that bridge when you come to it.* □ *He shouldn't worry about it now. He can cross that bridge when he comes to it.*

cross-examine someone to ask someone questions in great detail; to question a suspect or a witness at great length. □ *The police cross-examined the suspect for three hours.* □ *The lawyer plans to cross-examine the witness tomorrow morning.*

cross one's heart (and hope to die) to pledge or vow that the truth is being told. □ *It's true, cross my heart and hope to die.* □ *It's really true—cross my heart.*

cross swords (with someone) to enter into an argument with someone. (Not literal.) □ *I don't want to cross swords with Tom.* □ *The last time we crossed swords, we had a terrible time.*

crow flies, as the See *as the crow flies.*

crux of the matter the central issue of the matter. (*Crux* is an old word meaning "cross.") □ *All right, this is the crux of the matter.* □ *It's about time that we looked at the crux of the matter.*

cry before one is hurt to cry or complain before one is injured. □ *Bill always cries before he's hurt.* □ *There is no point in crying before one is hurt.*

cry bloody murder AND **scream bloody murder** to scream as if something very serious has happened. (To scream as if one had found the result of a bloody act of murder.) □ *Now that Bill is really hurt, he's screaming bloody murder.* □ *There is no point in crying bloody murder about the bill if you aren't going to pay it.*

cry one's eyes out to cry very hard. (Not literal.) □ *When we heard the news, we cried our eyes out with joy.* □ *She cried her eyes out after his death.*

cry over spilled milk to be unhappy about having done something that cannot be undone. (Usually viewed as a childish action. *Spilled* can also be spelled *spilt*.) □ *I'm sorry that you broke your bicycle, Tom. But there is nothing that can be done now. Don't cry over spilled milk.* □ *Ann is always crying over spilt milk.*

cry wolf to cry or complain about something when nothing is really wrong. □ *Pay no attention. She's just crying wolf again.* □ *Don't cry wolf too often. No one will come.*

cup of tea, not someone's See *not someone's cup of tea.*

Curiosity killed the cat. a proverb meaning that it is dangerous to be curious. □ *Don't ask so many questions, Billy. Curiosity killed the cat.* □ *Curiosity killed the cat. Mind your own business.*

curl someone's hair to frighten or alarm someone severely; to shock someone with sight, sound, or taste. (Also used literally.) □ *Don't ever sneak up on me like that again. You really curled my hair.* □ *The horror film curled my hair.*

curl up and die to retreat and die. □ *When I heard you say that, I could have curled up and died.* □ *No, it wasn't an illness. She just curled up and died.*

cut class to skip going to class. (Refers to high school or college classes.) □ *If Mary keeps cutting classes, she'll fail the course.* □ *I can't cut that class. I've missed too many already.*

cut off one's nose to spite one's face a phrase meaning that one harms oneself in trying to punish another person. (The phrase is variable in form, as shown in the examples.) □ *Billy loves the zoo, but he refused to go with his mother because he was mad at her. He cut off his nose to spite his face.* □ *Find a* *better way to be angry. It is silly to cut your nose off to spite your face.*

cut one's (own) throat   [for someone] to experience certain failure; to do damage to someone. (Also used literally.) □ *If I were to run for office, I'd just be cutting my throat.* □ *Judges who take bribes are cutting their own throats.*

cut someone or something (off) short   to end something before it is finished; to end one's speaking before one is finished. □ *We cut the picnic short because of the storm.* □ *I'm sorry to cut you off short, but I must go now.*

cut someone or something to the bone   **1.** to slice deep to a bone. (Literal.) □ *The knife cut John to the bone. He had to be sewed up.* □ *Cut each slice of ham to the bone. Then each slice will be as big as possible.* **2.** [with *something*] to cut down severely (on something). (Not literal.) □ *We cut our expenses to the bone and are still losing money.* □ *Congress had to cut the budget to the bone in order to balance it.*

cut someone's losses   to reduce someone's losses of money, goods, or other things of value. □ *I sold the stock as it went down, thus cutting my losses.* □ *He cut his losses by putting better locks on the doors. There were fewer robberies.* □ *The mayor's reputation suffered because of the scandal. He finally resigned to cut his losses.*

cut someone to the quick   to hurt someone's feelings very badly. (Can be used literally when *quick* refers to the tender flesh at the base of fingernails and toenails.) □ *Your criticism cut me to the quick.* □ *Tom's sharp words to Mary cut her to the quick.*

cut the ground out from under someone AND **cut out the ground from under someone**   to destroy the foundation of someone's plans or someone's argument. □ *The politician cut the ground out from under his opponent.* □ *Congress cut out the ground from under the president.*

D

dance to another tune to shift quickly to different behavior; to change one's behavior or attitude. □ *After being yelled at, Ann danced to another tune.* □ *A stern talking-to will make her dance to another tune.*

dash cold water on something See under *pour cold water on something.*

date back (to sometime) to extend back to a particular time; to have been alive at a particular time in the past. □ *My late grand-mother dated back to the Civil War.* □ *This record dates back to the sixties.* □ *How far do you date back?*

Davy Jones's locker, go to See *go to Davy Jones's locker.*

dead and buried gone forever. (Refers literally to persons and figuratively to ideas and other things.) □ *Now that Uncle Bill is dead and buried, we can read his will.* □ *That kind of thinking is dead and buried.*

dead as a dodo, as See *as dead as a dodo.*

dead as a doornail, as See *as dead as a doornail.*

dead heat, in a See *in a dead heat.*

dead to rights, have someone See *have someone dead to rights.*

dead to the world tired; exhausted; sleeping soundly. (Asleep and oblivious to what is going on in the rest of the world.) □ *I've had such a hard day. I'm really dead to the world.* □ *Look at her sleep. She's dead to the world.*

death on someone or something **1.** very effective in acting against someone or something; harmful to someone or something. □ *This road is terribly bumpy. It's death on tires and shock absorbers.* □ *The sergeant is death on poor unsuspecting soldiers.* □ *Johnny's mother said that he was just death on leather shoes.* **2.** [with *something*] accurate or deadly at doing something requiring skill or great effort. □ *John is death on curve balls. He's our best pitcher.* □ *The boxing champ is really death on those fast punches.* □ *Every single player on the opposite team is death on long shots.*

death's door, at See *at death's door.*

deep end, go off the See *go off the deep end.*

deep water, in See *in deep water.*

depth, beyond one's See *beyond one's depth.*

desert a sinking ship AND **leave a sinking ship** to leave a place, a person, or a situation when things become difficult or unpleasant. (Rats are said to be the first to leave a ship that is sinking.) □ *I hate to be the one to desert a sinking ship, but I can't stand it around here anymore.* □ *There goes Tom. Wouldn't you know he'd leave a sinking ship rather than stay around and try to help?*

devil and the deep blue sea, between the See *between the devil and the deep blue sea.*

devil of it, for the See *for the devil of it.*

diamond in the rough a valuable or potentially excellent person or thing hidden by an unpolished or rough exterior. □ *Ann looks like a stupid woman, but she's a fine person—a real diamond in* *the rough.* □ *That piece of property is a diamond in the rough. Someday it will be valuable.*

dibs on something, have   See *have dibs on something.*

die of a broken heart   **1.** to die of emotional distress. □ *I was not surprised to hear of her death. They say she died of a broken heart.* □ *In the movie, the heroine appeared to die of a broken heart, but the audience knew she was poisoned.* **2.** to suffer from emotional distress, especially from a failed romance. □ *Tom and Mary broke off their romance and both died of broken hearts.* □ *Please don't leave me. I know I'll die of a broken heart.*

die of boredom   to suffer from boredom; to be very bored. □ *No one has ever really died of boredom.* □ *We sat there and listened politely, even though we almost died of boredom.*

die on the vine   See under *wither on the vine.*

different as night and day, as   See *as different as night and day.*

dig some dirt up on someone AND **dig up some dirt on someone**   to find out something bad about someone. (This dirt is gossip.) □ *If you don't stop trying to dig some dirt up on me, I'll get a lawyer and sue you.* □ *The citizens' group dug up some dirt on the mayor and used it against her at election time.*

dirty one's hands   See under *get one's hands dirty.*

dishes, do the   See *do the dishes.*

distance, go the   See *go the distance.*

do a land-office business   to do a large amount of business in a short period of time. (As if selling land during a land rush.) □ *The ice-cream shop always does a land-office business on a hot day.* □ *The tax collector's office did a land-office business on the day that taxes were due.*

doghouse, in the   See *in the doghouse.*

dogs, go to the See *go to the dogs.*

doldrums, in the See *in the doldrums.*

dollar for dollar considering the amount of money involved; considering the cost. (Often seen in advertising.) □ *Dollar for dollar, you cannot buy a better car.* □ *Dollar for dollar, this laundry detergent washes cleaner and brighter than any other product on the market.*

Don't hold your breath. Do not stop breathing (while waiting for something to happen). □ *You think he'll get a job? Ha! Don't hold your breath.* □ *I'll finish building the fence as soon as I have time, but don't hold your breath.*

Don't let someone or something get you down. Do not allow yourself to be overcome by someone or something. □ *Don't let their constant teasing get you down.* □ *Don't let Tom get you down. He's not always unpleasant.*

Don't look a gift horse in the mouth. a proverb meaning that one should not expect perfect gifts. (Usually stated in the negative. Note the variation in the examples. The age of a horse and, therefore, its usefulness can be determined by looking at its teeth. It would be greedy to inspect the teeth of a horse given as a gift to make sure the horse is of the best quality.) □ *Don't complain. You shouldn't look a gift horse in the mouth.* □ *John complained that the television set he got for his birthday was black and white rather than color. He was told, "Don't look a gift horse in the mouth."*

doorstep, at someone's See *at someone's doorstep.*

doorstep, on someone's See *on someone's doorstep.*

dose of one's own medicine the same kind of treatment that one gives to other people. (Often with *get* or *have.*) □ *Sally never is very friendly. Someone is going to give her a dose of her own medicine someday.* □ *He didn't like getting a dose of his own medicine.*

do someone's heart good to make someone feel good emotionally. (Also used literally.) □ *It does my heart good to hear you talk that way.* □ *When she sent me a get-well card, it really did my heart good.*

do something by hand to do something with one's hands rather than with a machine. □ *The computer was broken so I had to do the calculations by hand.* □ *All this tiny stitching was done by hand. Machines cannot do this kind of work.*

do something hands down to do something easily and without opposition. (Without anyone raising a hand in opposition.) □ *The mayor won the election hands down.* □ *She was the choice of the people hands down.*

do the dishes to wash the dishes; to wash and dry the dishes. □ *Bill, you cannot go out and play until you've done the dishes.* □ *Why am I always the one who has to do the dishes?*

do the honors to act as host or hostess and serve one's guests by pouring drinks, slicing meat, making (drinking) toasts, etc. □ *All the guests were seated, and a huge juicy turkey sat on the table. Jane Thomas turned to her husband and said, "Bob, will you do the honors?" Mr. Jones smiled and began slicing thick slices of meat from the turkey.* □ *The mayor stood up and addressed the people who were still eating their salads. "I'm delighted to do the honors this evening and propose a toast to your friend and mine, Bill Jones. Bill, good luck and best wishes in your new job in Washington." And everyone sipped a bit of wine.*

dot, on the See *on the dot.*

down in the dumps sad or depressed. □ *I've been down in the dumps for the past few days.* □ *Try to cheer Jane up. She's down in the dumps for some reason.*

down in the mouth sad-faced; depressed and unsmiling. (Refers to a frown or sagging mouth.) □ *Since her dog died, Barbara has been down in the mouth.* □ *Bob has been down in the mouth since the car wreck.*

down the drain lost forever; wasted. (Also used literally.) □ *I just hate to see all that money go down the drain.* □ *Well, there goes the whole project, right down the drain.*

down to the wire at the very last minute; up to the very last instant. (Refers to a wire that marks the end of a horse race.) □ *I have to turn this in tomorrow, and I'll be working down to the wire.* □ *When we get down to the wire, we'll know better what to do.*

drain, down the See *down the drain.*

draw a blank **1.** to get no response; to find nothing. □ *I asked him about Tom's financial problems, and I just drew a blank.* □ *We looked in the files for an hour, but we drew a blank.* **2.** to fail to remember (something). □ *I tried to remember her telephone number, but I could only draw a blank.* □ *It was a very hard test with just one question to answer, and I drew a blank.*

draw a line between something and something else to separate two things; to distinguish or differentiate between two things. (The *a* can be replaced with *the*. Also used literally.) □ *It's necessary to draw a line between bumping into people and striking them.* □ *It's very hard to draw the line between slamming a door and just closing it loudly.*

draw blood **1.** to hit or bite (a person or an animal) and make a wound that bleeds. □ *The dog chased me and bit me hard, but it didn't draw blood.* □ *The boxer landed just one punch and drew blood immediately.* **2.** to anger or insult a person. □ *Sally screamed out a terrible insult at Tom. Judging by the look on his face, she really drew blood.* □ *Tom started yelling and cursing, trying to insult Sally. He wouldn't be satisfied until he had drawn blood, too.*

dream come true a wish or a dream that has become real. □ *Going to Hawaii is like having a dream come true.* □ *Having you for a friend is a dream come true.*

drink to excess   to drink too much alcohol; to drink alcohol continually. □ *Mr. Franklin drinks to excess.* □ *Some people drink to excess only at parties.*

drive a hard bargain   to work hard to negotiate prices or agreements in one's own favor. □ *I saved $200 by driving a hard bargain when I bought my new car.* □ *All right, sir, you drive a hard bargain. I'll sell you this car for $12,450.* □ *You drive a hard bargain, Jane, but I'll sign the contract.*

drive someone to the wall   See under *force someone to the wall.*

drop in one's tracks   to stop or collapse from exhaustion; to die suddenly. □ *If I keep working this way, I'll drop in my tracks.* □ *Uncle Bob was working in the garden and dropped in his tracks. We are all sorry that he's dead.*

drop of a hat, at the   See *at the drop of a hat.*

drop someone a few lines   See the following entry.

drop someone a line AND **drop someone a few lines**   to write a letter or a note to someone. (The *line* refers to lines of writing.) □ *I dropped Aunt Jane a line last Thanksgiving.* □ *She usually drops me a few lines around the first of the year.*

drop the ball   to make a blunder; to fail in some way. (Also literally, in sports: to drop a ball in error.) □ *Everything was going fine in the election until my campaign manager dropped the ball.* □ *You can't trust John to do the job right. He's always dropping the ball.*

drop the other shoe   to do the deed that completes something; to do the expected remaining part of something. (Refers to the removal of shoes at bedtime. One shoe is dropped, and then the process is completed when the second shoe drops.) □ *Mr. Franklin has left his wife. Soon he'll drop the other shoe and divorce her.* □ *Tommy has just failed three classes in school. We expect him to drop the other shoe and quit altogether any day now.*

drown one's sorrows   See the following entry.

drown one's troubles AND **drown one's sorrows**   to try to forget one's problems by drinking a lot of alcohol. □ *Bill is in the bar, drowning his troubles.* □ *Jane is at home, drowning her sorrows.*

drug on the market   on the market in great abundance; a glut on the market. □ *Right now, small computers are a drug on the market.* □ *Ten years ago, small transistor radios were a drug on the market.*

drum some business up AND **drum up some business**   to stimulate people to buy what you are selling. (As if someone were beating a drum to get the attention of customers.) □ *I need to do something to drum some business up.* □ *A little bit of advertising would drum up some business.*

duck takes to water, as a   See *as a duck takes to water.*

dumps, down in the   See *down in the dumps.*

Dutch, go   See *go Dutch.*

duty, off   See *off duty.*

duty, on   See *on duty.*

E

early bird gets the worm, The. See *The early bird gets the worm.*

Early to bed, early to rise(, makes a man healthy, wealthy, and wise). a proverb that claims that going to bed early and getting up early is good for you. (Sometimes said to explain why a person is going to bed early. The last part of the saying is sometimes left out.) □ *Tom left the party at ten o'clock, saying "Early to bed, early to rise, makes a man healthy, wealthy, and wise." □ I always get up at six o'clock. After all, early to bed, early to rise.*

earn one's keep to help out with chores in return for food and a place to live; to earn one's pay by doing what is expected. □ *I earn my keep at college by shoveling snow in the winter. □ Tom hardly earns his keep around here. He should be fired.*

ears (in something), up to one's See *up to one's ears (in something).*

earth, on See *on earth.*

ear to the ground, have one's See *have one's ear to the ground.*

easy as (apple) pie, as See *as easy as (apple) pie.*

easy as duck soup, as See *as easy as duck soup.*

easy come, easy go said to explain the loss of something that required only a small amount of effort to get in the first place. □

Ann found twenty dollars in the morning and spent it foolishly at noon. "Easy come, easy go," she said. □ *John spends his money as fast as he can earn it. With John it's easy come, easy go.*

Easy does it. Act with care. □ *Be careful with that glass vase. Easy does it!* □ *Now, now, Tom. Don't get angry. Easy does it.*

eat humble pie **1.** to act very humble when one is shown to be wrong. □ *I think I'm right, but if I'm wrong, I'll eat humble pie.* □ *You think you're so smart. I hope you have to eat humble pie.* **2.** to accept insults and humiliation. □ *John, stand up for your rights. You don't have to eat humble pie all the time.* □ *Beth seems quite happy to eat humble pie. She should stand up for her rights.*

eat like a bird to eat only small amounts of food; to peck at one's food. □ *Jane is very slim because she eats like a bird.* □ *Bill is trying to lose weight by eating like a bird.*

eat like a horse to eat large amounts of food. □ *No wonder he's so fat. He eats like a horse.* □ *John works like a horse and eats like a horse, so he never gets fat.*

eat one's cake and have it too See under *have one's cake and eat it too.*

eat one's hat a phrase telling the kind of thing that one would do if a very unlikely event really happens. (Always used with *if.* Never used literally.) □ *If we get there on time, I'll eat my hat.* □ *I'll eat my hat if you get a raise.* □ *He said he'd eat his hat if she got elected.*

eat one's heart out **1.** to be very sad (about someone or something). □ *Bill spent a lot of time eating his heart out after his divorce.* □ *Sally ate her heart out when she had to sell her house.* **2.** to be envious (of someone or something). □ *Do you like my new watch? Well, eat your heart out. It was the last one in the store.* □ *Don't eat your heart out about my new car. Go get one of your own.*

eat one's words to have to take back one's statements; to confess that one's predictions were wrong. □ *You shouldn't say that to me. I'll make you eat your words.* □ *John was wrong about the election and had to eat his words.*

eat out of someone's hands to do what someone else wants; to obey someone eagerly. (Often with *have*; see the examples.) □ *Just wait! I'll have everyone eating out of my hands. They'll do whatever I ask.* □ *The president has Congress eating out of his hands.* □ *A lot of people are eating out of his hands.*

eat someone out of house and home to eat a lot of food (in someone's home); to eat all the food in the house. □ *Billy has a huge appetite. He almost eats us out of house and home.* □ *When the kids come home from college, they always eat us out of house and home.*

egg on one's face, have See *have egg on one's face.*

element, out of one's See *out of one's element.*

eleventh hour, at the See *at the eleventh hour.*

empty-handed, come away See *come away empty-handed.*

empty-handed, go away See *go away empty-handed.*

end in itself for its own sake; toward its own ends; toward no purpose but its own. □ *For Bob, art is an end in itself. He doesn't hope to make any money from it.* □ *Learning is an end in itself. Knowledge does not have to have a practical application.*

end of one's rope, at the See *at the end of one's rope.*

end of one's tether, at the See *at the end of one's tether.*

end of the line See the following entry.

end of the road AND **end of the line** the end; the end of the whole process; death. (*Line* originally referred to railroad tracks.)

□ *Our house is at the end of the road.* □ *We rode the train to the end of the line.* □ *When we reach the end of the road on this project, we'll get paid.* □ *You've come to the end of the line. I'll not lend you another penny.* □ *When I reach the end of the road, I wish to be buried in a quiet place, near some trees.*

ends of the earth, to the See *to the ends of the earth.*

end up with the short end of the stick See under *get the short end of the stick.*

Enough is enough. That is enough, and there should be no more. □ *Stop asking for money! Enough is enough!* □ *I've heard all the complaining from you that I can take. Stop! Enough is enough!*

enter one's mind to come to one's mind; [for an idea or memory] to come into one's consciousness; to be thought of. □ *Leave you behind? The thought never even entered my mind.* □ *A very interesting idea just entered my mind. What if I ran for Congress?*

Every cloud has a silver lining. a proverb meaning that there is something good in every bad thing. □ *Jane was upset when she saw that all her flowers had died from the frost. But when she saw that the weeds had died too, she said, "Every cloud has a silver lining."* □ *Sally had a sore throat and had to stay home from school. When she learned she missed a math test, she said, "Every cloud has a silver lining."*

Every dog has its day. AND **Every dog has his day.** a proverb meaning that everyone will get a chance, even the lowliest. □ *Don't worry, you'll get chosen for the team. Every dog has its day.* □ *You may become famous someday. Every dog has his day.*

every living soul every person. □ *I expect every living soul to be there and be there on time.* □ *This is the kind of problem that affects every living soul.*

every minute counts AND **every moment counts** time is very important. □ *Doctor, please try to get here quickly. Every minute* *counts.* □ *When you take a test, you must work rapidly because every minute counts.* □ *When you're trying to meet a deadline, every moment counts.*

every (other) breath, with See *with every (other) breath.*

everything but the kitchen sink almost everything one can think of. □ *When Sally went off to college, she took everything but the kitchen sink.* □ *John orders everything but the kitchen sink when he goes out to dinner, especially if someone else is paying for it.*

everything from A to Z See the following entry.

everything from soup to nuts AND **everything from A to Z** almost everything one can think of. (The main entry is used especially when describing the many things served at a meal.) □ *For dinner we had everything from soup to nuts.* □ *In college I studied everything from soup to nuts.* □ *She mentioned everything from A to Z.*

expecting (a child) pregnant. (A euphemism.) □ *Tommy's mother is expecting a child.* □ *Oh, I didn't know she was expecting.*

eye for an eye, a tooth for a tooth, An. See *An eye for an eye, a tooth for a tooth.*

eye out (for someone or something), have an See *have an eye out (for someone or something).*

eyes bigger than one's stomach, have See *have eyes bigger than one's stomach.*

eyes in the back of one's head, have See *have eyes in the back of one's head.*

F

face the music to receive punishment; to accept the unpleasant results of one's actions. □ *Mary broke a dining-room window and had to face the music when her father got home.* □ *After failing a math test, Tom had to go home and face the music.*

fair-weather friend someone who is your friend only when things are going well for you. (This person will desert you when things go badly for you.) □ *Bill wouldn't help me with my homework. He's just a fair-weather friend.* □ *A fair-weather friend isn't much help in an emergency.*

fall down on the job to fail to do something properly; to fail to do one's job adequately. (Also used literally.) □ *The team kept losing because the coach was falling down on the job.* □ *Tom was fired because he fell down on the job.*

fall flat (on one's face) AND **fall flat (on its face)** to be completely unsuccessful. □ *I fell flat on my face when I tried to give my speech.* □ *The play fell flat on its face.* □ *My jokes fall flat most of the time.*

fall in(to) place to fit together; to become organized. □ *After we heard the whole story, things began to fall in place.* □ *When you get older, the different parts of your life begin to fall into place.*

fall short (of something) **1.** to lack something; to lack enough of something. □ *We fell short of money at the end of the month.* □ *When baking a cake, the cook fell short of eggs and had to go to the store for more.* **2.** to fail to achieve a goal. □ *We fell short of* *our goal of collecting a thousand dollars.* □ *Ann ran a fast race, but fell short of the record.*

Familiarity breeds contempt.   a proverb meaning that knowing a person closely for a long time leads to bad feelings. □ *Bill and his brothers are always fighting. As they say: "Familiarity breeds contempt."* □ *Mary and John were good friends for many years. Finally they got into a big argument and became enemies. That just shows that familiarity breeds contempt.*

familiar ring, have a   See *have a familiar ring.*

fan of someone, be a   See *be a fan of someone.*

far as it goes, as   See *as far as it goes.*

farm someone or something out AND **farm out someone or something**   **1.** [with *someone*] to send someone (somewhere) for care or development. □ *When my mother died, they farmed me out to my aunt and uncle.* □ *The team manager farmed out the baseball player to the minor leagues until he improved.* **2.** [with *something*] to send something (elsewhere) to be dealt with. □ *I farmed out various parts of the work to different people.* □ *Bill farmed his chores out to his brothers and sisters and went to a movie.*

fat is in the fire, The.   See *The fat is in the fire.*

fear of something, for   See *for fear of something.*

feast one's eyes (on someone or something)   to look at someone or something with pleasure, envy, or admiration. (As if such visions provided a feast of visual delight for one's eyes.) □ *Just feast your eyes on that beautiful juicy steak!* □ *Yes, feast your eyes. You won't see one like that again for a long time.*

feather in one's cap   an honor; a reward for something. □ *Getting a new client was really a feather in my cap.* □ *John earned a feather in his cap by getting an A in physics.*

feather one's (own) nest **1.** to decorate and furnish one's home in style and comfort. (Birds line their nests with feathers to make them warm and comfortable.) □ *Mr. and Mrs. Simpson have feathered their nest quite comfortably.* □ *It costs a great deal of money to feather one's nest these days.* **2.** to use power and prestige to provide for oneself selfishly. (Said especially of politicians who use their offices to make money for themselves.) □ *The mayor seemed to be helping people, but she was really feathering her own nest.* □ *The building contractor used a lot of public money to feather his nest.*

feed the kitty to contribute money. (The *kitty* is a name for a container into which money is put.) □ *Please feed the kitty. Make a contribution to help sick children.* □ *Come on, Bill. Feed the kitty. You can afford a dollar for a good cause.*

feel like a million (dollars) to feel well and healthy, both physically and mentally. (To feel like something unbelievably good.) □ *A quick swim in the morning makes me feel like a million dollars.* □ *What a beautiful day! It makes you feel like a million.*

feel like a new person to feel refreshed and renewed, especially after getting well or getting dressed up. □ *I bought a new suit, and now I feel like a new person.* □ *Bob felt like a new person when he got out of the hospital.*

feel out of place to feel that one does not belong in a place. □ *I feel out of place at formal dances.* □ *Bob and Ann felt out of place at the picnic, so they went home.*

feel something in one's bones AND **know something in one's bones** to sense something; to have an intuition about something. □ *The train will be late. I feel it in my bones.* □ *I failed the test. I know it in my bones.*

feet of clay, have See *have feet of clay.*

feet, on one's See *on one's feet.*

fell swoop, at one See *at one fell swoop.*

fell swoop, in one   See *in one fell swoop.*

fight someone or something hammer and tongs AND **fight someone or something tooth and nail; go at it hammer and tongs; go at it tooth and nail**   to fight against someone or something energetically and with great determination. (These phrases are old and refer to fighting with and without weapons.) □ *They fought against the robber tooth and nail.* □ *The dogs were fighting each other hammer and tongs.* □ *The mayor fought the new law hammer and tongs.* □ *We'll fight this zoning ordinance tooth and nail.*

fight someone or something tooth and nail   See the previous entry.

fill someone's shoes   to take the place of some other person and do that person's work satisfactorily. (As if you were wearing the other person's shoes, that is, filling the shoes with your feet.) □ *I don't know how we'll be able to do without you. No one can fill your shoes.* □ *It'll be difficult to fill Jane's shoes. She did her job very well.*

fill the bill   to be exactly the thing that is needed. □ *Ah, this steak is great. It really fills the bill.* □ *This new pair of shoes fills the bill nicely.*

Finders keepers(, losers weepers).   a phrase said when something is found. (A proverb meaning that the person who finds something gets to keep it. The person who loses it can only weep.) □ *John lost a quarter in the dining room yesterday. Ann found the quarter there today. Ann claimed that since she found it, it was hers. She said, "Finders keepers, losers weepers."* □ *John said, "I'll say finders keepers when I find something of yours!"*

find it in one's heart (to do something)   to have the courage or compassion to do something. □ *She couldn't find it in her heart to refuse to come home to him.* □ *I can't do it! I can't find it in my heart.*

find one's or something's way somewhere   **1.** [with *one's*] to discover the route to a place. □ *Mr. Smith found his way to the museum.* □ *Can you find your way home?* **2.** [with *something's*] to end up in a place. (This expression avoids accusing someone of moving the thing to the place.) □ *The money found its way into the mayor's pocket.* □ *The secret plans found their way into the enemy's hands.*

fine feather, in   See *in fine feather.*

fine kettle of fish   a real mess; an unsatisfactory situation. (Not meaningful literally.) □ *The dog has eaten the steak we were going to have for dinner. This is a fine kettle of fish!* □ *This is a fine kettle of fish. It's below freezing outside, and the furnace won't work.*

fine-tooth comb, go over something with a   See *go over something with a fine-tooth comb.*

finger in the pie, have one's   See *have one's finger in the pie.*

fingertips, have something at one's   See *have something at one's fingertips.*

fire, under   See *under fire.*

first and foremost   first and most important. (A cliché.) □ *First and foremost, I think you should work harder on your biology.* □ *Have this in mind first and foremost: Keep smiling!*

First come, first served.   The first people to arrive will be served first. (A cliché.) □ *They ran out of tickets before we got there. It was first come, first served, but we didn't know that.* □ *Please line up and take your turn. It's first come, first served.*

first of all   the very first thing; before anything else. (Similar expressions, "second of all" or "third of all," are said, but do not make a lot of sense.) □ *First of all, put your name on this piece of paper.* □ *First of all, we'll try to find a place to live.*

first thing (in the morning) before anything else in the morning. □ *Please call me first thing in the morning. I can't help you now.* □ *I'll do that first thing.*

first things first the most important things must be taken care of first. □ *It's more important to get a job than to buy new clothes. First things first!* □ *Do your homework now. Go out and play later. First things first.*

first water, of the See *of the first water.*

fish for a compliment to try to get someone to pay you a compliment. (As if one were tempting someone to utter a compliment.) □ *When she showed me her new dress, I could tell that she was fishing for a compliment.* □ *Tom was certainly fishing for a compliment when he modeled his fancy haircut for his friends.*

fishing expedition, go on a See *go on a fishing expedition.*

fish or cut bait either do the job you are supposed to be doing or quit and let someone else do it. (Attend to the job of fishing or move aside and prepare the bait for others more active in the task of fishing to use.) □ *Mary is doing much better on the job since her manager told her to fish or cut bait.* □ *The boss told Tom, "Quit wasting time! Fish or cut bait!"*

fish out of water, like a See *like a fish out of water.*

fish to fry, have other See *have other fish to fry.*

fit as a fiddle, as See *as fit as a fiddle.*

fit for a king totally suitable; suitable for royalty. (A cliché.) □ *What a delicious meal. It was fit for a king.* □ *Our room at the hotel was fit for a king.*

fit like a glove to fit very well; to fit tightly or snugly. □ *My new shoes fit like a glove.* □ *My new coat is a little tight. It fits like a glove.*

fit someone to a T   See under *suit someone to a T.*

fix someone's wagon   to punish someone; to get even with someone; to plot against someone. □ *If you ever do that again, I'll fix your wagon!* □ *Tommy! You clean up your room this instant, or I'll fix your wagon!* □ *He reported me to the boss, but I fixed his wagon. I knocked his lunch on the floor.*

flames, go up in   See *go up in flames.*

flash, in a   See *in a flash.*

flash in the pan   someone or something that draws a lot of attention for a very brief time. □ *I'm afraid that my success as a painter was just a flash in the pan.* □ *Tom had hoped to be a singer, but his career was only a flash in the pan.*

flat as a pancake, as   See *as flat as a pancake.*

flat broke   completely broke; with no money at all. □ *I spent my last dollar, and I'm flat broke.* □ *The bank closed its doors to the public. It was flat broke!*

flesh and blood   **1.** a living human body, especially with reference to its natural limitations; a human being. □ *This cold weather is more than flesh and blood can stand.* □ *Carrying 300 pounds is beyond mere flesh and blood.* **2.** the quality of being alive. □ *The paintings of this artist are lifeless. They lack flesh and blood.* □ *These ideas have no flesh and blood.* **3.** one's own relatives; one's own kin. □ *That's no way to treat one's own flesh and blood.* □ *I want to leave my money to my own flesh and blood.* □ *Grandmother was happier living with her flesh and blood.*

flesh, in the   See *in the flesh.*

float a loan   to get a loan; to arrange for a loan. □ *I couldn't afford to pay cash for the car, so I floated a loan.* □ *They needed money, so they had to float a loan.*

flying colors, with   See *with flying colors.*

fly in the face of someone or something AND **fly in the teeth of someone or something**   to disregard, defy, or show disrespect for someone or something. □ *John loves to fly in the face of tradition.* □ *Ann made it a practice to fly in the face of standard procedures.* □ *John finds great pleasure in flying in the teeth of his father.*

fly in the ointment   a small, unpleasant matter that spoils something; a drawback. □ *We enjoyed the play, but the fly in the ointment was not being able to find our car afterward.* □ *It sounds like a good idea, but there must be a fly in the ointment somewhere.*

fly in the teeth of someone or something   See under *fly in the face of someone or something.*

fly off the handle   to lose one's temper. □ *Every time anyone mentions taxes, Mrs. Brown flies off the handle.* □ *If she keeps flying off the handle like that, she'll have a heart attack.*

foam at the mouth   to be very angry. (Related to a "mad dog"—a dog with rabies—that foams at the mouth.) □ *Bob was raving— foaming at the mouth. I've never seen anyone so angry.* □ *Bill foamed at the mouth in anger.*

follow one's heart   to act according to one's feelings; to obey one's sympathetic or compassionate inclinations. □ *I couldn't decide what to do, so I just followed my heart.* □ *I trust that you will follow your heart in this matter.*

food for thought   something to think about. □ *I don't like your idea very much, but it's food for thought.* □ *Your lecture was very good. It contained much food for thought.*

fool and his money are soon parted, A.   See *A fool and his money are soon parted.*

foot-in-mouth disease, have   See *have foot-in-mouth disease.*

foot the bill to pay the bill; to pay (for something). □ *Let's go out and eat. I'll foot the bill.* □ *If the bank goes broke, don't worry. The government will foot the bill.*

force someone's hand to force a person to reveal plans, strategies, or secrets. (Refers to a handful of cards in card playing.) □ *We didn't know what she was doing until Tom forced her hand.* □ *We couldn't plan our game until we forced the other team's hand in the last play.*

force someone to the wall AND **drive someone to the wall** to push someone to an extreme position; to put someone into an awkward position. □ *He wouldn't tell the truth until we forced him to the wall.* □ *They don't pay their bills until you drive them to the wall.*

for fear of something out of fear for something; because of fear of something. □ *He doesn't drive for fear of an accident.* □ *They lock their doors for fear of being robbed.*

forgive and forget to forgive someone (for something) and forget that it ever happened. (A cliché.) □ *I'm sorry, John. Let's forgive and forget. What do you say?* □ *It was nothing. We'll just have to forgive and forget.*

fork money out (for something) AND **fork out money (for something)** to pay (perhaps unwillingly) for something. (Often mention is made about the amount of money. See the examples.) □ *I like that stereo, but I don't want to fork out a lot of money.* □ *Do you think I'm going to fork twenty dollars out for that book?* □ *I hate having to fork out money day after day.* □ *Forking money out to everyone is part of life in a busy economy.*

form an opinion to think up or decide on an opinion. (Note the variations in the examples.) □ *I don't know enough about the issue to form an opinion.* □ *Don't tell me how to think! I can form my own opinion.* □ *I don't form opinions without careful consideration.*

for the devil of it AND **for the heck of it; for the hell of it**   just for fun; because it is slightly evil; for no good reason. (Some people may object to the word *hell*.) □ *We filled their garage with leaves just for the devil of it.* □ *Tom tripped Bill for the heck of it.* □ *John picked a fight with Tom just for the hell of it.*

for the heck of it   See the previous entry.

for the odds to be against one   for things to be against one generally; for one's chances to be slim. □ *You can give it a try, but the odds are against you.* □ *I know the odds are against me, but I wish to run in the race anyway.*

for the record   so that (one's own version of) the facts will be known; so there will be a record of a particular fact. (This often is said when there are reporters present.) □ *I'd like to say—for the record—that at no time have I ever accepted a bribe from anyone.* □ *For the record, I've never been able to get anything done around city hall without bribing someone.*

foul play   illegal activity; bad practices. □ *The police investigating the death suspect foul play.* □ *Each student got an A on the test, and the teacher imagined it was the result of foul play.*

free and easy   casual. □ *John is so free and easy. How can anyone be so relaxed?* □ *Now, take it easy. Just act free and easy. No one will know you're nervous.*

free as a bird, as   See *as free as a bird.*

free-for-all   a disorganized fight or contest involving everyone; a brawl. □ *The picnic turned into a free-for-all after midnight.* □ *The race started out in an organized manner, but ended up being a free-for-all.*

friend in need is a friend indeed, A.   See *A friend in need is a friend indeed.*

from hand to hand   from one person to a series of other persons; passed from one hand to another. □ *The book traveled from* *hand to hand until it got back to its owner.* □ *By the time the baby had been passed from hand to hand, it was crying.*

from pillar to post   from one place to a series of other places; (figuratively) from person to person, as with gossip. (A cliché.) □ *My father was in the army, and we moved from pillar to post year after year.* □ *After I told one person my secret, it went quickly from pillar to post.*

from rags to riches   from poverty to wealth; from modesty to elegance. □ *The princess used to be quite poor. She certainly moved from rags to riches.* □ *After I inherited the money, I went from rags to riches.*

from start to finish   from the beginning to the end; throughout. □ *I disliked the whole business from start to finish.* □ *Mary caused problems from start to finish.*

from stem to stern   from one end to another. (Refers to the front and back ends of a ship. Also used literally in reference to ships.) □ *Now, I have to clean the house from stem to stern.* □ *I polished my car carefully from stem to stern.*

from the bottom of one's heart   sincerely. □ *When I returned the lost kitten to Mrs. Brown, she thanked me from the bottom of her heart.* □ *Oh, thank you! I'm grateful from the bottom of my heart.*

from the ground up   from the beginning; from start to finish. (Used literally in reference to building a house or other building.) □ *We must plan our sales campaign carefully from the ground up.* □ *Sorry, but you'll have to start all over again from the ground up.*

from the word go   from the beginning; from the very start of things. (Actually from the uttering of the word *go*.) □ *I knew about the problem from the word go.* □ *She was failing the class from the word go.*

from top to bottom from the highest point to the lowest point; throughout. □ *I have to clean the house from top to bottom.* □ *We need to replace our elected officials from top to bottom.*

frying pan into the fire, out of the See *out of the frying pan into the fire.*

full as a tick, as See *as full as a tick.*

full swing, in See *in full swing.*

fun and games playing around; doing worthless things; activities that are a waste of time. □ *All right, Bill, the fun and games are over. It's time to get down to work.* □ *This isn't a serious course. It's nothing but fun and games.*

funny as a crutch, as See *as funny as a crutch.*

further ado, without See *without further ado.*

G

gas, out of See *out of gas.*

get a black eye (Also with *have*. Note: *Get* can be replaced with *have*. Note variations in the examples. *Get* usually means to become, to acquire, or to cause. *Have* usually means to possess, to be, or to have resulted in.) **1.** to get a bruise near the eye from being struck. □ *I got a black eye from walking into a door.* □ *I have a black eye where John hit me.* **2.** to have one's character or reputation harmed. □ *Mary got a black eye because of her complaining.* □ *The whole group now has a black eye.* ALSO: **give someone a black eye 1.** to hit someone near the eye so that a dark bruise appears. □ *John became angry and gave me a black eye.* **2.** to harm the character or reputation of someone. □ *The constant complaining gave the whole group a black eye.*

get a clean bill of health [for someone] to be pronounced healthy by a physician. (Also with *have*. See the note at **get a black eye.**) □ *Sally got a clean bill of health from the doctor.* □ *Now that Sally has a clean bill of health, she can go back to work.* ALSO: **give someone a clean bill of health** [for a doctor] to pronounce someone well and healthy. □ *The doctor gave Sally a clean bill of health.*

get (all) dolled up to dress (oneself) up. (Usually used for females, but not necessarily.) □ *I have to get all dolled up for the dance tonight.* □ *I just love to get dolled up in my best clothes.*

get a load off one's feet AND **take a load off one's feet** to sit down; to enjoy the results of sitting down. □ *Come in, John. Sit* *down and take a load off your feet.* □ *Yes, I need to get a load off my feet. I'm really tired.*

get a load off one's mind to say what one is thinking. □ *He sure talked a long time. I guess he had to get a load off his mind.* □ *You aren't going to like what I'm going to say, but I have to get a load off my mind.*

get along (on a shoestring) to be able to afford to live on very little money. □ *For the last two years, we have had to get along on a shoestring.* □ *With so little money, it's hard to get along.*

get a lump in one's throat to have the feeling of something in one's throat—as if one were going to cry. (Also with *have*. See the note at *get a black eye*.) □ *Whenever they play the national anthem, I get a lump in my throat.* □ *I have a lump in my throat because I'm frightened.*

get a word in edgewise AND **get a word in edgeways** to manage to say something when other people are talking and ignoring you. (Often in the negative. As if one were trying to fit in or squeeze in one's contribution to a conversation.) □ *It was such an exciting conversation that I could hardly get a word in edgewise.* □ *Mary always talks so fast that nobody can get a word in edgeways.*

get cold feet to become timid or frightened; to have one's feet seem to freeze with fear. (Also with *have*. See the note at *get a black eye*.) □ *I usually get cold feet when I have to speak in public.* □ *John got cold feet and wouldn't run in the race.* □ *I can't give my speech now. I have cold feet.*

get down to brass tacks to begin to talk about important things. □ *Let's get down to brass tacks. We've wasted too much time chatting.* □ *Don't you think that it's about time to get down to brass tacks?*

get down to business AND **get down to work** to begin to get serious; to begin to negotiate or conduct business. □ *All right, everyone. Let's get down to business. There has been enough* *playing around.* □ *When the president and vice president arrive, we can get down to business.* □ *They're here. Let's get down to work.*

get down to work   See the previous entry.

get fresh (with someone)   to become overly bold or impertinent. □ *When I tried to kiss Mary, she slapped me and shouted, "Don't get fresh with me!"* □ *I can't stand people who get fresh.*

get goose bumps AND **get goose pimples**   [for someone's skin] to feel prickly or become bumpy due to fear or excitement. (Also with *have.* See the note at *get a black eye.* For one's flesh to become like the flesh of a plucked goose. Very few Americans have ever seen a plucked goose.) □ *When he sings, I get goose bumps.* □ *I never get goose pimples.* □ *That really scared her. Now she's got goose pimples.*

get goose pimples   See the previous entry.

get in someone's hair   to bother or irritate someone. (Not usually literal.) □ *Billy is always getting in his mother's hair.* □ *I wish you'd stop getting in my hair.*

get into the swing of things   to join into the routine or the activities. (Refers to the rhythm of routinized activity.) □ *Come on, Bill. Try to get into the swing of things.* □ *John just couldn't seem to get into the swing of things.*

get off scot-free   See under *go scot-free.*

get one's ducks in a row   to put one's affairs in order; to get things ready. (Informal or slang. As if one were lining up wooden ducks to shoot them one by one, as in a carnival game.) □ *You can't hope to go into a company and sell something until you get your ducks in a row.* □ *As soon as you people get your ducks in a row, we'll leave.*

get one's feet on the ground   to get firmly established or reestablished. (Also with *have.* See the note at *get a black eye.*) □

He's new at the job, but soon he'll get his feet on the ground. □ *Her productivity will improve after she gets her feet on the ground again.* □ *Don't worry about Sally. She has her feet on the ground.* ALSO: **keep one's feet on the ground** to remain firmly established. □ *Sally will have no trouble keeping her feet on the ground.*

get one's feet wet to begin something; to have one's first experience of something. (As if one were wading into water.) □ *Of course he can't do the job right. He's hardly got his feet wet yet.* □ *I'm looking forward to learning to drive. I can't wait to get behind the steering wheel and get my feet wet.*

get one's fill of someone or something to receive enough of someone or something. (Also with *have*. See the note at *get a black eye*.) □ *You'll soon get your fill of Tom. He can be quite a pest.* □ *I can never get my fill of shrimp. I love it.* □ *Three weeks of visiting grandchildren is enough. I've had my fill of them.*

get one's fingers burned to have a bad experience. (Also used literally.) □ *I tried that once before and got my fingers burned. I won't try it again.* □ *If you go swimming and get your fingers burned, you won't want to swim again.*

get one's foot in the door to achieve a favorable position (for further action); to take the first step in a process. (People selling things from door to door used to block the door with a foot, so it could not be closed on them. Also with *have*. See the note at *get a black eye*.) □ *I think I could get the job if I could only get my foot in the door.* □ *It pays to get your foot in the door. Try to get an appointment with the boss.* □ *I have a better chance now that I have my foot in the door.*

get one's hands dirty AND **dirty one's hands; soil one's hands** to become involved with something illegal; to do a shameful thing; to do something that is beneath one. □ *The mayor would never get his hands dirty by giving away political favors.* □ *I will not dirty my hands by breaking the law.* □ *Sally felt that to talk to the hobo was to soil her hands.*

get one's head above water   to get ahead of one's problems; to catch up with one's work or responsibilities. (Also used literally. Also with *have*. See the note at *get a black eye*.) □ *I can't seem to get my head above water. Work just keeps piling up.* □ *I'll be glad when I have my head above water.* ALSO: **keep one's head above water**   to stay ahead of one's responsibilities. □ *Now that I have more space to work in, I can easily keep my head above water.*

get one's just deserts   to get what one deserves. □ *I feel better now that Jane got her just deserts. She really insulted me.* □ *Bill got back exactly the treatment that he gave out. He got his just deserts.*

get one's second wind   (Also with *have*. See the note at *get a black eye*.) **1.** [for someone] to achieve stability in breathing after brief exertion. □ *John was having a hard time running until he got his second wind.* □ *Bill had to quit the race because he never got his second wind.* □ *"At last," thought Ann, "I have my second wind. Now I can really swim fast."* **2.** to become more active or productive (after starting off slowly). □ *I usually get my second wind early in the afternoon.* □ *Mary is a better worker now that she has her second wind.*

get one's teeth into something   to start on something seriously, especially a difficult task. (Also used literally in reference to eating.) □ *Come on, Bill. You have to get your teeth into your biology.* □ *I can't wait to get my teeth into this problem.*

get on someone's nerves   to irritate someone. □ *Please stop whistling. It's getting on my nerves.* □ *All this arguing is getting on their nerves.*

get on the bandwagon AND **jump on the bandwagon**   to join the popular side (of an issue); to take a popular position. □ *You really should get on the bandwagon. Everyone else is.* □ *Jane has always had her own ideas about things. She's not the kind of person to jump on the bandwagon.*

get out of the wrong side of the bed   See under *get up on the wrong side of the bed.*

get second thoughts about someone or something   to have doubts about someone or something. (Also with *have.* See the note at *get a black eye.*) □ *I'm beginning to get second thoughts about Tom.* □ *Tom is getting second thoughts about it, too.* □ *We now have second thoughts about going to Canada.*

get (someone) off the hook   to free someone from an obligation; to help someone out of an awkward situation. □ *Thanks for getting me off the hook. I didn't want to attend that meeting.* □ *I couldn't get off the hook by myself.*

get someone over a barrel AND **get someone under one's thumb**   to put someone at one's mercy; to get control over someone. (Also with *have.* See the note at *get a black eye.*) □ *He got me over a barrel, and I had to do what he said.* □ *Ann will do exactly what I say. I've got her over a barrel.* □ *All right, John. You've got me under your thumb. What do you want me to do?*

get someone's back up   See the following entry.

get someone's dander up AND **get someone's back up; get someone's hackles up; get someone's Irish up**   to make someone get angry. (Also with *have.* See the note at *get a black eye.*) □ *Now, don't get your dander up. Calm down.* □ *Bob had his Irish up all day yesterday. I don't know what was wrong.* □ *She really got her back up when I asked her for money.* □ *Now, now, don't get your hackles up. I didn't mean any harm.*

get someone's ear   to get someone to listen (to you); to have someone's attention. (Also with *have.* See the note at *get a black eye.* Not literal.) □ *He got my ear and talked for an hour.* □ *While I have your ear, I'd like to tell you about something I'm selling.*

get someone's eye   See under *catch someone's eye.*

get someone's hackles up   See under *get someone's dander up.*

get someone's Irish up   See under *get someone's dander up.*

get someone under one's thumb   See under *get someone over a barrel.*

get something into someone's thick head   See under *get something through someone's thick skull.*

get something off one's chest   to tell something that has been bothering you. (Also with *have.* See the note at *get a black eye.*) □ *I have to get this off my chest. I broke your window with a stone.* □ *I knew I'd feel better when I had that off my chest.*

get something off (the ground)   to get something started. □ *I can relax after I get this project off the ground.* □ *You'll have a lot of free time when you get the project off.*

get something sewed up   (Also with *have.* See the note at *get a black eye.*) **1.** to have something stitched together (by someone). (Literal.) □ *I want to get this tear sewed up now.* □ *I'll have this hole sewed up tomorrow.* **2.** AND **get something wrapped up**   to have something settled or finished. (Also with *have.*) □ *I'll take the contract to the mayor tomorrow morning. I'll get the whole deal sewed up by noon.* □ *Don't worry about the car loan. I'll have it sewed up in time to make the purchase.* □ *I'll get the loan wrapped up, and you'll have the car this week.*

get something straight   to understand something clearly. (Also with *have.* See the note at *get a black eye.*) □ *Now get this straight. You're going to fail history.* □ *Let me get this straight. I'm supposed to go there in the morning?* □ *Let me make sure I have this straight.*

get something through someone's thick skull AND **get something into someone's thick head**   to make someone understand something; to get some information into someone's head. □ *He can't seem to get it through his thick skull.* □ *If I could get this into my thick head once, I'd remember it.*

get something under one's belt (Also with *have*. See the note at *get a black eye*.) **1.** to eat or drink something. (This means the food goes into one's stomach and is under one's belt.) □ *I'd feel a lot better if I had a cool drink under my belt.* □ *Come in out of the cold and get a nice warm meal under your belt.* **2.** to learn something well; to assimilate some information. (Not literal. The knowledge is in one's mind and nowhere near the belt.) □ *I have to study tonight. I have to get a lot of algebra under my belt.* □ *Now that I have my lessons under my belt, I can rest easy.*

get something under way to get something started. (Also with *have*. See the note at *get a black eye*. Originally nautical.) □ *The time has come to get this meeting under way.* □ *Now that the president has the meeting under way, I can relax.*

get something wrapped up See under *get something sewed up*.

get stars in one's eyes to be obsessed with show business; to be stagestruck. (Also with *have*. See the note at *get a black eye*. Refers to stardom, as in the stars of Hollywood or New York.) □ *Many young people get stars in their eyes at this age.* □ *Ann has stars in her eyes. She wants to go to Hollywood.*

get the benefit of the doubt to receive a judgment in your favor when the evidence is neither for you nor against you. (Also with *have*. See the note at *get a black eye*.) □ *I was right between a B and an A. I got the benefit of the doubt—an A.* □ *I thought I should have had the benefit of the doubt, but the judge made me pay a fine.* ALSO: **give someone the benefit of the doubt** □ *I'm glad the teacher gave me the benefit of the doubt.* □ *Please, judge. Give me the benefit of the doubt.*

get the blues to become sad or depressed; to become melancholy. (Also with *have*. See the note at *get a black eye*.) □ *You'll have to excuse Bill. He has the blues tonight.* □ *I get the blues every time I hear that song.*

get the final word See under *get the last word*.

get the hang of something to learn how to do something; to learn how something works. (Also with *have*. See the note at *get a black eye*.) □ *As soon as I get the hang of this computer, I'll be able to work faster.* □ *Now that I have the hang of starting the car in cold weather, I won't have to get up so early.*

get the inside track to get the advantage (over someone) because of special connections, special knowledge, or favoritism. (Also with *have*. See the note at *get a black eye*.) □ *If I could get the inside track, I could win the contract.* □ *The boss likes me. Since I have the inside track, I'll probably be the new office manager.*

get the jump on someone to do something before someone; to get ahead of someone. (Also with *have*. See the note at *get a black eye*.) □ *I got the jump on Tom and got a place in line ahead of him.* □ *We'll have to work hard to get the contract, because they have the jump on us.*

get the last laugh to laugh at or ridicule someone who has laughed at or ridiculed you; to put someone in the same bad position that you were once in. (Also with *have*. See the note at *get a black eye*.) □ *John laughed when I got a D on the final exam. I got the last laugh, though. He failed the course.* □ *Mr. Smith said I was foolish when I bought an old building. I had the last laugh when I sold it a month later for twice what I paid for it.*

get the last word AND **get the final word** to get to make the final point (in an argument); to get to make the final decision (in some matter). (Also with *have*. See the note at *get a black eye*.) □ *The boss gets the last word in hiring.* □ *Why do you always have to have the final word in an argument?*

get the message See under *get the word.*

get the nod to get chosen. (Also with *have*. See the note at *get a black eye*.) □ *The boss is going to pick the new sales manager. I think Ann will get the nod.* □ *I had the nod for captain of the team, but I decided not to do it.*

get the red-carpet treatment to receive very special treatment; to receive royal treatment. (This refers—sometimes literally—to the rolling out of a clean red carpet for someone to walk on.) □ *I love to go to fancy stores where I get the red-carpet treatment.* □ *The queen expects to get the red-carpet treatment wherever she goes.* ALSO: **give someone the red-carpet treatment** to give someone very special treatment; to give someone royal treatment. □ *We always give the queen the red-carpet treatment when she comes to visit.* ALSO: **roll out the red carpet for someone** to provide special treatment for someone. □ *There's no need to roll out the red carpet for me.* □ *We rolled out the red carpet for the king and queen.*

get the runaround to receive a series of excuses, delays, and referrals. □ *You'll get the runaround if you ask to see the manager.* □ *I hate it when I get the runaround.* ALSO: **give someone the runaround** to give someone a series of excuses, delays, and referrals. □ *If you ask to see the manager, they'll give you the runaround.*

get the shock of one's life to receive a serious (emotional) shock. (Also with *have*. See the note at *get a black eye.*) □ *I opened the telegram and got the shock of my life.* □ *I had the shock of my life when I won $5,000.*

get the short end of the stick AND **end up with the short end of the stick** to end up with less (than someone else); to end up cheated or deceived. (Also with *have*. See the note at *get a black eye.*) □ *Why do I always get the short end of the stick? I want my fair share!* □ *She's unhappy because she has the short end of the stick again.* □ *I hate to end up with the short end of the stick.*

get the upper hand (on someone) to get into a position superior to someone; to get the advantage of someone. (Also with *have*. See the note at *get a black eye.*) □ *John is always trying to get the upper hand on someone.* □ *He never ends up having the upper hand, though.*

get the word AND **get the message** to receive an explanation; to receive the final and authoritative explanation. (Also with *have.* See the note at *get a black eye.*) □ *I'm sorry, I didn't get the word. I didn't know the matter had been settled.* □ *Now that I have the message, I can be more effective in answering the customers' questions.*

get time to catch one's breath to find enough time to relax or behave normally. (Also with *have.* See the note at *get a black eye.*) □ *When things slow down around here, I'll get time to catch my breath.* □ *Sally was so busy she didn't even have time to catch her breath.*

get to first base (with someone or something) AND **reach first base (with someone or something)** to make a major advance with someone or something. (*First base* refers to baseball.) □ *I wish I could get to first base with this business deal.* □ *John adores Sally, but he can't even reach first base with her. She won't even speak to him.* □ *He smiles and acts friendly, but he can't get to first base.*

get to one's feet to stand up. □ *On a signal from the director, the singers got to their feet.* □ *I was so weak, I could hardly get to my feet.*

get to the bottom of something to get an understanding of the causes of something. □ *We must get to the bottom of this problem immediately.* □ *There is clearly something wrong here, and I want to get to the bottom of it.*

get to the heart of the matter to get to the essentials of a matter. □ *We have to stop wasting time and get to the heart of the matter.* □ *You've been very helpful. You really seem to be able to get to the heart of the matter.*

get to the point See under *come to the point.*

get two strikes against one to get several things against one; to be in a position where success is unlikely. (From baseball, where one is "out" after three strikes. Also with *have.* See the note at *get a black eye.*) □ *Poor Bob got two strikes against him when* *he tried to explain where he was last night.* □ *I can't win. I've got two strikes against me before I start.*

get under someone's skin to bother or irritate someone. (Refers to an irritant such as an insect or chemical that penetrates the skin.) □ *John is so annoying. He really gets under my skin.* □ *I know he's bothersome, but don't let him get under your skin.* □ *This kind of problem gets under my skin.*

get up enough nerve (to do something) to get brave enough to do something. □ *I could never get up enough nerve to sing in public.* □ *I'd do it if I could get up enough nerve, but I'm shy.*

get up on the wrong side of the bed AND **get out of the wrong side of the bed** to get up in the morning in a bad mood. (As if the choice of the side of the bed makes a difference in one's humor.) □ *What's wrong with you? Did you get up on the wrong side of the bed today?* □ *Excuse me for being grouchy. I got out of the wrong side of the bed.*

get wind of something to hear about something; to receive information about something. (The *wind* may be someone's breath or words, but more likely it refers to catching the scent of something in the wind long in advance of its appearance.) □ *I just got wind of your marriage. Congratulations.* □ *Wait until the boss gets wind of this. Somebody is going to get in trouble.*

get worked up about something See the following entry.

get worked up (over something) AND **get worked up about something** to get excited or emotionally distressed about something. □ *Please don't get worked up over this matter.* □ *They get worked up about these things very easily.* □ *I try not to get worked up.*

gild the lily to add ornament or decoration to something that is pleasing in its original state; to attempt to improve something that is already fine the way it is. (Often refers to flattery or exaggeration. The lily is considered beautiful enough as it is. Gilding it—covering it with gold—is overdoing it.) □ *Your house has* *lovely brickwork. Don't paint it. That would be gilding the lily.* □ *Oh, Sally. You're beautiful the way you are. You don't need makeup. You would be gilding the lily.*

gird (up) one's loins to get ready; to prepare oneself (for something). (A cliché. Means essentially to dress oneself in preparation for something. From biblical references.) □ *Well, I guess I had better gird up my loins and go to work.* □ *Somebody has to do something about the problem. Why don't you gird your loins and do something?*

give a good account of oneself to do (something) well or thoroughly. □ *John gave a good account of himself when he gave his speech last night.* □ *Mary was not hungry, and she didn't give a good account of herself at dinner.*

give as good as one gets to give as much as one receives; to pay someone back in kind. (Usually in the present tense.) □ *John can take care of himself in a fight. He can give as good as he gets.* □ *Sally usually wins a formal debate. She gives as good as she gets.*

give credit where credit is due to give credit to someone who deserves it; to acknowledge or thank someone who deserves it. (A cliché.) □ *We must give credit where credit is due. Thank you very much, Sally.* □ *Let's give credit where credit is due. Mary is the one who wrote the report, not Jane.*

Give one an inch, and one will take a mile. AND **If you give one an inch, one will take a mile.** a proverb meaning that a person who is granted a little of something (such as a reprieve or lenience) will want more. □ *I told John he could turn in his paper one day late, but he turned it in three days late. Give him an inch, and he'll take a mile.* □ *First we let John borrow our car for a day. Now he wants to go on a two-week vacation. If you give him an inch, he'll take a mile.*

give one an inch, one will take a mile, If you. See the previous entry.

give one one's freedom to set someone free; to divorce someone. (Usually euphemistic for *divorce.*) □ *Mrs. Brown wanted to give her husband his freedom.* □ *Well, Tom, I hate to break it to you this way, but I have decided to give you your freedom.*

give oneself airs to act conceited or superior. □ *Sally is always giving herself airs. You'd think she had royal blood.* □ *Come on, John. Don't act so haughty. Stop giving yourself airs.*

give one's right arm (for someone or something) to be willing to give something of great value for someone or something. (Never literal.) □ *I'd give my right arm for a nice cool drink.* □ *I'd give my right arm to be there.* □ *Tom really admires John. Tom would give his right arm for John.*

give someone a black eye See under *get a black eye.*

give someone a buzz See under *give someone a ring.*

give someone a clean bill of health See under *get a clean bill of health.*

give someone a piece of one's mind to bawl someone out; to tell someone off. (Actually to give someone a helping of what one is thinking about.) □ *I've had enough from John. I'm going to give him a piece of my mind.* □ *Sally, stop it, or I'll give you a piece of my mind.*

give someone a ring AND **give someone a buzz** to call someone on the telephone. (*Ring* and *buzz* refer to the bell in a telephone.) □ *Nice talking to you. Give me a ring sometime.* □ *Give me a buzz when you're in town.*

give someone or something a wide berth to keep a reasonable distance from someone or something; to steer clear of someone or something. (Originally referred to sailing ships.) □ *The dog we are approaching is very mean. Better give it a wide berth.* □ *Give Mary a wide berth. She's in a very bad mood.*

give someone the benefit of the doubt See under *get the benefit of the doubt.*

give someone the eye to look at someone in a way that communicates romantic interest. (Not literal.) □ *Ann gave John the eye. It really surprised him.* □ *Tom kept giving Sally the eye. She finally left.*

give someone the red-carpet treatment See under *get the red-carpet treatment.*

give someone the runaround See under *get the runaround.*

give someone the shirt off one's back to be very generous or solicitous to someone. □ *Tom really likes Bill. He'd give Bill the shirt off his back.* □ *John is so friendly that he'd give anyone the shirt off his back.*

give someone tit for tat to give someone something equal to what was given you; to exchange a series of things, one by one, with someone. □ *They gave me the same kind of difficulty that I gave them. They gave me tit for tat.* □ *He punched me, so I punched him. Every time he hit me, I hit him. I just gave him tit for tat.*

give something a lick and a promise to do something poorly— quickly and carelessly. □ *John! You didn't clean your room! You just gave it a lick and a promise.* □ *This time, Tom, comb your hair. It looks as if you just gave it a lick and a promise.*

give the bride away [for a bride's father] to accompany the bride to the groom in a wedding ceremony. □ *Mr. Brown is ill. Who'll give the bride away?* □ *In the traditional wedding ceremony, the bride's father gives the bride away.*

give the devil his due AND **give the devil her due** to give your foe proper credit (for something). (A cliché. This usually refers to a person who has acted evil—like the devil.) □ *She's generally impossible, but I have to give the devil her due. She cooks a ter-*

rific cherry pie. □ *John may cheat on his taxes and yell at his wife, but he keeps his car polished. I'll give the devil his due.*

give up the ghost to die; to release one's spirit. (A cliché. Considered literary or humorous.) □ *The old man sighed, rolled over, and gave up the ghost.* □ *I'm too young to give up the ghost.*

go about one's business to mind one's business; to move elsewhere and mind one's own business. □ *Leave me alone! Just go about your business!* □ *I have no more to say. I would be pleased if you would go about your business.*

go against the grain to go against the natural direction or inclination. (Refers to the lay of the grain of wood. Against the grain is perpendicular to the lay of the grain.) □ *Don't expect me to help you cheat. That goes against the grain.* □ *Would it go against the grain for you to call in sick for me?*

go along for the ride to accompany (someone) for the pleasure of riding along; to accompany someone for no special reason. □ *Join us. You can go along for the ride.* □ *I don't really need to go to the grocery store, but I'll go along for the ride.* □ *We're having a little party next weekend. Nothing fancy. Why don't you come along for the ride?*

go and never darken my door again to go away and not come back. (A cliché.) □ *The heroine of the drama told the villain never to darken her door again.* □ *She touched the back of her hand to her forehead and said, "Go and never darken my door again!"*

go (a)round the bend 1. to go around a turn or a curve; to make a turn or a curve. □ *You'll see the house you're looking for as you go round the bend.* □ *John waved to his father until the car went round the bend.* 2. to go crazy; to lose one's mind. □ *If I don't get some rest, I'll go round the bend.* □ *Poor Bob. He has been having trouble for a long time. He finally went around the bend.*

go away empty-handed   to depart with nothing. □ *I hate for you to go away empty-handed, but I cannot afford to contribute any money.* □ *They came hoping for some food, but they had to go away empty-handed.*

go back on one's word   to break a promise that one has made. □ *I hate to go back on my word, but I won't pay you $100 after all.* □ *Going back on your word makes you a liar.*

go down in history   to be remembered as historically important. (A cliché.) □ *Bill is so great. I'm sure that he'll go down in history.* □ *This is the greatest party of the century. I bet it'll go down in history.*

go Dutch   to share the cost of a meal or some other event. □ JANE: *Let's go out and eat.* MARY: *Okay, but let's go Dutch.* □ *It's getting expensive to have Sally for a friend. She never wants to go Dutch.*

go in one ear and out the other   [for something] to be heard and then forgotten. (Not literal.) □ *Everything I say to you seems to go in one ear and out the other. Why don't you pay attention?* □ *I can't concentrate. Things people say to me just go in one ear and out the other.*

go into a nosedive AND **take a nosedive**   **1.** [for an airplane] to dive suddenly toward the ground, nose first. □ *It was a bad day for flying, and I was afraid we'd go into a nosedive.* □ *The small plane took a nosedive. The pilot was able to bring it out at the last minute, so the plane didn't crash.* **2.** to go into a rapid emotional or financial decline, or a decline in health. □ *Our profits took a nosedive last year.* □ *After he broke his hip, Mr. Brown's health went into a nosedive, and he never recovered.*

go into a tailspin   **1.** [for an airplane] to lose control and spin to the earth, nose first. □ *The plane shook and then suddenly went into a tailspin.* □ *The pilot was not able to bring the plane out of the tailspin, and it crashed into the sea.* **2.** [for someone] to become disoriented or panicked; [for someone's life] to fall apart. □ *Although John was a great success, his life went into a tailspin.*

It took him a year to get straightened out. □ *After her father died, Mary's world fell apart, and she went into a tailspin.*

go into one's song and dance about something   to start giving one's usual or typical explanations and excuses about something. (A cliché. *One's* can be replaced by *the same old.* Does not involve singing or dancing.) □ *Please don't go into your song and dance about how you always tried to do what was right.* □ *John went into his song and dance about how he won the war all by himself.* □ *He always goes into the same old song and dance every time he makes a mistake.*

go like clockwork   to progress with regularity and dependability. (Refers more to mechanical works in general than to clocks.) □ *The building project is progressing nicely. Everything is going like clockwork.* □ *The elaborate pageant was a great success. It went like clockwork from start to finish.*

good as done, as   See *as good as done.*

good as gold, as   See *as good as gold.*

good condition, in   See *in good condition.*

good head on one's shoulders, have a   See *have a good head on one's shoulders.*

good shape, in   See *in good shape.*

go off the deep end AND **jump off the deep end**   to become deeply involved (with someone or something) before one is ready; to follow one's emotions into a situation. (Refers to going into a swimming pool at the deep end—rather than the shallow end—and finding oneself in deep water. Applies especially to falling in love.) □ *Look at the way Bill is looking at Sally. I think he's about to go off the deep end.* □ *Now, John, I know you really want to go to Australia, but don't go jumping off the deep end. It isn't all perfect there.*

go on a fishing expedition to attempt to discover information. (Also used literally. As if one were sending bait into the invisible depths of a body of water trying to catch something, but nothing in particular.) □ *We are going to have to go on a fishing expedition to try to find the facts.* □ *One lawyer went on a fishing expedition in court, and the other lawyer objected.*

go, on the See *on the go.*

go (out) on strike [for a group of people] to quit working at their jobs until certain demands are met. □ *If we don't have a contract by noon tomorrow, we'll go out on strike.* □ *The entire work force went on strike at noon today.*

go overboard **1.** to fall off or out of a boat or ship. □ *My fishing pole just went overboard. I'm afraid it's lost.* □ *That man just went overboard. I think he jumped.* **2.** to do too much; to be extravagant. □ *Look, Sally, let's have a nice party, but don't go overboard. It doesn't need to be fancy.* □ *Okay, you can buy a big comfortable car, but don't go overboard.*

go over someone's head [for the intellectual content of something] to be too difficult for someone to understand. (As if it flew over one's head rather than entering into one's store of knowledge.) □ *All that talk about computers went over my head.* □ *I hope my lecture didn't go over the students' heads.*

go over something with a fine-tooth comb AND **search something with a fine-tooth comb** to search through something very carefully. (As if one were searching for something very tiny lost in some kind of fiber.) □ *I can't find my calculus book. I went over the whole place with a fine-tooth comb.* □ *I searched this place with a fine-tooth comb and didn't find my ring.*

go over with a bang [for something] to be funny or entertaining. (Refers chiefly to jokes or stage performances.) □ *The play was a success. It really went over with a bang.* □ *That's a great joke. It went over with a bang.*

go scot-free AND **get off scot-free**   to go unpunished; to be acquitted of a crime. (This *scot* is an old word meaning "tax" or "tax burden.") □ *The thief went scot-free.* □ *Jane cheated on the test and got caught, but she got off scot-free.*

go stag   to go to an event (which is meant for couples) without a member of the opposite sex. (Originally referred only to males.) □ *Is Tom going to take you, or are you going stag?* □ *Bob didn't want to go stag, so he took his sister to the party.*

go the distance   to do the whole amount; to play the entire game; to run the whole race. (Originally sports use.) □ *That horse runs fast. I hope it can go the distance.* □ *This is going to be a long, hard project. I hope I can go the distance.*

go the limit   to do as much as possible. □ *What do I want on my hamburger? Go the limit!* □ *Don't hold anything back. Go the limit.*

go through channels   to proceed by consulting the proper persons or offices. (*Channels* refers to the route a piece of business must take through a hierarchy or a bureaucracy.) □ *If you want an answer to your questions, you'll have to go through channels.* □ *If you know the answers, why do I have to go through channels?*

go through the motions   to make a feeble effort to do something; to do something insincerely. □ *Jane isn't doing her best. She's just going through the motions.* □ *Bill was supposed to be raking the yard, but he was just going through the motions.*

go through the roof   to go very high; to reach a very high degree (of something). (Not literal in this sense.) □ *It's so hot! The temperature is going through the roof.* □ *Mr. Brown got so angry he almost went through the roof.*

go to bat for someone   to support or help someone. (From the use of a substitute batter in baseball.) □ *I tried to go to bat for Bill, but he said he didn't want any help.* □ *I heard them gossiping about Sally, so I went to bat for her.*

go to Davy Jones's locker   to go to the bottom of the sea. (Thought of as a nautical expression.) □ *My camera fell overboard and went to Davy Jones's locker.* □ *My uncle was a sailor. He went to Davy Jones's locker during a terrible storm.*

go to pot AND **go to the dogs**   to go to ruin; to deteriorate. □ *My whole life seems to be going to pot.* □ *My lawn is going to pot. I had better weed it.* □ *The government is going to the dogs.*

go to rack and ruin AND **go to wrack and ruin**   to become ruined. (The words *rack* and *wrack* mean "wreckage" and are found only in this expression.) □ *That lovely old house on the corner is going to go to rack and ruin.* □ *My lawn is going to wrack and ruin.*

go to seed   See under *run to seed.*

go to someone's head   to make someone conceited; to make someone overly proud. □ *You did a fine job, but don't let it go to your head.* □ *He let his success go to his head, and soon he became a complete failure.*

go to the dogs   See under *go to pot.*

go to the wall   to fail or be defeated after being pushed to the extreme. □ *We really went to the wall on that deal.* □ *The company went to the wall because of that contract. Now it's broke.*

go to town   to work hard or fast. (Also used literally.) □ *Look at all those ants working. They are really going to town.* □ *Come on, you guys! Let's go to town. We have to finish this job before noon.*

go to wrack and ruin   See under *go to rack and ruin.*

go up in flames AND **go up in smoke**   to burn up; to be consumed in flames. □ *The whole museum went up in flames.* □ *My paintings—my whole life's work—went up in flames.* □ *What a shame for all that to go up in smoke.*

go up in smoke See the previous entry.

grain, go against the See *go against the grain.*

green thumb, have a See *have a green thumb.*

green with envy envious; jealous. (A cliché. Not literal.) □ *When Sally saw me with Tom, she turned green with envy. She likes him a lot.* □ *I feel green with envy whenever I see you in your new car.*

grin and bear it to endure something unpleasant in good humor. □ *There is nothing you can do but grin and bear it.* □ *I hate having to work for rude people. I guess I have to grin and bear it.*

grind to a halt to slow to a stop; to run down. □ *By the end of the day, the factory had ground to a halt.* □ *The car ground to a halt, and we got out to stretch our legs.*

grit one's teeth to grind one's teeth together in anger or determination. □ *I was so mad, all I could do was stand there and grit my teeth.* □ *All through the race, Sally was gritting her teeth. She was really determined.*

ground up, from the See *from the ground up.*

gun for someone to be looking for someone, presumably to harm them with a gun. (Originally from western and gangster movies.) □ *The coach is gunning for you. I think he's going to bawl you out.* □ *I've heard that the sheriff is gunning for me, so I'm getting out of town.*

gutter, in the See *in the gutter.*

H

hail-fellow-well-met friendly to everyone; falsely friendly to everyone. (Usually said of males.) □ *Yes, he's friendly, sort of hail-fellow-well-met.* □ *He's not a very sincere person. Hail-fellow-well-met—you know the type.* □ *What a pain he is! Good old Mr. Hail-fellow-well-met. What a phony!*

hair of the dog that bit one a drink of liquor taken when one has a hangover; a drink of liquor taken when one is recovering from drinking too much liquor. (This has nothing to do with dogs or hair.) □ *Oh, I'm miserable. I need some of the hair of the dog that bit me.* □ *That's some hangover you've got there, Bob. Here, drink this. It's some of the hair of the dog that bit you.*

hair's breadth, by a See *by a hair's breadth.*

hale and hearty well and healthy. □ *Doesn't Ann look hale and hearty?* □ *I don't feel hale and hearty. I'm really tired.*

Half a loaf is better than none. a proverb meaning that having part of something is better than having nothing. □ *When my raise was smaller than I wanted, Sally said, "Half a loaf is better than none."* □ *People who keep saying "Half a loaf is better than none" usually have as much as they need.*

halfhearted (about someone or something), be See *be half-hearted (about someone or something).*

half-mast, at See *at half-mast.*

hand, do something by See *do something by hand.*

hand, have something at   See *have something at hand.*

hand in glove (with someone)   very close to someone. □ *John is really hand in glove with Sally.* □ *The teacher and the principal work hand in glove.*

hand in the till, have one's   See *have one's hand in the till.*

handle someone with kid gloves   to be very careful with a touchy person; to deal with someone who is very difficult. □ *Bill has become so sensitive. You really have to handle him with kid gloves.* □ *You don't have to handle me with kid gloves. I can take it.*

hand, out of   See *out of hand.*

hand over fist   [for money and merchandise to be exchanged] very rapidly. □ *What a busy day. We took in money hand over fist.* □ *They were buying things hand over fist.*

hand over hand   [moving] one hand after the other (again and again). □ *Sally pulled in the rope hand over hand.* □ *The man climbed the rope hand over hand.*

hands down, do something   See *do something hands down.*

hands full (with someone or something), have one's   See *have one's hands full (with someone or something).*

hands, have someone or something in one's   See *have someone or something in one's hands.*

hands tied, have one's   See *have one's hands tied.*

hand tied behind one's back, with one   See *with one hand tied behind one's back.*

hand to hand, from   See *from hand to hand.*

hang by a hair AND **hang by a thread** to be in an uncertain position; to depend on something very insubstantial for support. (Also with *on,* as in the second example.) □ *Your whole argument is hanging by a thread.* □ *John isn't failing geometry, but he's just hanging on by a hair.*

hang by a thread See the previous entry.

hanging over one's head, have something See *have something hanging over one's head.*

hang in the balance to be in an undecided state; to be between two equal possibilities. □ *The prisoner stood before the judge with his life hanging in the balance.* □ *This whole issue will have to hang in the balance until Jane gets back from her vacation.*

Hang on! be prepared for fast or rough movement. □ *Hang on! Here we go!* □ *The airplane passengers suddenly seemed weightless. Someone shouted, "Hang on!"*

hang on someone's every word to listen carefully to everything someone says. □ *He gave a great lecture. We hung on his every word.* □ *Look at the way John hangs on Mary's every word. He must be in love with her.*

Hang on to your hat! AND **Hold on to your hat!** "Grasp your hat"; "Prepare for a sudden surprise or shock." □ *What a windy day. Hang on to your hat!* □ *Here we go! Hold on to your hat!* □ *Are you ready to hear the final score? Hang on to your hat! We won ten to nothing!*

hang someone in effigy to hang a dummy or some other figure of a hated person. □ *They hanged the dictator in effigy.* □ *The angry mob hanged the president in effigy.*

happy as a clam, as See *as happy as a clam.*

happy as a lark, as See *as happy as a lark.*

hard-and-fast rule a strict rule. □ *It's a hard-and-fast rule that you must be home by midnight.* □ *You should have your project completed by the end of the month, but it's not a hard-and-fast rule.*

hard as nails, as See *as hard as nails.*

hardly have time to breathe to be very busy. □ *This was such a busy day. I hardly had time to breathe.* □ *They made him work so hard that he hardly had time to breathe.*

hard on someone's heels following someone very closely; following very closely to someone's heels. □ *I ran as fast as I could, but the dog was still hard on my heels.* □ *Here comes Sally, and John is hard on her heels.*

Haste makes waste. a proverb meaning that time gained in doing something rapidly and carelessly will be lost when one has to do the thing over again correctly. □ *Now, take your time. Haste makes waste.* □ *Haste makes waste, so be careful as you work.*

hat, be old See *be old hat.*

hate someone's guts to hate someone very much. (Informal and rude.) □ *Oh, Bob is terrible. I hate his guts!* □ *You may hate my guts for saying so, but I think you're getting gray hair.*

haul someone over the coals See under *rake someone over the coals.*

have a bee in one's bonnet to have an idea or a thought remain in one's mind; to have an obsession. (The bee is a thought that is inside one's head, which is inside a bonnet.) □ *I have a bee in my bonnet that you'd be a good manager.* □ *I had a bee in my bonnet about swimming. I couldn't stop wanting to go swimming.* ALSO: **put a bee in someone's bonnet** to give someone an idea (about something). □ *Somebody put a bee in my bonnet that we should go to a movie.* □ *Who put a bee in your bonnet?*

have a big mouth to be a gossiper; to be a person who tells secrets. (This mouth is too loud or is heard by too many people.) □ *Mary has a big mouth. She told Bob what I was getting him for his birthday.* □ *You shouldn't say things like that about people all the time. Everyone will say you have a big mouth.*

have a bone to pick (with someone) to have a matter to discuss with someone; to have something to argue about with someone. □ *Hey, Bill. I've got a bone to pick with you. Where is the money you owe me?* □ *I had a bone to pick with her, but she was so sweet that I forgot about it.* □ *You always have a bone to pick.*

have a brush with something to have a brief contact with something; to have an experience with something. (Especially with the law. Sometimes a *close* brush.) □ *Ann had a close brush with the law. She was nearly arrested for speeding.* □ *When I was younger, I had a brush with scarlet fever, but I got over it.*

have a chip on one's shoulder to be tempting someone to an argument or a fight. (An invitation to a fight can be expressed as an invitation to knock a chip off someone's shoulder, which would be sufficient provocation for a fight. A person who goes about seeming to have such a chip is always daring someone to fight or argue.) □ *Who are you mad at? You always seem to have a chip on your shoulder.* □ *John's had a chip on his shoulder ever since he got his speeding ticket.*

have a close call See the following entry.

have a close shave AND **have a close call** to have a narrow escape from something dangerous. □ *What a close shave I had! I nearly fell off the roof when I was working there.* □ *I almost got struck by a speeding car. It was a close shave.*

have a familiar ring [for a story or an explanation] to sound familiar. □ *Your excuse has a familiar ring. Have you done this before?* □ *This term paper has a familiar ring. I think it has been copied.*

have a good head on one's shoulders to have common sense; to be sensible and intelligent. □ *Mary doesn't do well in school, but she's got a good head on her shoulders.* □ *John has a good head on his shoulders and can be depended on to give good advice.*

have a green thumb to have the ability to grow plants well. (Not literal.) □ *Just look at Mr. Simpson's garden. He has a green thumb.* □ *My mother has a green thumb when it comes to house plants.*

have a heart to be compassionate; to be generous and forgiving; to have an especially compassionate heart. □ *Oh, have a heart! Give me some help!* □ *If Ann had a heart, she'd have made us feel more welcome.*

have a heart of gold to be generous, sincere, and friendly. (Not literal. To have a wonderful character and personality.) □ *Mary is such a lovely person. She has a heart of gold.* □ *You think Tom stole your watch? Impossible! He has a heart of gold.*

have a heart of stone to be cold, unfeeling, and unfriendly. (Not literal.) □ *Sally has a heart of stone. She never even smiles.* □ *The slave driver in the play had a heart of stone. He was an ideal villain.*

have a lot going (for one) to have many things working to one's benefit. □ *Jane is so lucky. She has a lot going for her.* □ *She has a good job and a nice family. She has a lot going.*

have a low boiling point to anger easily. □ *Be nice to John. He's upset and has a low boiling point.* □ *Mr. Jones sure has a low boiling point. I hardly said anything, and he got angry.*

have an ax to grind to have something to complain about. □ *Tom, I need to talk to you. I have an ax to grind.* □ *Bill and Bob went into the other room to argue. They had an ax to grind.*

have an eye out (for someone or something) AND **keep an eye out (for someone or something)** to watch for the arrival or appearance of someone or something. (The *an* can be replaced by *one's*.) □ *Please try to have an eye out for the bus.* □ *Keep an eye out for rain.* □ *Have your eye out for a raincoat on sale.* □ *Okay. I'll keep my eye out.*

have an in (with someone) to have a way to request a special favor from someone; to have influence with someone. (The *in* is a noun.) □ *Do you have an in with the mayor? I have to ask him a favor.* □ *Sorry, I don't have an in, but I know someone who does.*

have an itchy palm AND **have an itching palm** to be in need of a tip; to tend to ask for tips; to crave money. (As if placing money in the palm would stop the itching.) □ *All the waiters at that restaurant have itchy palms.* □ *The cab driver was troubled by an itching palm. But he refused to carry my bags, and I gave him nothing.*

have a price on one's head to be wanted by the authorities, who have offered a reward for one's capture. (Not literal. Usually limited to western and gangster movies. As if the presentation of one's head would produce payment or reward.) □ *We captured a thief who had a price on his head, and the sheriff gave us the reward.* □ *The crook was so mean, he turned in his own brother, who had a price on his head.*

have a scrape (with someone or something) to come into contact with someone or something; to have a small battle with someone or something. □ *I had a scrape with the county sheriff.* □ *John and Bill had a scrape, but they are friends again now.*

have a soft spot in one's heart for someone or something to be fond of someone or something. □ *John has a soft spot in his* *heart for Mary.* □ *I have a soft spot in my heart for chocolate cake.*

have a sweet tooth   to desire to eat many sweet foods—especially candy and pastries. (As if a certain tooth had a craving for sweets.) □ *I have a sweet tooth, and if I don't watch it, I'll really get fat.* □ *John eats candy all the time. He must have a sweet tooth.*

have a weakness for someone or something   to be unable to resist someone or something; to be fond of someone or something; to be (figuratively) powerless against someone or something. □ *I have a weakness for chocolate.* □ *John has a weakness for Mary. I think he's in love.*

have bats in one's belfry   to be slightly crazy. (The belfry—a bell tower—represents one's head or brains. The bats represent an infestation of confusion.) □ *Poor old Tom has bats in his belfry.* □ *Don't act so silly, John. People will think you have bats in your belfry.*

have clean hands   to be guiltless. (As if the guilty person would have bloody hands.) □ *Don't look at me. I have clean hands.* □ *The police took him in, but let him go again because he had clean hands.*

have dibs on something AND **put one's dibs on something**   to reserve something for oneself; to claim something for oneself. □ *I have dibs on the last piece of cake.* □ *John put his dibs on the last piece again. It isn't fair.*

have egg on one's face   to be embarrassed because of an error that is obvious to everyone. (Rarely literal.) □ *Bob has egg on his face because he wore jeans to the party and everyone else wore formal clothing.* □ *John was completely wrong about the weather for the picnic. It snowed! Now he has egg on his face.*

have eyes bigger than one's stomach   See under *one's eyes are bigger than one's stomach.*

have eyes in the back of one's head   to seem to be able to sense what is going on outside of one's vision. (Not literal.) □ *My teacher seems to have eyes in the back of her head.* □ *My teacher doesn't need to have eyes in the back of his head. He watches us very carefully.*

have feet of clay   [for a strong person] to have a defect of character. □ *All human beings have feet of clay. No one is perfect.* □ *Sally was popular and successful. She was nearly fifty before she learned that she, too, had feet of clay.*

have foot-in-mouth disease   to embarrass oneself through a silly blunder. (This is a parody on *foot-and-mouth disease* or *hoof-and-mouth disease,* which affects cattle and deer.) □ *I'm sorry I keep saying stupid things. I guess I have foot-in-mouth disease.* □ *Yes, you really have foot-in-mouth disease tonight.*

have mixed feelings (about someone or something)   to be uncertain about someone or something. □ *I have mixed feelings about Bob. Sometimes I think he likes me; other times I don't.* □ *I have mixed feelings about my trip to England. I love the people, but the climate upsets me.* □ *Yes, I also have mixed feelings.*

have money to burn   to have lots of money; to have more money than one needs; to have enough money that some can be wasted. □ *Look at the way Tom buys things. You'd think he had money to burn.* □ *If I had money to burn, I'd just put it in the bank.*

have one's back to the wall   to be in a defensive position. □ *He'll have to give in. He has his back to the wall.* □ *How can I bargain when I've got my back to the wall?*

have one's cake and eat it too AND **eat one's cake and have it too**   to enjoy both having something and using it up.   (Usually stated in the negative.) □ *Tom wants to have his cake and eat it too. It can't be done.* □ *Don't buy a car if you want to walk and stay healthy. You can't eat your cake and have it too.*

have one's ear to the ground AND **keep one's ear to the ground**   to listen carefully, hoping to get advance warning of something. (Not literal. As if one were listening for the sound of distant horses' hoofs pounding on the ground.) □ *John had his ear to the ground, hoping to find out about new ideas in computers.* □ *His boss told him to keep his ear to the ground so that he'd be the first to know of a new idea.*

have one's finger in the pie to be involved in something. (Not literal.) □ *I like to have my finger in the pie so I can make sure things go my way.* □ *As long as John has his finger in the pie, things will happen slowly.*

have one's hand in the till to be stealing money from a company or an organization. (The till is a cash box or drawer.) □ *Mr. Jones had his hand in the till for years before he was caught.* □ *I think that the new clerk has her hand in the till. There is cash missing every morning.*

have one's hands full (with someone or something) to be busy or totally occupied with someone or something. □ *I have my hands full with my three children.* □ *You have your hands full with the store.* □ *We both have our hands full.*

have one's hands tied to be prevented from doing something. □ *I can't help you. I was told not to, so I have my hands tied.* □ *John can help. He doesn't have his hands tied.*

have one's head in the clouds to be unaware of what is going on. □ *"Bob, do you have your head in the clouds?" said the teacher.* □ *She walks around all day with her head in the clouds. She must be in love.*

have one's heart in one's mouth to feel strongly emotional about someone or something. □ *"Gosh, Mary," said John, "I have my heart in my mouth whenever I see you."* □ *My heart is in my mouth whenever I hear the national anthem.* ALSO: **one's heart is in one's mouth** [for one] to feel strongly emotional. □ *It was a touching scene. My heart was in my mouth the whole time.*

have one's heart set on something to be desiring and expecting something. □ *Jane has her heart set on going to London.* □ *Bob will be disappointed. He had his heart set on going to college this year.* □ *His heart is set on it.* ALSO: **set one's heart on something** to become determined about something. □ *Jane set her heart on going to London.* ALSO: **one's heart is set on something** to desire and expect something. □ *Jane's heart is set on going to London.*

have one's nose in a book to be reading a book; to read books all the time. □ *Bob has his nose in a book every time I see him.* □ *His nose is always in a book. He never gets any exercise.*

have one's tail between one's legs to be frightened or cowed. (Refers to a frightened dog. Also used literally with dogs.) □ *John seems to lack courage. Whenever there is an argument, he has his tail between his legs.* □ *You can tell that the dog is frightened because it has its tail between its legs.* ALSO: **one's tail is between one's legs** one is acting frightened or cowed. □ *He should have stood up and argued, but—as usual—his tail was between his legs.*

have one's words stick in one's throat to be so overcome by emotion that one can hardly speak. □ *I sometimes have my words stick in my throat.* □ *John said that he never had his words stick in his throat.* ALSO: **one's words stick in one's throat** to find it difficult to speak because of emotion. □ *My words stick in my throat whenever I try to say something kind or tender.*

have other fish to fry to have other things to do; to have more important things to do. (*Other* can be replaced by *bigger, better, more important,* etc. The literal sense is not used.) □ *I can't take time for your problem. I have other fish to fry.* □ *I won't waste time on your question. I have bigger fish to fry.*

have someone dead to rights to have proven someone unquestionably guilty. □ *The police burst in on the robbers while they were at work. They had the robbers dead to rights.* □ *All right,*

Tom! I've got you dead to rights! Get your hands out of the cookie jar.

have someone in one's pocket to have control over someone. □ *Don't worry about the mayor. She'll cooperate. I've got her in my pocket.* □ *John will do just what I tell him. I've got him and his brother in my pocket.*

have someone or something in one's hands to have control of or responsibility for someone or something. (*Have* can be replaced with *leave* or *put*.) □ *You have the whole project in your hands.* □ *The boss put the whole project in your hands.* □ *I have to leave the baby in your hands while I go to the doctor.*

have something at hand See the following entry.

have something at one's fingertips AND **have something at hand** to have something within (one's) reach. (*Have* can be replaced with *keep*.) □ *I have a dictionary at my fingertips.* □ *I try to have everything I need at hand.* □ *I keep my medicine at my fingertips.*

have something hanging over one's head to have something bothering or worrying one; to have a deadline worrying one. (Also used literally.) □ *I keep worrying about getting drafted. I hate to have something like that hanging over my head.* □ *I have a history paper that is hanging over my head.*

have something in stock to have merchandise available and ready for sale. □ *Do you have extra large sizes in stock?* □ *Of course, we have all sizes and colors in stock.*

have something to spare to have more than enough of something. □ *Ask John for some firewood. He has firewood to spare.* □ *Do you have any candy to spare?*

have the right-of-way to possess the legal right to occupy a particular space on a public roadway. □ *I had a traffic accident yesterday, but it wasn't my fault. I had the right-of-way.* □ *Don't pull out onto a highway if you don't have the right-of-way.*

have the shoe on the other foot to experience the opposite situation (from a previous situation). (Also with *be* instead of *have*. See the examples.) □ *I used to be a student, and now I'm the teacher. Now I have the shoe on the other foot.* □ *You were mean to me when you thought I was cheating. Now that I have caught you cheating, the shoe is on the other foot.*

have the time of one's life to have a very good time; to have the most exciting time in one's life. □ *What a great party! I had the time of my life.* □ *We went to Florida last winter and had the time of our lives.*

have too many irons in the fire to be doing too many things at once. (A cliché. As if a blacksmith had more things get hot in the fire than could possibly be dealt with.) □ *Tom had too many irons in the fire and missed some important deadlines.* □ *It's better if you don't have too many irons in the fire.*

head and shoulders above someone or something to be clearly superior to someone. (Often with *stand,* as in the examples.) □ *This wine is head and shoulders above that one.* □ *John stands head and shoulders above Bob.*

head, go over someone's See *go over someone's head.*

head, go to someone's See *go to someone's head.*

head, in over one's See *in over one's head.*

head in the clouds, have one's See *have one's head in the clouds.*

head, on someone's See *on someone's head.*

head, out of one's See *out of one's head.*

heart and soul, with all one's See *with all one's heart and soul.*

heart good, do someone's See *do someone's heart good.*

heart, have a   See *have a heart.*

heart in one's mouth, have one's   See *have one's heart in one's mouth.*

heart of gold, have a   See *have a heart of gold.*

heart of stone, have a   See *have a heart of stone.*

heart set on something, have one's   See *have one's heart set on something.*

heat, in   See *in heat.*

heck of it, for the   See *for the heck of it.*

heels of something, on the   See *on the heels of something.*

He laughs best who laughs last.   See the following entry.

He who laughs last, laughs longest. AND **He laughs best who laughs last.**   a proverb meaning that whoever succeeds in making the last move or pulling the last trick has the most enjoyment. □ *Bill had pulled many silly tricks on Tom. Finally Tom pulled a very funny trick on Bill and said, "He who laughs last, laughs longest."* □ *Bill pulled another, even bigger trick on Tom, and said, laughing, "He laughs best who laughs last."*

hide one's head in the sand   See under *bury one's head in the sand.*

hide one's light under a bushel   to conceal one's good ideas or talents. (A biblical theme.) □ *Jane has some good ideas, but she doesn't speak very often. She hides her light under a bushel.* □ *Don't hide your light under a bushel. Share your gifts with other people.*

high as a kite, as   See *as high as a kite.*

high as the sky, as   See *as high as the sky.*

high man on the totem pole the person at the top of the hierarchy; the person in charge of an organization. (See also *low man on the totem pole.*) □ *I don't want to talk to a secretary. I demand to talk to the high man on the totem pole.* □ *Who's in charge around here? Who's high man on the totem pole?*

hill, over the See *over the hill.*

history, go down in See *go down in history.*

hit a happy medium See under *strike a happy medium.*

hit a snag to run into a problem. □ *We've hit a snag with the building project.* □ *I stopped working on the roof when I hit a snag.*

hit a sour note See under *strike a sour note.*

hit bottom to reach the lowest or worst point. □ *Our profits have hit bottom. This is our worst year ever.* □ *When my life hit bottom, I began to feel much better. I knew that if there was going to be any change, it would be for the better.*

hitch a ride See under *thumb a ride.*

hit someone between the eyes to become completely apparent; to surprise or impress someone. (Also with *right,* as in the examples. Also used literally.) □ *Suddenly, it hit me right between the eyes. John and Mary were in love.* □ *Then—as he was talking—the exact nature of the evil plan hit me between the eyes.*

hit (someone) like a ton of bricks to surprise, startle, or shock someone. □ *Suddenly, the truth hit me like a ton of bricks.* □ *The sudden tax increase hit like a ton of bricks. Everyone became angry.*

hit the bull's-eye 1. to hit the center area of a circular target. (Literal.) □ *The archer hit the bull's-eye three times in a row.* □ *I didn't hit the bull's-eye even once.* 2. to achieve the goal perfectly.

☐ *Your idea really hit the bull's-eye. Thank you!* ☐ *Jill has a lot of insight. She knows how to hit the bull's-eye.*

hit the nail (right) on the head   to do exactly the right thing; to do something in the most effective and efficient way. (A cliché.) ☐ *You've spotted the flaw, Sally. You hit the nail on the head.* ☐ *Bob doesn't say much, but every now and then he hits the nail right on the head.*

hit the spot   to be exactly right; to be refreshing. ☐ *This cool drink really hits the spot.* ☐ *That was a delicious meal, dear. It hit the spot.*

hold one's end (of the bargain) up AND **hold up one's end (of the bargain)**   to do one's part as agreed; to attend to one's responsibilities as agreed. ☐ *Tom has to learn to cooperate. He must hold up his end of the bargain.* ☐ *If you don't hold your end up, the whole project will fail.*

hold one's ground   See under *stand one's ground.*

hold one's head up AND **hold up one's head**   to have one's self-respect; to retain or display one's dignity. ☐ *I've done nothing wrong. I can hold my head up in public.* ☐ *I'm so embarrassed and ashamed. I'll never be able to hold up my head again.*

hold one's own   to do as well as anyone else. ☐ *I can hold my own in a footrace any day.* ☐ *She was unable to hold her own, and she had to quit.*

hold one's peace   to remain silent. ☐ *Bill was unable to hold his peace any longer. "Don't do it!" he cried.* ☐ *Quiet, John. Hold your peace for a little while longer.*

hold one's temper   See under *keep one's temper.*

hold one's tongue   to refrain from speaking; to refrain from saying something unpleasant. (Not literal.) ☐ *I felt like scolding her, but I held my tongue.* ☐ *Hold your tongue, John. You can't talk to me that way.*

Hold on to your hat! See under *Hang on to your hat!*

hold out the olive branch to offer to end a dispute and be friendly; to offer reconciliation. (The olive branch is a symbol of peace and reconciliation. A biblical reference.) □ *Jill was the first to hold out the olive branch after our argument.* □ *I always try to hold out the olive branch to someone I have hurt. Life is too short for a person to bear grudges for very long.*

hold the fort to take care of a place, such as a store or one's home. (From western movies.) □ *I'm going next door to visit Mrs. Jones. You stay here and hold the fort.* □ *You should open the store at eight o'clock and hold the fort until I get there at ten o'clock.*

hold true [for something] to be true; (for something) to remain true. □ *Does this rule hold true all the time?* □ *Yes, it holds true no matter what.*

hold water, not See *not hold water.*

hole in one **1.** an instance of hitting a golf ball into a hole in only one try. (From the game of golf.) □ *John made a hole in one yesterday.* □ *I've never gotten a hole in one.* **2.** an instance of succeeding the first time. □ *It worked the first time I tried it—a hole in one.* □ *Bob got a hole in one on that sale. A lady walked in the door, and he sold her a car in five minutes.*

hole, in the See *in the hole.*

hole, out of the See *out of the hole.*

honeymoon is over, The. See *The honeymoon is over.*

honor, on one's See *on one's honor.*

honors, do the See *do the honors.*

honor someone's check to accept someone's personal check. □ *The clerk at the store wouldn't honor my check. I had to pay* *cash.* □ *The bank didn't honor your check when I tried to deposit it. Please give me cash.*

hope against all hope   to have hope even when the situation appears to be hopeless. □ *We hope against all hope that she'll see the right thing to do and do it.* □ *There is little point in hoping against all hope, except that it makes you feel better.*

horizon, on the   See *on the horizon.*

horn in (on someone)   to attempt to displace someone. □ *I'm going to ask Sally to the party. Don't you dare try to horn in on me!* □ *I wouldn't think of horning in.*

horns of a dilemma, on the   See *on the horns of a dilemma.*

horse of a different color   See the following entry.

horse of another color AND **horse of a different color**   another matter altogether. □ *I was talking about the tree, not the bush. That's a horse of another color.* □ *Gambling is not the same as investing in the stock market. It's a horse of a different color.*

hot under the collar   very angry. (A cliché.) □ *The boss was really hot under the collar when you told him you lost the contract.* □ *I get hot under the collar every time I think about it.*

hour, on the   See *on the hour.*

house, on the   See *on the house.*

huff, in a   See *in a huff.*

hump, over the   See *over the hump.*

hungry as a bear, as   See *as hungry as a bear.*

I

(ifs, ands, or) buts about it, no   See *no (ifs, ands, or) buts about it.*

If the shoe fits, wear it.   a proverb meaning that you should pay attention to something if it applies to you. □ *Some people here need to be quiet. If the shoe fits, wear it.* □ *This doesn't apply to everyone. If the shoe fits, wear it.*

if worst comes to worst   in the worst possible situation; if things really get bad. (A cliché.) □ *If worst comes to worst, we'll hire someone to help you.* □ *If worst comes to worst, I'll have to borrow some money.*

If you give one an inch, one will take a mile.   See under *Give one an inch, and one will take a mile.*

in a dead heat   finishing a race at exactly the same time; tied. (Here, *dead* means "exact" or "total.") □ *The two horses finished the race in a dead heat.* □ *They ended the contest in a dead heat.*

in a flash   quickly; immediately. □ *I'll be there in a flash.* □ *It happened in a flash. Suddenly my wallet was gone.*

in a huff   in an angry or offended manner. (*In* can be replaced with *into*. See the examples.) □ *He heard what we had to say, then left in a huff.* □ *She came in a huff and ordered us to bring her something to eat.* □ *She gets into a huff very easily.*

in a mad rush in a hurry; in a busy rush. □ *I ran around all day today in a mad rush, looking for a present for Bill.* □ *Why are you always in a mad rush?*

in a (tight) spot caught in a problem; in a difficult position. (*In* can be replaced with *into.* See the examples.) □ *Look, John, I'm in a tight spot. Can you lend me twenty dollars?* □ *I'm in a spot too. I need $300.* □ *I have never gotten into a tight spot.*

in a vicious circle in a situation in which the solution of one problem leads to a second problem, and the solution of the second problem brings back the first problem, etc. (*In* can be replaced with *into.* See the examples.) □ *Life is so strange. I seem to be in a vicious circle most of the time.* □ *I put lemon in my tea to make it sour, then sugar to make it sweet. I'm in a vicious circle.* □ *Don't let your life get into a vicious circle.*

in a world of one's own aloof; detached; self-centered. (*In* can be replaced with *into.* See the examples.) □ *John lives in a world of his own. He has very few friends.* □ *Mary walks around in a world of her own, but she's very intelligent.* □ *When she's thinking, she drifts into a world of her own.*

in bad faith without sincerity; with bad or dishonest intent; with duplicity. □ *It appears that you acted in bad faith and didn't live up to the terms of our agreement.* □ *If you do things in bad faith, you'll get a bad reputation.*

in bad sorts in a bad humor. □ *Bill is in bad sorts today. He's very grouchy.* □ *I try to be extra nice to people when I'm in bad sorts.*

in bad taste AND **in poor taste** rude; vulgar; obscene. □ *Mrs. Franklin felt that your joke was in bad taste.* □ *We found the play to be in poor taste, so we walked out in the middle of the second act.*

in black and white official, in writing or printing. (Said of something, such as an agreement or a statement, that has been recorded in writing. *In* can be replaced with *into.* See the examples.)

□ *I have it in black and white that I'm entitled to three weeks of vacation each year.* □ *It says right here in black and white that oak trees make acorns.* □ *Please put the agreement into black and white.*

in broad daylight publicly visible in the daytime. □ *The thief stole the car in broad daylight.* □ *There they were, selling drugs in broad daylight.*

inch by inch one inch at a time; little by little. □ *Traffic moved along inch by inch.* □ *Inch by inch, the snail moved across the stone.*

inch of one's life, within an See *within an inch of one's life.*

in creation See under *on earth.*

in deep water in a dangerous or vulnerable situation; in a serious situation; in trouble. (As if one were swimming in or fell into water that is over one's head. *In* can be replaced with *into.* See the examples.) □ *John is having trouble with his taxes. He's in deep water.* □ *Bill is in deep water in algebra class. He's almost failing.* □ *He really got himself into deep water.*

in fine feather in good humor; in good health. (A cliché. *In* can be replaced with *into.* See the examples. Refers to a healthy and therefore beautiful bird.) □ *Hello, John. You appear to be in fine feather.* □ *Of course I'm in fine feather. I get lots of sleep.* □ *Good food and lots of sleep put me into fine feather.*

in full swing in progress; operating or running without restraint. (*In* can be replaced with *into.* See the examples.) □ *We can't leave now! The party is in full swing.* □ *Our program to help the starving people is in full swing. You should see results soon.* □ *Just wait until our project gets into full swing.*

in good condition See the following entry.

in good shape AND **in good condition** physically and functionally sound and sturdy. (Used for both people and things. *In* can be replaced with *into.* See the examples.) □ *This car isn't in good shape.* □ *I'd like to have one that's in better condition.* □ *Mary is in good condition. She works hard to keep healthy.* □ *You have to make an effort to get into good shape.*

in heat in a period of sexual excitement; in estrus. (Estrus is the period of time in which females are most willing to breed. See also *in season.* This expression is usually used for animals. It has been used for humans in a joking sense. *In* can be replaced with *into.* See the examples.) □ *Our dog is in heat.* □ *She goes into heat every year at this time.* □ *When my dog is in heat, I have to keep her locked in the house.*

in less than no time very quickly. □ *I'll be there in less than no time.* □ *Don't worry. This won't take long. It'll be over with in less than no time.*

in mint condition in perfect condition. (Refers to the perfect state of a coin that has just been minted. *In* can be replaced with *into.* See the examples.) □ *This is a fine car. It runs well and is in mint condition.* □ *We went through a house in mint condition and decided to buy it.* □ *We put our house into mint condition before we sold it.*

in name only nominally; not actual, only by terminology. □ *The president is head of the country in name only. Congress makes the laws.* □ *Mr. Smith is the boss of the Smith Company in name only. Mrs. Smith handles all the business affairs.*

innocent as a lamb, as See *as innocent as a lamb.*

in no mood to do something not to feel like doing something; to wish not to do something. □ *I'm in no mood to cook dinner tonight.* □ *Mother is in no mood to put up with our arguing.*

in nothing flat in exactly no time at all. □ *Of course I can get there in a hurry. I'll be there in nothing flat.* □ *We covered the distance between New York and Philadelphia in nothing flat.*

in one ear and out the other   [for something to be] ignored; [for something to be] unheard or unheeded. (A cliché. *In* can be replaced with *into*. See the examples.) □ *Everything I say to you goes into one ear and out the other!* □ *Bill just doesn't pay attention. Everything is in one ear and out the other.*

in one fell swoop   See under *at one fell swoop*.

in one's birthday suit   naked; nude. (In the "clothes" in which one was born. *In* can be replaced with *into*. See the examples.) □ *I've heard that John sleeps in his birthday suit.* □ *We used to go down to the river and swim in our birthday suits.* □ *You have to get into your birthday suit to bathe.*

in one's mind's eye   in one's mind. (Refers to visualizing something in one's mind.) □ *In my mind's eye, I can see trouble ahead.* □ *In her mind's eye, she could see a beautiful building beside the river. She decided to design such a building.*

in one's or its prime   at one's or its peak or best time. □ *Our dog —which is in its prime—is very active.* □ *The program ended in its prime when we ran out of money.* □ *I could work long hours when I was in my prime.*

in one's right mind   sane; rational and sensible. (Often in the negative.) □ *That was a stupid thing to do. You're not in your right mind.* □ *You can't be in your right mind! That sounds crazy!*

in one's second childhood   being interested in things or people that normally interest children. □ *My father bought himself a toy train, and my mother said he was in his second childhood.* □ *Whenever I go to the river and throw stones, I feel as though I'm in my second childhood.*

in one's spare time   in one's extra time; in the time not reserved for doing something else. □ *I write novels in my spare time.* □ *I'll try to paint the house in my spare time.*

in over one's head with more difficulties than one can manage. □ *Calculus is very hard for me. I'm in over my head.* □ *Ann is too busy. She's really in over her head.*

in poor taste See under *in bad taste.*

in print [for a book] to be available for sale. (Compare to *out of print.*) □ *I think I can get that book for you. It's still in print.* □ *This is the only book in print on this subject.*

in rags in worn-out and torn clothing. □ *Oh, look at my clothing. I can't go to the party in rags!* □ *I think the new casual fashions make you look as if you're in rags.*

in round figures See the following entry.

in round numbers AND **in round figures** as an estimated number; a figure that has been rounded off to the closest whole number. (*In* can be replaced with *into.* See the examples.) □ *Please tell me in round numbers what it'll cost.* □ *I don't need the exact amount. Just give it to me in round figures.*

ins and outs of something the correct and successful way to do something; the special things that one needs to know to do something. □ *I don't understand the ins and outs of politics.* □ *Jane knows the ins and outs of working with computers.*

in season **1.** currently available for selling. (Some foods and other things are available only at certain seasons. *In* can be replaced with *into,* especially when used with *come.* See the examples.) □ *Oysters are available in season.* □ *Strawberries aren't in season in January.* □ *When do strawberries come into season?* **2.** legally able to be caught or hunted. □ *Catfish are in season all year round.* □ *When are salmon in season?* **3.** [of a dog] in estrus; *in heat.* □ *My dog is in season every year at this time.* □ *When my dog is in season, I have to keep her locked in the house.*

in seventh heaven in a very happy state. (A cliché. This is the highest heaven, where God exists.) □ *Ann was really in seventh* heaven when she got a car of her own. □ *I'd be in seventh heaven if I had a million dollars.*

in short order   very quickly. □ *I can straighten out this mess in short order.* □ *The people came in and cleaned the place up in short order.*

in short supply   scarce. (*In* can be replaced with *into*. See the examples.) □ *Fresh vegetables are in short supply in the winter.* □ *Yellow cars are in short supply because everyone likes them and buys them.* □ *At this time of the year, fresh vegetables go into short supply.*

in stock   readily available, as with goods in a store. □ *I'm sorry, I don't have that in stock. I'll have to order it for you.* □ *We have all our Christmas merchandise in stock now.*

in the air   everywhere; all about. (Also used literally.) □ *There is such a feeling of joy in the air.* □ *We felt a sense of tension in the air.*

in the bargain   in addition to what was agreed on. (*In* can be replaced with *into*. See the examples.) □ *I bought a car, and they threw an air conditioner into the bargain.* □ *When I bought a house, I asked the seller to include the furniture in the bargain.*

in the black   not in debt; in a financially profitable condition. (Refers to writing figures in black rather than in red, which would indicate a debit. See also **in the red**. *In* can be replaced with *into*. See the examples.) □ *I wish my accounts were in the black.* □ *Sally moved the company into the black.*

in the blood AND **in one's blood**   built into one's personality or character. (Actually in the genes, not the blood.) □ *John's a great runner. It's in his blood.* □ *The whole family is very athletic. It's in the blood.*

in the bullpen   [for a baseball pitcher to be] in a special place near a baseball playing field, warming up to pitch. (*In* can be replaced with *into*. See the examples.) □ *You can tell who is pitching next* *by seeing who is in the bullpen.* □ *Our best pitcher just went into the bullpen. He'll be pitching soon.*

in the cards in the future. □ *Well, what do you think is in the cards for tomorrow?* □ *I asked the boss if there was a raise in the cards for me.*

in the doghouse in trouble; in (someone's) disfavor. (*In* can be replaced with *into*. See the examples. As if a person would be sent outside for misbehavior—as one might send a dog from the comforts of the house to the discomforts of the yard.) □ *I'm really in the doghouse. I was late for an appointment.* □ *I hate being in the doghouse all the time. I don't know why I can't stay out of trouble.*

in the doldrums sluggish; inactive; in low spirits. (*In* can be replaced with *into*. See the examples.) □ *He's usually in the doldrums in the winter.* □ *I had some bad news yesterday, which put me into the doldrums.*

in the flesh really present; in person. □ *I've heard that the queen is coming here in the flesh.* □ *Is she really here? In the flesh?* □ *I've wanted a color television for years, and now I've got one right here in the flesh.*

in the gutter [for a person to be] in a low state; depraved. (*In* can be replaced with *into*. See the examples.) □ *You had better straighten out your life, or you'll end up in the gutter.* □ *His bad habits put him into the gutter.*

in the hole in debt. (*In* can be replaced with *into*. See the examples. Also used literally.) □ *I'm $200 in the hole.* □ *Our finances end up in the hole every month.*

in the know knowledgeable. (*In* can be replaced with *into*. See the examples.) □ *Let's ask Bob. He's in the know.* □ *I have no knowledge of how to work this machine. I think I can get into the know very quickly though.*

in the lap of luxury in luxurious surroundings. (A cliché. *In* can be replaced with *into*. See the examples.) □ *John lives in the lap of luxury because his family is very wealthy.* □ *When I retire, I'd like to live in the lap of luxury.*

in the limelight AND **in the spotlight** at the center of attention. (*In* can be replaced with *into*. See the examples. The literal sense is also used. *Limelight* is an obsolete type of spotlight, and the word occurs only in this phrase.) □ *John will do almost anything to get himself into the limelight.* □ *I love being in the spotlight.* □ *All elected officials spend a lot of time in the limelight.*

in the line of duty as part of the expected (military or police) duties. □ *When soldiers fight people in a war, it's in the line of duty.* □ *Police officers have to do things they may not like in the line of duty.*

in the long run over a long period of time; ultimately. (A cliché.) □ *We'd be better off in the long run buying one instead of renting one.* □ *In the long run, we'd be happier in the South.*

in the money 1. wealthy. □ *John is really in the money. He's worth millions.* □ *If I am ever in the money, I'll be generous.* 2. in the winning position in a race or contest. (As if one had won the prize money.) □ *I knew when Jane came around the final turn that she was in the money.* □ *The horses coming in first, second, and third are said to be in the money.*

in the nick of time just in time; at the last possible instant; just before it's too late. (A cliché.) □ *The doctor arrived in the nick of time. The patient's life was saved.* □ *I reached the airport in the nick of time.*

in the pink (of condition) in very good health; in very good condition, physically and emotionally. (*In* can be replaced with *into*. See the examples.) □ *The garden is lovely. All the flowers are in the pink of condition.* □ *Jane has to exercise hard to get into the pink of condition.* □ *I'd like to be in the pink, but I don't have the time.*

in the prime of life in the best and most productive period of one's life. (*In* can be replaced with *into*. See the examples.) □ *The good health of one's youth can carry over into the prime of life.* □ *He was struck down by a heart attack in the prime of life.*

in the public eye publicly; visible to all; conspicuous. (*In* can be replaced with *into*. See the examples.) □ *Elected officials find themselves constantly in the public eye.* □ *The mayor made it a practice to get into the public eye as much as possible.*

in the red in debt. (Refers to writing debit figures in red ink rather than in black ink. See also *in the black. In* can be replaced with *into*. See the examples.) □ *My accounts are in the red at the end of every month.* □ *It's easy to get into the red if you don't pay close attention to the amount of money you spend.*

in the right on the moral or legal side of an issue; on the right side of an issue. □ *I felt I was in the right, but the judge ruled against me.* □ *It's hard to argue with Jane. She always believes that she's in the right.*

in the same boat in the same situation; having the same problem. (A cliché. *In* can be replaced with *into*. See the examples.) □ TOM: *I'm broke. Can you lend me twenty dollars?* BILL: *Sorry. I'm in the same boat.* □ *Jane and Mary are in the same boat. They both have been called for jury duty.*

in the same breath [stated or said] almost at the same time; as part of the same thought or conversation. □ *He told me I was lazy, but then in the same breath he said I was doing a good job.* □ *The teacher said that the students were working hard and, in the same breath, that they were not working hard enough.*

in the spotlight See under *in the limelight.*

in the twinkling of an eye very quickly. (A biblical reference.) □ *In the twinkling of an eye, the deer had disappeared into the forest.* □ *I gave Bill ten dollars and, in the twinkling of an eye, he spent it.*

in the wind about to happen. (Also used literally.) □ *There are some major changes in the wind. Expect these changes to happen soon.* □ *There is something in the wind. We'll find out what it is soon.*

in the world See under *on earth.*

in the wrong on the wrong or illegal side of an issue; guilty or in error. □ *I felt she was in the wrong, but the judge ruled in her favor.* □ *It's hard to argue with Jane. She always believes that everyone else is in the wrong.*

in two shakes of a lamb's tail very quickly. (A cliché.) □ *I'll be there in two shakes of a lamb's tail.* □ *In two shakes of a lamb's tail, the bird flew away.*

itchy palm, have an See *have an itchy palm.*

It never rains but it pours. a proverb meaning that a lot of bad things tend to happen at the same time. □ *The car won't start, the stairs broke, and the dog died. It never rains but it pours.* □ *Everything seems to be going wrong at the same time. It never rains but it pours.*

J

Johnny-come-lately someone who joins in (something) after it is under way. □ *Don't pay any attention to Sally. She's just a Johnny-come-lately and doesn't know what she's talking about.* □ *We've been here for thirty years. Why should some Johnny-come-lately tell us what to do?*

Johnny-on-the-spot someone who is in the right place at the right time. □ *Here I am, Johnny-on-the-spot. I told you I would be here at 12:20.* □ *Bill is late again. You can hardly call him Johnny-on-the-spot.*

jump off the deep end See under *go off the deep end.*

jump on the bandwagon See under *get on the bandwagon.*

jump out of one's skin to react strongly to shock or surprise. (Usually with *nearly, almost,* etc. Never used literally.) □ *Oh! You really scared me. I nearly jumped out of my skin.* □ *Bill was so startled he almost jumped out of his skin.*

jump the gun to start before the starting signal. (Originally used in sports contests that are started by firing a gun.) □ *We all had to start the race again because Jane jumped the gun.* □ *When we took the test, Tom jumped the gun and started early.*

jump the track **1.** [for something] to fall or jump off the rails or guides. (Usually said about a train.) □ *The train jumped the track, causing many injuries to the passengers.* □ *The engine jumped the track, but the other cars stayed on.* **2.** to change suddenly from one thing, thought, plan, or activity to another. □

The entire project jumped the track, and we finally had to give up. □ *John's mind jumped the track while he was in the play, and he forgot his lines.*

just what the doctor ordered exactly what is required, especially for health or comfort. (A cliché.) □ *That meal was delicious, Bob. Just what the doctor ordered.* □ BOB: *Would you like something to drink?* MARY: *Yes, a cold glass of water would be just what the doctor ordered.*

K

keep a civil tongue (in one's head) to speak decently and politely. (Also with *have.*) □ *Please, John. Don't talk like that. Keep a civil tongue in your head.* □ *John seems unable to keep a civil tongue.* □ *He'd be welcome here if he had a civil tongue in his head.*

keep an eye out (for someone or something) See under *have an eye out (for someone or something).*

keep a stiff upper lip to be cool and unmoved by unsettling events. (Also with *have.* See the note at *keep a straight face.*) □ *John always keeps a stiff upper lip.* □ *Now, Billy, don't cry. Keep a stiff upper lip.* □ *Bill can take it. He has a stiff upper lip.*

keep a straight face to make one's face stay free from laughter. (*Keep* can be replaced with *have.* Note: *Keep* implies the exercise of effort, and *have* simply means to possess.) □ *It's hard to keep a straight face when someone tells a funny joke.* □ *I knew it was John who played the trick. He couldn't keep a straight face.* □ *John didn't have a straight face.*

keep body and soul together to feed, clothe, and house oneself. (A cliché.) □ *I hardly have enough money to keep body and soul together.* □ *How the old man was able to keep body and soul together is beyond me.*

keep late hours to stay up or stay out until very late; to work late. □ *I'm always tired because I keep late hours.* □ *If I didn't keep late hours, I wouldn't sleep so late in the morning.*

keep one's ear to the ground See under *have one's ear to the ground.*

keep one's eye on the ball **1.** to watch or follow the ball carefully, especially when one is playing a ball game; to follow the details of a ball game very carefully. □ *John, if you can't keep your eye on the ball, I'll have to take you out of the game.* □ *"Keep your eye on the ball," the coach roared at the players.* **2.** to remain alert to the events occurring around one. □ *If you want to get along in this office, you're going to have to keep your eye on the ball.* □ *Bill would do better in his classes if he would just keep his eye on the ball.*

keep one's feet on the ground See under *get one's feet on the ground.*

keep one's head above water See under *get one's head above water.*

keep one's nose to the grindstone See under *put one's nose to the grindstone.*

keep one's temper AND **hold one's temper** not to get angry; to hold back an expression of anger. □ *She should have learned to keep her temper when she was a child.* □ *Sally got thrown off the team because she couldn't hold her temper.*

keep one's weather eye open to watch for something (to happen); to be on the alert (for something); to be on guard. □ *Some trouble is brewing. Keep your weather eye open.* □ *Try to be more alert. Learn to keep your weather eye open.*

keep one's word to uphold one's promise. □ *I told her I'd be there to pick her up, and I intend to keep my word.* □ *Keeping one's word is necessary in the legal profession.*

keep someone in stitches to cause someone to laugh loud and hard, over and over. (Also with *have.* See the note at *keep a straight face.*) □ *The comedian kept us in stitches for nearly an* *hour.* □ *The teacher kept the class in stitches, but the students didn't learn anything.*

keep someone on tenterhooks   to keep someone anxious or in suspense. (Also with *have.* See the note at *keep a straight face.*) □ *Please tell me now. Don't keep me on tenterhooks any longer!* □ *Now that we have her on tenterhooks, shall we let her worry, or shall we tell her?*

keep someone or something hanging in midair   See under *leave someone or something hanging in midair.*

keep someone or something in mind AND **bear someone or something in mind**   to remember and think about someone or something. □ *When you're driving a car, you must bear this in mind at all times: Keep your eyes on the road.* □ *As you leave home, keep your family in mind.*

keep someone posted   to keep someone informed (of what is happening); to keep someone up to date. □ *If the price of corn goes up, I need to know. Please keep me posted.* □ *Keep her posted about the patient's status.*

keep something to oneself   to keep something a secret. (Notice the use of *but* in the examples.) □ *I'm quitting my job, but please keep that to yourself.* □ *Keep it to yourself, but I'm quitting my job.* □ *John is always gossiping. He can't keep anything to himself.*

keep something under one's hat   to keep something a secret; to keep something in one's mind (only). (If the secret stays under your hat, it stays in your mind. Note the use of *but* in the examples.) □ *Keep this under your hat, but I'm getting married.* □ *I'm getting married, but keep it under your hat.*

keep something under wraps   to keep something concealed (until some future time). □ *We kept the plan under wraps until after the election.* □ *The automobile company kept the new model under wraps until most of the old models had been sold.*

keep the home fires burning to keep things going at one's home or other central location. (A cliché.) □ *My uncle kept the home fires burning when my sister and I went to school.* □ *The manager stays at the office and keeps the home fires burning while I'm out selling our products.*

keep the wolf from the door to maintain oneself at a minimal level; to keep from starving, freezing, etc. (A cliché.) □ *I don't make a lot of money, just enough to keep the wolf from the door.* □ *We have a small amount of money saved, hardly enough to keep the wolf from the door.*

keep up (with the Joneses) to stay financially even with one's peers; to work hard to get the same amount of material goods that one's friends and neighbors have. □ *Mr. and Mrs. Brown bought a new car simply to keep up with the Joneses.* □ *Keeping up with the Joneses can take all your money.*

keep up (with the times) to stay in fashion; to keep up with the news; to be contemporary or modern. □ *I try to keep up with the times. I want to know what's going on.* □ *I bought a whole new wardrobe because I want to keep up with the times.* □ *Sally learns all the new dances. She likes to keep up.*

kick up a fuss AND **kick up a row; kick up a storm** to become a nuisance; to misbehave and disturb (someone). (*Row* rhymes with *cow*. Note the variations in the examples.) □ *The customer kicked up such a fuss about the food that the manager came to apologize.* □ *I kicked up such a row that they kicked me out.*

kick up a row See the previous entry.

kick up a storm See under *kick up a fuss*.

kick up one's heels to act frisky; to be lively and have fun. □ *I like to go to an old-fashioned square dance and really kick up my heels.* □ *For an old man, your uncle is really kicking up his heels.*

kill the fatted calf to prepare an elaborate banquet (in someone's honor). (From the biblical story recounting the return of the prodigal son.) □ *When Bob got back from college, his parents killed the fatted calf and threw a great party.* □ *Sorry this meal isn't much, John. We didn't have time to kill the fatted calf.*

kill the goose that laid the golden egg   a proverb concerning the destruction of the source of one's good fortune. (Based on an old fable.) □ *If you fire your best office worker, you'll be killing the goose that laid the golden egg.* □ *He sold his computer, which was like killing the goose that laid the golden egg.*

kill time   to waste time. □ *Stop killing time. Get to work!* □ *We went over to the record shop just to kill time.*

kill two birds with one stone   to solve two problems with one so-lution. (A cliché.) □ *John learned the words to his part in the play while peeling potatoes. He was killing two birds with one stone.* □ *I have to cash a check and make a payment on my bank loan. I'll kill two birds with one stone by doing them both in one trip to the bank.*

kiss and make up   to forgive (someone) and be friends again. (Also used literally.) □ *They were very angry, but in the end they kissed and made up.* □ *I'm sorry. Let's kiss and make up.*

kiss of death   an act that puts an end to someone or something. □ *The mayor's veto was the kiss of death for the new law.* □ *Fainting on stage was the kiss of death for my acting career.*

kiss something good-bye   to anticipate or experience the loss of something. (Not literal.) □ *If you leave your camera on a park bench, you can kiss it good-bye.* □ *You kissed your wallet good-bye when you left it in the store.*

knit one's brow   to wrinkle one's brow, especially by frowning. □ *The woman knit her brow and asked us what we wanted from her.* □ *While he read his book, John knit his brow occasionally. He must not have agreed with what he was reading.*

knock on wood   a phrase said to cancel out imaginary bad luck. (The same as British "touch wood.") □ *My stereo has never*

given me any trouble—*knock on wood*. □ *We plan to be in Flor-*
ida by tomorrow evening—knock on wood.

knock someone for a loop See under *throw someone for a*
loop.

know all the tricks of the trade to possess the skills and knowledge necessary to do something. (Also without *all*.) □ *Tom can*
repair car engines. He knows the tricks of the trade. □ *If I knew*
all the tricks of the trade, I could be a better plumber.

know enough to come in out of the rain, not See *not know*
enough to come in out of the rain.

know, in the See *in the know.*

know one's ABCs to know the alphabet; to know the most basic
things (about something). □ *Bill can't do it. He doesn't even*
know his ABCs. □ *You can't expect to write novels when you*
don't even know your ABCs.

know someone by sight to know the name and recognize the
face of someone. □ *I've never met the man, but I know him by*
sight. □ BOB: *Have you ever met Mary?* JANE: *No, but I know*
her by sight.

know someone from Adam, not See *not know someone from*
Adam.

know someone or something like a book See under *know*
someone or something like the palm of one's hand.

know someone or something like the back of one's hand See
the following entry.

know someone or something like the palm of one's hand AND
know someone or something like the back of one's hand;
know someone or something like a book to know someone
or something very well. □ *Of course I know John. I know him*
like the back of my hand. □ *I know him like a book.*

know something from memory to have memorized something so that one does not have to consult a written version; to know something well from seeing it very often. □ *Mary didn't need the script because she knew the play from memory.* □ *The conductor went through the entire concert without music. He knew it from memory.*

know something in one's bones See under *feel something in one's bones.*

know something inside out to know something thoroughly; to know about something thoroughly. □ *I know my geometry inside out.* □ *I studied and studied for my driver's test until I knew the rules inside out.*

know the ropes to know how to do something. □ *I can't do the job because I don't know the ropes.* □ *Ask Sally to do it. She knows the ropes.* ALSO: **show someone the ropes** to tell or show someone how something is to be done. □ *Since this was my first day on the job, the manager spent a lot of time showing me the ropes.*

know the score AND **know what's what** to know the facts; to know the facts about life and its difficulties. (Also used literally.) □ *Bob is so naive. He sure doesn't know the score.* □ *I know what you're trying to do. Oh, yes, I know what's what.*

know what's what See the previous entry.

know which side one's bread is buttered on to know what is most advantageous for one. (A cliché.) □ *He'll do it if his boss tells him to. He knows which side his bread is buttered on.* □ *Since John knows which side his bread is buttered on, he'll be there on time.*

L

land-office business, do a See *do a land-office business.*

lap of luxury, in the See *in the lap of luxury.*

last but not least last in sequence, but not last in importance. (An overused cliché. Often said in introductions.) □ *The speaker said, "And now, last but not least, I'd like to present Bill Smith, who will give us some final words." □ And last but not least, here is the loser of the race.*

last legs, on someone's or something's See *on someone's or something's last legs.*

last minute, at the See *at the last minute.*

laughing matter, no See *no laughing matter.*

laugh out of the other side of one's mouth to change sharply from happiness to sadness. (A cliché.) □ *Now that you know the truth, you'll laugh out of the other side of your mouth. □ He was so proud that he won the election. He's laughing out of the other side of his mouth since they recounted the ballots and found out that he lost.*

laugh up one's sleeve to laugh secretly; to laugh quietly to oneself. □ *Jane looked very serious, but I knew she was laughing up her sleeve. □ I told Sally that her dress was darling, but I was laughing up my sleeve because her dress was too small.*

law unto oneself one who makes one's own laws or rules; one who sets one's own standards of behavior. □ *You can't get Bill to follow the rules. He's a law unto himself.* □ *Jane is a law unto herself. She's totally unwilling to cooperate.*

lay a finger on someone or something to touch someone or something, even slightly, even with a finger. (Usually in the negative.) □ *Don't you dare lay a finger on my pencil. Go get your own!* □ *If you lay a finger on me, I'll scream.*

lay an egg to give a bad performance. (Also used literally, but only with birds.) □ *The cast of the play really laid an egg last night.* □ *I hope I don't lay an egg when it's my turn to sing.*

lay down the law **1.** to state firmly what the rules are (for something). (A cliché.) □ *Before the meeting, the boss laid down the law. We all knew exactly what to do.* □ *The way she laid down the law means that I'll remember her rules.* **2.** to scold someone for misbehaving. □ *When the teacher caught us, he really laid down the law.* □ *Poor Bob. He really got it when his mother laid down the law.*

lay it on thick AND **pour it on thick; spread it on thick** to exaggerate praise, excuses, or blame. □ *Sally was laying it on thick when she said that Tom was the best singer she had ever heard.* □ *After Bob finished making his excuses, Sally said that he was pouring it on thick.* □ *Bob always spreads it on thick.*

lay one's cards on the table See under *put one's cards on the table.*

lay something on the line See under *put something on the line.*

lay something to waste AND **lay waste to something** to destroy something (literally or figuratively). □ *The invaders laid the village to waste.* □ *The kids came in and laid waste to my clean house.*

lay waste to something See the previous entry.

lead a dog's life AND **live a dog's life**   to lead a miserable life. □ *Poor Jane really leads a dog's life.* □ *I've been working so hard. I'm tired of living a dog's life.*

lead someone down the garden path   to deceive someone. (A cliché.) □ *Now, be honest with me. Don't lead me down the garden path.* □ *That cheater really led her down the garden path.*

lead someone on a merry chase   to lead someone in a purposeless pursuit. □ *What a waste of time. You really led me on a merry chase.* □ *Jane led Bill on a merry chase trying to find an antique lamp.*

lead the life of Riley   to live in luxury. (No one knows who Riley is.) □ *If I had a million dollars, I could live the life of Riley.* □ *The treasurer took our money to Mexico, where he lived the life of Riley until the police caught him.*

leaps and bounds, by   See *by leaps and bounds.*

learn something from the bottom up   to learn something thoroughly, from the very beginning; to learn all aspects of something, even the most lowly. □ *I learned my business from the bottom up.* □ *I started out sweeping the floors and learned everything from the bottom up.*

leave a bad taste in someone's mouth   [for someone or something] to leave a bad feeling or memory with someone. (Also used literally.) □ *The whole business about the missing money left a bad taste in his mouth.* □ *It was a very nice party, but something about it left a bad taste in my mouth.* □ *I'm sorry that Bill was there. He always leaves a bad taste in my mouth.*

leave a sinking ship   See under *desert a sinking ship.*

leave no stone unturned   to search in all possible places. (A cliché. As if one might find something under a rock.) □ *Don't worry. We'll find your stolen car. We'll leave no stone unturned.* □ *In searching for a nice place to live, we left no stone unturned.*

leave one to one's fate to abandon someone to whatever may happen—possibly death or some other unpleasant event. □ *We couldn't rescue the miners, and we were forced to leave them to their fate.* □ *Please don't try to help. Just go away and leave me to my fate.*

leave someone for dead to abandon someone as being dead. (The abandoned person may actually be alive.) □ *He looked so bad that they almost left him for dead.* □ *As the soldiers turned —leaving the enemy captain for dead—the captain fired at them.*

leave someone high and dry **1.** to leave someone unsupported and unable to maneuver; to leave someone helpless. (Refers to a boat stranded on land or on a reef.) □ *All my workers quit and left me high and dry.* □ *All the children ran away and left Billy high and dry to take the blame for the broken window.* **2.** to leave someone without any money at all. □ *Mrs. Franklin took all the money out of the bank and left Mr. Franklin high and dry.* □ *Paying the bills always leaves me high and dry.*

leave someone holding the bag to leave someone to take all the blame; to leave someone appearing guilty. □ *They all ran off and left me holding the bag. It wasn't even my fault.* □ *It was the mayor's fault, but he wasn't left holding the bag.*

leave someone in peace to stop bothering someone; to go away and leave someone in peace. (Does not necessarily mean to go away from a person.) □ *Please go—leave me in peace.* □ *Can't you see that you're upsetting her? Leave her in peace.*

leave someone in the lurch to leave someone waiting for or anticipating your actions. □ *Where were you, John? You really left me in the lurch.* □ *I didn't mean to leave you in the lurch. I thought we had canceled our meeting.*

leave someone or something hanging in midair to suspend dealing with someone or something; to leave someone or something waiting to be finished or continued. (Also used literally.) □ *She left her sentence hanging in midair.* □ *She left us hanging in midair when she paused.* □ *Tell me the rest of the story. Don't* *leave me hanging in midair.* □ *Don't leave the story hanging in midair.* ALSO: **keep someone or something hanging in midair** to maintain someone or something waiting to be completed or continued. □ *Please don't keep us hanging in midair.*

left field, out in See *out in left field.*

leg to stand on, not have a See *not have a leg to stand on.*

lend an ear (to someone) to listen to someone. □ *Lend an ear to John. Hear what he has to say.* □ *I'd be delighted to lend an ear. I find great wisdom in everything John has to say.*

lend oneself or itself to something [for someone or something] to be adaptable to something; [for someone or something] to be useful for something. □ *This room doesn't lend itself to bright colors.* □ *John doesn't lend himself to casual conversation.*

less than no time, in See *in less than no time.*

Let bygones be bygones. a proverb meaning that one should forget the problems of the past. (Also a cliché.) □ *Okay, Sally, let bygones be bygones. Let's forgive and forget.* □ *Jane was unwilling to let bygones be bygones. She still won't speak to me.*

let grass grow under one's feet to do nothing; to stand still. (A cliché.) □ *Mary doesn't let the grass grow under her feet. She's always busy.* □ *Bob is too lazy. He's letting the grass grow under his feet.*

let off steam AND **blow off steam** to release excess energy or anger. (Also used literally.) □ *Whenever John gets a little angry, he blows off steam.* □ *Don't worry about John. He's just letting off steam.*

let one's hair down AND **let down one's hair** to become more intimate and begin to speak frankly. □ *Come on, Jane, let your hair down and tell me all about it.* □ *I have a problem. Do you mind if I let down my hair?*

Let sleeping dogs lie. a proverb meaning that one should not search for trouble or that one should leave well enough alone. (A cliché.) □ *Don't mention that problem with Tom again. It's almost forgotten. Let sleeping dogs lie.* □ *You'll never be able to reform Bill. Leave him alone. Let sleeping dogs lie.*

let someone off (the hook) to release someone from a responsibility. □ *Please let me off the hook for Saturday. I have other plans.* □ *Okay, I'll let you off.*

let something slide to neglect something. □ *John let his lessons slide.* □ *Jane doesn't let her work slide.*

let something slide by See the following entry.

let something slip by AND **let something slide by** **1.** to forget or miss an important time or date. □ *I'm sorry I just let your birthday slip by.* □ *I let it slide by accidentally.* **2.** to waste a period of time. □ *You wasted the whole day by letting it slip by.* □ *We were having fun, and we let the time slide by.*

let the cat out of the bag AND **spill the beans** to reveal a secret or a surprise by accident. (Two clichés.) □ *When Bill glanced at the door, he let the cat out of the bag. We knew then that he was expecting someone to arrive.* □ *We are planning a surprise party for Jane. Don't let the cat out of the bag.* □ *It's a secret. Try not to spill the beans.*

let the chance slip by to lose the opportunity (to do something). □ *When I was younger, I wanted to become a doctor, but I let the chance slip by.* □ *Don't let the chance slip by. Do it now!*

level, on the See *on the level*.

lie through one's teeth to lie boldly, obviously, and with no remorse. (A cliché.) □ *I knew she was lying through her teeth, but I didn't want to say so just then.* □ *I'm not lying through my teeth! I never do!*

life of the party the type of person who is lively and helps make a party fun and exciting. □ *Bill is always the life of the party. Be sure to invite him.* □ *Bob isn't exactly the life of the party, but he's polite.*

light as a feather, as See *as light as a feather.*

light, out like a See *out like a light.*

like a bat out of hell with great speed and force. (A cliché. Use caution with the word *hell.*) □ *Did you see her leave? She left like a bat out of hell.* □ *The car sped down the street like a bat out of hell.*

like a bolt out of the blue suddenly and without warning. (A cliché. Refers to a bolt of lightning coming out of a clear blue sky.) □ *The news came to us like a bolt out of the blue.* □ *Like a bolt out of the blue, the boss came and fired us all.*

like a bump on a log unresponsive; immobile. (A cliché.) □ *I spoke to him, but he just sat there like a bump on a log.* □ *Don't stand there like a bump on a log. Give me a hand!*

like a fish out of water awkward; in a foreign or unaccustomed environment. (A cliché.) □ *At a formal dance, John is like a fish out of water.* □ *Mary was like a fish out of water at the bowling tournament.*

like a sitting duck AND **like sitting ducks** unguarded; unsuspecting and unaware. (A cliché. The second phrase is the plural form. Refers to floating rather than flying ducks.) □ *He was waiting there like a sitting duck—a perfect target for a mugger.* □ *The soldiers were standing at the top of the hill like sitting ducks. It's a wonder they weren't all killed.*

like a three-ring circus chaotic; exciting and busy. (A cliché.) □ *Our household is like a three-ring circus on Monday mornings.* □ *This meeting is like a three-ring circus. Quiet down and listen!*

like looking for a needle in a haystack   engaged in a hopeless search. (A cliché.) □ *Trying to find a white dog in the snow is like looking for a needle in a haystack.* □ *I tried to find my lost contact lens on the beach, but it was like looking for a needle in a haystack.*

likely as not, as   See *as likely as not.*

like water off a duck's back   easily; without any apparent effect. (A cliché.) □ *Insults rolled off John like water off a duck's back.* □ *The bullets had no effect on the steel door. They fell away like water off a duck's back.*

limelight, in the   See *in the limelight.*

limit, go the   See *go the limit.*

line of duty, in the   See *in the line of duty.*

little bird told me, a   See *a little bird told me.*

little by little   slowly, a bit at a time. □ *Little by little, he began to understand what we were talking about.* □ *The snail crossed the stone little by little.*

little knowledge is a dangerous thing, A.   See *A little knowledge is a dangerous thing.*

live a dog's life   See under *lead a dog's life.*

live and let live   not to interfere with other people's business or preferences. (A cliché.) □ *I don't care what they do! Live and let live, I always say.* □ *Your parents are strict. Mine just live and let live.*

live beyond one's means   to spend more money than one can afford. □ *The Browns are deeply in debt because they are living beyond their means.* □ *I keep a budget so that I don't live beyond my means.*

live by one's wits   to survive by being clever. □ *When you're in the kind of business I'm in, you have to live by your wits.* □ *John was orphaned at the age of ten and grew up living by his wits.*

live from hand to mouth   to live in poor circumstances. □ *When both my parents were out of work, we lived from hand to mouth.* □ *We lived from hand to mouth during the war. Things were very difficult.*

live in an ivory tower   to be aloof from the realities of living. (*Live* can be replaced by several expressions meaning to dwell or spend time, as in the examples. Academics are often said to live in ivory towers.) □ *If you didn't spend so much time in your ivory tower, you'd know what people really think!* □ *Many professors are said to live in ivory towers. They don't know what the real world is like.*

live off the fat of the land   to grow one's own food; to live on stored-up resources or abundant resources. (A cliché.) □ *If I had a million dollars, I'd invest it and live off the fat of the land.* □ *I'll be happy to retire soon and live off the fat of the land.* □ *Many farmers live off the fat of the land.*

live out of a suitcase   to live briefly in a place, never unpacking one's luggage. □ *I hate living out of a suitcase. For my next vacation, I want to go to just one place and stay there the whole time.* □ *We were living out of suitcases in a motel while they repaired the damage the fire caused to our house.*

live within one's means   to spend no more money than one has. □ *We have to struggle to live within our means, but we manage.* □ *John is unable to live within his means.*

lock horns (with someone)   to get into an argument with someone. (Like bulls or stags fighting.) □ *Let's settle this peacefully. I don't want to lock horns with the boss.* □ *The boss doesn't want to lock horns either.*

lock, stock, and barrel everything. □ *We had to move everything out of the house—lock, stock, and barrel.* □ *We lost everything—lock, stock, and barrel—in the fire.*

loggerheads, at See *at loggerheads.*

long for this world, not See *not long for this world.*

long haul, over the See *over the long haul.*

long run, in the See *in the long run.*

Long time no see. not to have seen someone for a long time. □ *Hello, John. Long time no see.* □ *When John and Mary met on the street, they both said, "Long time no see."*

look as if butter wouldn't melt in one's mouth to appear to be cold and unfeeling (despite any information to the contrary). □ *Sally looks as if butter wouldn't melt in her mouth. She can be so cruel.* □ *What a sour face. He looks as if butter wouldn't melt in his mouth.*

look daggers at someone to give someone a dirty look. (As if one's line of vision were daggers aimed at someone.) □ *Tom must have been mad at Ann from the way he was looking daggers at her.* □ *Don't you dare look daggers at me. Don't even look cross-eyed at me!*

looking for a needle in a haystack, like See *like looking for a needle in a haystack.*

look like a million dollars to look very good. (A cliché.) □ *Oh, Sally, you look like a million dollars.* □ *Your new hairdo looks like a million dollars.*

look like the cat that swallowed the canary to appear as if one had just had a great success. (A cliché. Cats sometimes seem to appear guilty for bad things they have done.) □ *After the meeting John looked like the cat that swallowed the canary. I knew he* *must have been a success.* □ *What happened? You look like the cat that swallowed the canary.*

look the other way to ignore (something) on purpose. (Also used literally.) □ *John could have prevented the problem, but he looked the other way.* □ *By looking the other way, he actually made the problem worse.*

loose ends, at See *at loose ends.*

lord it over someone to dominate someone; to direct and control someone. □ *Mr. Smith seems to lord it over his wife.* □ *The boss lords it over everyone in the office.*

lose face to lose status; to become less respectable. □ *John is more afraid of losing face than losing money.* □ *Things will go better if you can explain to him where he was wrong without making him lose face.*

lose heart to lose one's courage or confidence. □ *Now, don't lose heart. Keep trying.* □ *What a disappointment! It's enough to make one lose heart.*

lose one's grip **1.** to lose one's grasp (of something). □ *I'm holding on to the rope as tightly as I can. I hope I don't lose my grip.* □ *This hammer is slippery. Try not to lose your grip.* **2.** to lose control (over something). □ *I can't seem to run things the way I used to. I'm losing my grip.* □ *They replaced the board of directors because it was losing its grip.*

lose one's temper to become angry. □ *Please don't lose your temper. It's not good for you.* □ *I'm sorry that I lost my temper.*

lose one's train of thought to forget what one was talking or thinking about. □ *Excuse me, I lost my train of thought. What was I talking about?* □ *You made the speaker lose her train of thought.*

lost in thought busy thinking. □ *I'm sorry, I didn't hear what you said. I was lost in thought.* □ *Bill—lost in thought as always —went into the wrong room.*

lot going (for one), have a See *have a lot going (for one).*

love at first sight love established when two people first see one another. (A cliché.) □ *Bill was standing at the door when Ann opened it. It was love at first sight.* □ *It was love at first sight when they met, but it didn't last long.*

lovely weather for ducks rainy weather. (A cliché.) □ BOB: *Not very nice out today, is it?* BILL: *It's lovely weather for ducks.* □ *I don't like this weather, but it's lovely weather for ducks.*

low boiling point, have a See *have a low boiling point.*

lower one's sights to set one's goals lower. □ *Even though you get frustrated, don't lower your sights.* □ *I shouldn't lower my sights. If I work hard, I can do what I want.*

lower one's voice to speak more softly. □ *Please lower your voice, or you'll disturb the people who are working.* □ *He wouldn't lower his voice, so everyone heard what he said.*

lower the boom on someone to scold or punish someone severely; to crack down on someone. (Originally nautical.) □ *If Bob won't behave better, I'll have to lower the boom on him.* □ *The teacher lowered the boom on the whole class because one student misbehaved.*

low man on the totem pole the least important person. (See also *high man on the totem pole.*) □ *I was the last to find out because I'm low man on the totem pole.* □ *I can't be of any help. I'm low man on the totem pole.*

luck, out of See *out of luck.*

luck out of something to get out of some responsibility or task by sheer luck. □ *He lucked out of having to take calculus.* □ *I hoped I would luck out of jury duty, but I had to serve on a three-week long case.*

luck, press one's See *push one's luck.*

luck, push one's See *push one's luck.*

luck would have it, as See *as luck would have it.*

lunch, out to See *out to lunch.*

M

mad as a hatter, as   See *as mad as a hatter.*

mad as a hornet, as   See *as mad as a hornet.*

mad as a March hare, as   See *as mad as a March hare.*

mad as a wet hen, as   See *as mad as a wet hen.*

mad rush, in a   See *in a mad rush.*

make a beeline for someone or something   to head straight toward someone or something. (Also used literally for bees in flight.) □ *Billy came into the kitchen and made a beeline for the cookies.* □ *After the game, we all made a beeline for John, who was serving cold drinks.*

make a clean breast of something   to confess something. □ *You'll feel better if you make a clean breast of it. Now tell us what happened.* □ *I was forced to make a clean breast of the whole affair.*

make a go of it   to make something work out all right. □ *It's a tough situation, but Ann is trying to make a go of it.* □ *We don't like living here, but we have to make a go of it.*

make a great show of something   to make something obvious; to do something in a showy fashion. □ *Ann made a great show of wiping up the drink that John spilled.* □ *Jane displayed her irritation at our late arrival by making a great show of serving the cold dinner.*

make a hit (with someone or something) to please someone. □ *The singer made a hit with the audience.* □ *She was afraid she wouldn't make a hit.* □ *John made a hit with my parents last evening.*

make a long story short to bring a story to an end. (A cliché. A formula that introduces a summary of a story or a joke.) □ *And —to make a long story short—I never got back the money that I lent him.* □ *If I can make a long story short, let me say that everything worked out fine.*

make a mountain out of a molehill to make a major issue out of a minor one; to exaggerate the importance of something. (A cliché.) □ *Come on, don't make a mountain out of a molehill. It's not that important.* □ *Mary is always making mountains out of molehills.*

make a nuisance of oneself to be a constant bother. □ *I'm sorry to make a nuisance of myself, but I do need an answer to my question.* □ *Stop making a nuisance of yourself and wait your turn.*

make a run for it to run fast to get away or get somewhere. □ *When the guard wasn't looking, the prisoner made a run for it.* □ *In the baseball game, the player on first base made a run for it, but he didn't make it to second base.*

make a silk purse out of a sow's ear to create something of value out of something of no value. (A cliché. Often in the negative.) □ *Don't bother trying to fix up this old bicycle. You can't make a silk purse out of a sow's ear.* □ *My mother made a lovely jacket out of an old coat. She succeeded in making a silk purse out of a sow's ear.*

make cracks (about someone or something) to ridicule or make jokes about someone or something. □ *Please stop making cracks about my haircut. It's the new style.* □ *Some people can't help making cracks. They are just rude.*

make fast work of someone or something See under *make short work of someone or something.*

make free with someone or something See under *take liberties with someone or something.*

make good money to earn a large amount of money. (Here, *good* means plentiful.) □ *Ann makes good money at her job.* □ *I don't know what she does, but she makes good money.*

Make hay while the sun is shining. a proverb meaning that you should make the most of good times. □ *There are lots of people here now. You should try to sell them soda pop. Make hay while the sun is shining.* □ *Go to school and get a good education while you're young. Make hay while the sun is shining.*

make life miserable for someone to make someone unhappy over a long period of time. □ *My shoes are tight, and they are making life miserable for me.* □ *Jane's boss is making life miserable for her.*

make light of something to treat something as if it were unimportant or humorous. □ *I wish you wouldn't make light of his problems. They're quite serious.* □ *I make light of my problems, and that makes me feel better.*

make oneself at home to make oneself comfortable as if one were in one's own home. □ *Please come in and make yourself at home.* □ *I'm glad you're here. During your visit, just make yourself at home.*

make short work of someone or something AND **make fast work of someone or something** to finish with someone or something quickly. □ *I made short work of Tom so I could leave the office to play golf.* □ *Billy made fast work of his dinner so he could go out and play.*

make someone or something tick to cause someone or something to run or function. (Usually with *what*. Originally the kind of thing that would be said about a clock or a watch.) □ *I don't* *know what makes it tick.* □ *What makes John tick? I just don't understand him.* □ *I took apart the radio to find out what made it tick.*

make someone's blood boil to make someone very angry. □ *It just makes my blood boil to think of the amount of food that gets wasted around here.* □ *Whenever I think of that dishonest mess, it makes my blood boil.*

make someone's blood run cold to shock or horrify someone. □ *The terrible story in the newspaper made my blood run cold.* □ *I could tell you things about prisons that would make your blood run cold.*

make someone's hair stand on end to cause someone to be very frightened. □ *The horrible scream made my hair stand on end.* □ *The ghost story made our hair stand on end.*

make someone's head spin See the following entry.

make someone's head swim AND **make someone's head spin** **1.** to make someone dizzy or disoriented. □ *Riding in your car makes my head spin.* □ *Breathing the gas made my head swim.* **2.** to confuse or overwhelm someone. □ *All these numbers make my head swim.* □ *The physics lecture made my head spin.*

make someone's mouth water to make someone hungry (for something); to cause someone to salivate. (Also used literally.) □ *That beautiful salad makes my mouth water.* □ *Talking about food makes my mouth water.*

make someone the scapegoat for something to make someone take the blame for something. □ *They made Tom the scapegoat for the whole affair. It wasn't all his fault.* □ *Don't try to make me the scapegoat. I'll tell who really did it.*

make something from scratch to make something by starting with the basic ingredients. □ *We made the cake from scratch,* *using no prepared ingredients.* □ *I didn't have a ladder, so I made one from scratch.*

make something up out of whole cloth AND **make up something out of whole cloth**   to create a story or a lie from no facts at all. (A cliché.) □ *I don't believe you. I think you made that up out of whole cloth.* □ *Ann made up her explanation out of whole cloth. There was not a bit of truth in it.*

make the feathers fly   See the following entry.

make the fur fly AND **make the feathers fly**   to cause a fight or an argument. □ *When your mother gets home and sees what you've done, she'll really make the fur fly.* □ *When those two get together, they'll make the feathers fly. They hate each other.*

make the grade   to be satisfactory; to be what is expected. □ *I'm sorry, but your work doesn't exactly make the grade.* □ *This meal doesn't just make the grade. It is excellent.*

make up for lost time   to do much of something; to do something fast. □ *Because we took so long eating lunch, we have to drive faster to make up for lost time. Otherwise we won't arrive on time.* □ *At the age of sixty, Bill learned to play golf. Now he plays every day. He's making up for lost time.*

march to a different drummer   to believe in a different set of principles. (A cliché.) □ *John is marching to a different drummer, and he doesn't come to our parties anymore.* □ *Since Sally started marching to a different drummer, she has had a lot of great new ideas.*

market, on the   See *on the market.*

means, beyond one's   See *beyond one's means.*

meet one's end   to die. □ *The dog met his end under the wheels of a car.* □ *I don't intend to meet my end until I'm 100 years old.*

meet one's match to meet one's equal. □ *John played tennis with Bill yesterday, and it looks as if John has finally met his match.* □ *Listen to Jane and Mary argue. I always thought that Jane was loud, but she has finally met her match.*

meet someone halfway to offer to compromise with someone. □ *No, I won't give in, but I'll meet you halfway.* □ *They settled the argument by agreeing to meet each other halfway.*

melt in one's mouth to taste very good; [for food] to be very rich and satisfying. (A cliché.) □ *This cake is so good it'll melt in your mouth.* □ *John said that the food didn't exactly melt in his mouth.*

mend (one's) fences to restore good relations (with someone). (Also used literally.) □ *I think I had better get home and mend my fences. I had an argument with my daughter this morning.* □ *Sally called up her uncle to apologize and try to mend fences.*

mend, on the See *on the mend.*

mention something in passing to mention something casually; to mention something while talking about something else. □ *He just happened to mention in passing that the mayor had resigned.* □ *John mentioned in passing that he was nearly eighty years old.*

mill, been through the See *been through the mill.*

millstone about one's neck a continual burden or handicap. □ *This huge and expensive house is a millstone about my neck.* □ *Bill's inability to read is a millstone about his neck.*

mind one's own business to attend only to the things that concern one. □ *Leave me alone, Bill. Mind your own business.* □ *I'd be fine if John would mind his own business.*

mind one's p's and q's to mind one's manners; to pay attention to small details of behavior. (From an old caution to children learning the alphabet or to typesetters to watch carefully for the difference between *p* and *q*.) □ *When we go to the mayor's re-*

ception, please mind your p's and q's. □ *I always mind my p's and q's when I eat at a restaurant with white tablecloths.*

mind, on one's   See *on one's mind.*

mind, out of one's   See *out of one's mind.*

mind's eye, in one's   See *in one's mind's eye.*

mint condition, in   See *in mint condition.*

Missouri, be from   See *be from Missouri.*

miss (something) by a mile   to fail to hit something by a great distance. (A cliché.) □ *Ann shot the arrow and missed the target by a mile.* □ *"Good grief, you missed by a mile," shouted Sally.*

miss the point   to fail to understand the point, purpose, or intent. □ *I'm afraid you missed the point. Let me explain it again.* □ *You keep explaining, and I keep missing the point.*

mixed feelings (about someone or something), have   See *have mixed feelings (about someone or something).*

Money burns a hole in someone's pocket.   someone spends as much money as possible. (As if the money were trying as hard as possible to get out.) □ *Sally can't seem to save anything. Money burns a hole in her pocket.* □ *If money burns a hole in your pocket, you never have any for emergencies.*

money, in the   See *in the money.*

money is no object   it does not matter how much something costs. □ *Please show me your finest automobile. Money is no object.* □ *I want the finest earrings you have. Don't worry about how much they cost because money is no object.*

Money is the root of all evil.   a proverb meaning that money is the basic cause of all wrongdoing. □ *Why do you work so hard to make money? It will just cause you trouble. Money is the root* *of all evil.* □ *Any thief in prison can tell you that money is the root of all evil.*

money talks   money gives one power and influence to help get things done or get one's own way. □ *Don't worry. I have a way of getting things done. Money talks.* □ *I can't compete against rich old Mrs. Jones. She'll get her way because money talks.*

money to burn, have   See *have money to burn.*

mood to do something, in no   See *in no mood to do something.*

motions, go through the   See *go through the motions.*

mouth, down in the   See *down in the mouth.*

move heaven and earth to do something   to make a major effort to do something. (A cliché. Not literal.) □ *"I'll move heaven and earth to be with you, Mary," said Bill.* □ *I had to move heaven and earth to get there on time.*

move, on the   See *on the move.*

move up (in the world)   to advance (oneself) and become successful. □ *The harder I work, the more I move up in the world.* □ *Keep your eye on John. He's really moving up.*

much ado about nothing   a lot of excitement about nothing. (A cliché. This is the title of a play by Shakespeare. Do not confuse *ado* with *adieu.*) □ *All the commotion about the new tax law turned out to be much ado about nothing.* □ *Your promises always turn out to be much ado about nothing.*

N

name only, in   See *in name only.*

nape of the neck, by the   See *by the nape of the neck.*

neck and neck   exactly even, especially in a race or a contest. □ *John and Tom finished the race neck and neck.* □ *Mary and Ann were neck and neck in the spelling contest. Their scores were tied.*

neck (in something), up to one's   See *up to one's neck (in something).*

neither fish nor fowl   not any recognizable thing. (A cliché.) □ *The car that they drove up in was neither fish nor fowl. It must have been made out of spare parts.* □ *This proposal is neither fish nor fowl. I can't tell what you're proposing.*

neither hide nor hair   no sign or indication (of someone or something). (A cliché.) □ *We could find neither hide nor hair of him. I don't know where he is.* □ *There has been no one here—neither hide nor hair—for the last three days.*

nerve, of all the   See *of all the nerve.*

new lease on life   a renewed and revitalized outlook on life; a new start in living. (A cliché.) □ *Getting the job offer was a new lease on life.* □ *When I got out of the hospital, I felt as if I had a new lease on life.*

nick of time, in the   See *in the nick of time.*

nip and tuck almost even; almost tied. □ *The horses ran nip and tuck for the first half of the race. Then my horse pulled ahead.* □ *In the football game last Saturday, both teams were nip and tuck throughout the game.*

nip something in the bud to put an end to something at an early stage. (A cliché. As if one were pinching the flowering bud from an annoying plant.) □ *John is getting into bad habits, and it's best to nip them in the bud.* □ *There was trouble in the classroom, but the teacher nipped it in the bud.*

no (ifs, ands, or) buts about it absolutely no discussion, dissension, or doubt about something. (A cliché.) □ *I want you there exactly at eight, no ifs, ands, or buts about it.* □ *This is the best television set available for the money, no buts about it.*

no laughing matter a serious matter. (A cliché.) □ *Be serious. This is no laughing matter.* □ *This disease is no laughing matter. It's quite deadly.*

none the worse for wear no worse because of use or effort. □ *I lent my car to John. When I got it back, it was none the worse for wear.* □ *I had a hard day today, but I'm none the worse for wear.*

nosedive, go into a See *go into a nosedive.*

nose in a book, have one's See *have one's nose in a book.*

no skin off someone's nose See the following entry.

no skin off someone's teeth AND **no skin off someone's nose** no difficulty for someone; no concern of someone. (A cliché.) □ *It's no skin off my nose if she wants to act that way.* □ *She said it was no skin off her teeth if we wanted to sell the house.*

no spring chicken not young (anymore). □ *I don't get around very well anymore. I'm no spring chicken, you know.* □ *Even though John is no spring chicken, he still plays tennis twice a week.*

not able to see the forest for the trees allowing many details of a problem to obscure the problem as a whole. (A cliché. *Not able to* is often expressed as *can't*.) □ *The solution is obvious. You missed it because you can't see the forest for the trees.* □ *She suddenly realized that she hadn't been able to see the forest for the trees.*

not born yesterday experienced; knowledgeable in the ways of the world. □ *I know what's going on. I wasn't born yesterday.* □ *Sally knows the score. She wasn't born yesterday.*

not have a leg to stand on [for an argument or a case] to have no support. □ *You may think you're in the right, but you don't have a leg to stand on.* □ *My lawyer said I didn't have a leg to stand on, so I shouldn't sue the company.*

nothing but skin and bones AND **all skin and bones** very thin or emaciated. □ *Bill has lost so much weight. He's nothing but skin and bones.* □ *That old horse is all skin and bones. I won't ride it.*

nothing flat, in See *in nothing flat.*

Nothing ventured, nothing gained. a proverb meaning that you cannot achieve anything if you do not try. □ *Come on, John. Give it a try. Nothing ventured, nothing gained.* □ *I felt as if I had to take the chance. Nothing ventured, nothing gained.*

not hold water to make no sense; to be illogical. (Said of ideas, arguments, etc., not people. It means that the idea has holes in it.) □ *Your argument doesn't hold water.* □ *This scheme won't work because it won't hold water.*

not know enough to come in out of the rain to be very stupid. (A cliché.) □ *Bob is so stupid he doesn't know enough to come in out of the rain.* □ *You can't expect very much from somebody who doesn't know enough to come in out of the rain.*

not know someone from Adam not to know someone at all. (A cliché.) □ *I wouldn't recognize John if I saw him. I don't know* *him from Adam.* □ *What does she look like? I don't know her from Adam.*

not long for this world to be about to die. (A cliché.) □ *Our dog is nearly twelve years old and not long for this world.* □ *I'm so tired. I think I'm not long for this world.*

not open one's mouth AND **not utter a word** not to say anything at all; not to tell something (to anyone). □ *Don't worry, I'll keep your secret. I won't even open my mouth.* □ *Have no fear. I won't utter a word.* □ *I don't know how they found out. I didn't even open my mouth.*

not set foot somewhere not to go somewhere. □ *I wouldn't set foot in John's room. I'm very angry with him.* □ *He never set foot here.*

not show one's face not to appear (somewhere). □ *After what she said, she had better not show her face around here again.* □ *If I don't say I'm sorry, I'll never be able to show my face again.*

not sleep a wink not to sleep at all; not to close one's eyes in sleep even as long as it takes to blink. □ *I couldn't sleep a wink last night.* □ *Ann hasn't been able to sleep a wink for a week.*

not someone's cup of tea not something one prefers. (A cliché.) □ *Playing cards isn't her cup of tea.* □ *Sorry, that's not my cup of tea.*

not up to scratch AND **not up to snuff** not adequate. □ *Sorry, your paper isn't up to scratch. Please do it over again.* □ *The performance was not up to snuff.*

not up to snuff See the previous entry.

not utter a word See under *not open one's mouth*.

O

odd man out   an unusual or atypical person or thing. □ *I'm odd man out because I'm not wearing a tie.* □ *You had better learn to work a computer unless you want to be odd man out.*

odds to be against one, for the   See *for the odds to be against one.*

of all the nerve   how shocking; how dare (someone). (The speaker is exclaiming that someone is being very cheeky or rude.) □ *How dare you talk to me that way! Of all the nerve!* □ *Imagine anyone coming to a formal dance in jeans. Of all the nerve!*

off base   unrealistic; inexact; wrong. (Also used literally in baseball.) □ *I'm afraid you're off base when you state that this problem will take care of itself.* □ *You're way off base!*

off-color   **1.** not the exact color (that one wants). □ *The book cover used to be red, but now it's a little off-color.* □ *The wall was painted off-color. I think it was meant to be orange.* **2.** rude, vulgar, or impolite. □ *That joke you told was off-color and embarrassed me.* □ *The nightclub act was a bit off-color.*

off duty   not working at one's job. □ *I'm sorry, I can't talk to you until I'm off duty.* □ *The police officer couldn't help me because he was off duty.*

off the air   not broadcasting (a radio or television program). □ *The radio audience won't hear what you say when you're off the air.* □ *When the performers were off the air, the director told them how well they had done.*

off the record unofficial; informal. □ *This is off the record, but I disagree with the mayor on this matter.* □ *Although she said her comments were off the record, the newspaper published them anyway.*

off the top of one's head [to state something] rapidly and without having to think or remember. □ *I can't think of the answer off the top of my head.* □ *Jane can tell you the correct amount off the top of her head.*

off to a running start with a good, fast beginning, possibly a head start. □ *I got off to a running start in math this year.* □ *The horses got off to a running start.*

of the first water of the finest quality. (Originally a measurement of the quality of a pearl.) □ *This is a very fine pearl—a pearl of the first water.* □ *Tom is of the first water—a true gentleman.*

on active duty in battle or ready to go into battle. (Military.) □ *The soldier was on active duty for ten months.* □ *That was a long time to be on active duty.*

on all fours on one's hands and knees. □ *I dropped a contact lens and spent an hour on all fours looking for it.* □ *The baby can walk, but is on all fours most of the time anyway.*

on a waiting list [for someone's name to be] on a list of people waiting for an opportunity to do something. (*A* can be replaced with *the*.) □ *I couldn't get a seat on the plane, but I got on a waiting list.* □ *There is no room for you, but we can put your name on the waiting list.*

once in a blue moon very rarely. (A cliché.) □ *I seldom go to a movie—maybe once in a blue moon.* □ *I don't go into the city except once in a blue moon.*

on cloud nine very happy. □ *When I got my promotion, I was on cloud nine.* □ *When the check came, I was on cloud nine for days.*

on duty   at work; currently doing one's work. □ *I can't help you now, but I'll be on duty in about an hour.* □ *Who is on duty here? I need some help.*

on earth AND **in creation; in the world**   how amazing!; of all things! (Used as an intensifier after *who, what, when, where, how, which.*) □ *What on earth do you mean?* □ *How in creation do you expect me to do that?* □ *Who in the world do you think you are?* □ *When on earth do you expect me to do this?*

one ear and out the other, go in   See *go in one ear and out the other.*

one ear and out the other, in   See *in one ear and out the other.*

One good turn deserves another.   a proverb meaning that a good deed should be repaid with another good deed. □ *If he does you a favor, you should do him a favor. One good turn deserves another.* □ *Glad to help you out. One good turn deserves another.*

one in a hundred   See under *one in a thousand.*

one in a million   See the following entry.

one in a thousand AND **one in a hundred; one in a million**   unique; one of a very few. □ *He's a great guy. He's one in million.* □ *Mary's one in a hundred—such a hard worker.*

One man's meat is another man's poison.   a proverb meaning that one person's preference may be disliked by another person. □ *John just loves his new fur hat, but I think it is horrible. Oh, well, one man's meat is another man's poison.* □ *The neighbors are very fond of their dog even though it's ugly, loud, and smelly. I guess one man's meat is another man's poison.*

One's bark is worse than one's bite.   a proverb meaning that one may threaten, but not do much damage. □ *Don't worry about Bob. He won't hurt you. His bark is worse than his bite.* □

She may scream and yell, but have no fear. Her bark is worse than her bite.

one's better half one's spouse. (Usually refers to a wife.) □ *I think we'd like to come for dinner, but I'll have to ask my better half.* □ *I have to go home now to my better half. We are going out tonight.*

one's days are numbered [for someone] to face death or dismissal. (A cliché.) □ *If I don't get this contract, my days are numbered at this company.* □ *Uncle Tom has a terminal disease. His days are numbered.*

one's desk, away from See *away from one's desk.*

one's eyes are bigger than one's stomach [for one] to take more food than one can eat. □ *I can't eat all this. I'm afraid that my eyes were bigger than my stomach.* □ *Try to take less food. Your eyes are bigger than your stomach at every meal.* ALSO: **have eyes bigger than one's stomach** to have a desire for more food than one could possibly eat. □ *I know I have eyes bigger than my stomach, so I won't take a lot of food.*

one's heart is in one's mouth See under *have one's heart in one's mouth.*

one's heart is set on something See under *have one's heart set on something.*

one's number is up one's time to die—or to suffer some other unpleasantness—has come. □ *John is worried. He thinks his number is up.* □ *When my number is up, I hope it all goes fast.*

one's song and dance about something, go into See *go into one's song and dance about something.*

one's tail is between one's legs See under *have one's tail between one's legs.*

one's words stick in one's throat See under *have one's words stick in one's throat.*

on one's feet **1.** standing up; standing on one's feet. □ *Get on your feet. They are playing the national anthem.* □ *I've been on my feet all day, and they hurt.* **2.** well and healthy, especially after an illness. □ *I hope to be back on my feet next week.* □ *I can help out as soon as I'm back on my feet.*

on one's honor on one's solemn oath; promised sincerely. □ *On my honor, I'll be there on time.* □ *He promised on his honor that he'd pay me back next week.*

on one's mind occupying one's thoughts; currently being thought about. □ *You've been on my mind all day.* □ *Do you have something on your mind? You look so serious.*

on one's toes alert. □ *You have to be on your toes if you want to be in this business.* □ *My boss keeps me on my toes.*

on pins and needles anxious; in suspense. (A cliché.) □ *I've been on pins and needles all day, waiting for you to call with the news.* □ *We were on pins and needles until we heard that your plane landed safely.*

on second thought having given something more thought; having reconsidered something. □ *On second thought, maybe you should sell your house and move into an apartment.* □ *On second thought, let's not go to a movie.*

on someone's doorstep See under *at someone's doorstep.*

on someone's head on someone's own self. (Usually with *blame*. *On* can be replaced with *upon*.) □ *All the blame fell on their heads.* □ *I don't think that all the criticism should be on my head.*

on someone's or something's last legs for someone or something to be almost finished. □ *This building is on its last legs. It* *should be torn down.* □ *I feel as if I'm on my last legs. I'm really tired.*

on someone's say-so   on someone's authority; with someone's permission. □ *I can't do it on your say-so. I'll have to get a written request.* □ BILL: *I canceled the contract with the A.B.C. Company.* BOB: *On whose say-so?*

on someone's shoulders   on someone's own self. (Usually with *responsibility. On* can be replaced with *upon*.) □ *Why should all the responsibility fall on my shoulders?* □ *She carries a tremendous amount of responsibility on her shoulders.*

on target   on schedule; exactly as predicted. □ *Your estimate of the cost was right on target.* □ *My prediction was not on target.*

on the air   broadcasting (a radio or television program). □ *The radio station came back on the air shortly after the storm.* □ *We were on the air for two hours.*

on the average   generally; usually. □ *On the average, you can expect about a 10 percent failure.* □ *This report looks okay, on the average.*

on the bench   **1.** directing a session of court. (Said of a judge.) □ *I have to go to court tomorrow. Who's on the bench?* □ *It doesn't matter who's on the bench. You'll get a fair hearing.* **2.** sitting, waiting for a chance to play in a game. (In sports, such as basketball, football, soccer, etc.) □ *Bill is on the bench now. I hope he gets to play.* □ *John played during the first quarter, but now he's on the bench.*

on the block   **1.** on a city block. □ *John is the biggest kid on the block.* □ *We had a party on the block last weekend.* **2.** on sale at auction; on the auction block. □ *We couldn't afford to keep up the house, so it was put on the block to pay the taxes.* □ *That's the finest painting I've ever seen on the block.*

on the button   exactly right; in exactly the right place; at exactly the right time. ☐ *That's it! You're right on the button.* ☐ *He got here at one o'clock on the button.*

on the contrary   [as the] opposite. ☐ *I'm not ill. On the contrary, I'm very healthy.* ☐ *She's not in a bad mood. On the contrary, she's as happy as a lark.*

on the dot   at exactly the right time. ☐ *I'll be there at noon on the dot.* ☐ *I expect to see you here at eight o'clock on the dot.*

on the go   busy; moving about busily. ☐ *I'm usually on the go all day long.* ☐ *I hate being on the go all the time.*

on the heels of something   soon after something. ☐ *There was a rainstorm on the heels of the windstorm.* ☐ *The team held a victory celebration on the heels of their winning season.*

on the horizon   soon to happen. (Also used literally.) ☐ *You never know what's on the horizon.* ☐ *Who can tell what's on the horizon?*

on the horns of a dilemma   having to decide between two things, people, etc.; balanced between one choice and another. ☐ *Mary found herself on the horns of a dilemma. She didn't know which to choose.* ☐ *I make up my mind easily. I'm not on the horns of a dilemma very often.*

on the hour   at each hour on the hour mark. ☐ *I have to take this medicine every hour on the hour.* ☐ *I expect to see you there on the hour, not one minute before and not one minute after.*

on the house   [something that is] given away free by a merchant. (Also used literally.) ☐ *"Here," said the waiter, "have a cup of coffee on the house."* ☐ *I went to a restaurant last night. I was the ten thousandth customer, so my dinner was on the house.*

on the level   honest; dependably open and fair. (Also with strictly.) ☐ *How can I be sure you're on the level?* ☐ *You can trust Sally. She's on the level.*

on the market available for sale; offered for sale. □ *I had to put my car on the market.* □ *This is the finest home computer on the market.*

on the mend getting well; healing. □ *My cold was terrible, but I'm on the mend now.* □ *What you need is some hot chicken soup. Then you'll really be on the mend.*

on the move moving; happening busily. □ *What a busy day. Things are really on the move at the store.* □ *When all the buffalo were on the move across the plains, it must have been very exciting.*

on the QT quietly; secretly. □ *The company president was making payments to his wife on the QT.* □ *The mayor accepted a bribe on the QT.*

on the spot **1.** at exactly the right place; at exactly the right time. □ *It's noon, and I'm glad you're all here on the spot. Now we can begin.* □ *I expect you to be on the spot when and where trouble arises.* **2.** in trouble; in a difficult situation. □ *There is a problem in the department I manage, and I'm really on the spot.* □ *I hate to be on the spot when it's not my fault.*

on the spur of the moment suddenly; spontaneously. □ *We decided to go on the spur of the moment.* □ *I had to leave town on the spur of the moment.*

on the tip of one's tongue about to be said; almost remembered. (As if a word were about to leap from one's tongue and be spoken.) □ *I have his name right on the tip of my tongue. I'll think of it in a second.* □ *John had the answer on the tip of his tongue, but Ann said it first.*

on the wagon not drinking alcohol; no longer drinking alcohol. (Also used literally. Refers to a "water wagon.") □ *None for me, thanks. I'm on the wagon.* □ *Look at John. I don't think he's on the wagon anymore.*

on the wrong track going the wrong way; following the wrong set of assumptions. (Also used literally for trains, hounds, etc.) □ *You'll never get the right answer. You're on the wrong track.* □ *They won't get it figured out because they are on the wrong track.*

on thin ice in a risky situation. □ *If you try that you'll really be on thin ice. That's too risky.* □ *If you don't want to find yourself on thin ice, you must be sure of your facts.* ALSO: **skate on thin ice** to be in a risky situation. (Also used literally.) □ *I try to stay well informed so I don't end up skating on thin ice when the teacher asks me a question.*

on tiptoe standing or walking on the front part of the feet (the balls of the feet) with no weight put on the heels. (This is done to gain height or to walk quietly.) □ *I had to stand on tiptoe in order to see over the fence.* □ *I came in late and walked on tiptoe so I wouldn't wake anybody up.*

on top victorious over something; famous or notorious for something. □ *I have to study day and night to keep on top.* □ *Bill is on top in his field.*

on top of the world feeling wonderful; glorious; ecstatic. (A cliché.) □ *Wow, I feel on top of the world.* □ *Since he got a new job, he's on top of the world.*

on trial being tried in court. □ *My sister is on trial today, so I have to go to court.* □ *They placed the suspected thief on trial.*

on vacation away, taking a vacation; on holiday. □ *Where are you going on vacation this year?* □ *I'll be away on vacation for three weeks.*

open a can of worms to uncover a set of problems; to create unnecessary complications. (*Can of worms* means "mess." Also with *open up* and with various modifiers such as *new, whole, another,* as in the examples.) □ *Now you are opening a whole new can of worms.* □ *How about cleaning up this mess before you open up a new can of worms?*

open one's heart (to someone) to reveal one's inmost thoughts to someone. □ *I always open my heart to my spouse when I have a problem.* □ *It's a good idea to open your heart every now and then.*

open one's mouth, not See *not open one's mouth.*

open Pandora's box to uncover a lot of unsuspected problems. (A cliché.) □ *When I asked Jane about her problems, I didn't know I had opened Pandora's box.* □ *You should be cautious with people who are upset. You don't want to open Pandora's box.*

order, out of See *out of order.*

other side of the tracks the poorer part of a town, often near the railroad tracks. (Especially with *from the* or *live on the.*) □ *Who cares if she's from the other side of the tracks?* □ *I came from a poor family—we lived on the other side of the tracks.*

ounce of prevention is worth a pound of cure, An. See *An ounce of prevention is worth a pound of cure.*

out and about able to go out and travel around; well enough to go out. □ *Beth has been ill, but now she's out and about.* □ *As soon as I feel better, I'll be able to get out and about.*

out cold AND **out like a light** unconscious. □ *I fell and hit my head. I was out cold for about a minute.* □ *Tom fainted! He's out like a light!*

out in left field offbeat; unusual and eccentric. □ *Sally is a lot of fun, but she's sort of out in left field.* □ *What a strange idea. It's really out in left field.*

out like a light See under *out cold.*

out of a clear blue sky AND **out of the blue** suddenly; without warning. (A cliché.) □ *Then, out of a clear blue sky, he told me* *he was leaving.* □ *Mary appeared on my doorstep out of the blue.*

out of all proportion   of an exaggerated proportion; of an unrealistic proportion compared to something else; (figuratively) lopsided. (The *all* can be left out.) □ *This problem has grown out of all proportion.* □ *Yes, this thing is way out of proportion.* ALSO: **blow something out of all proportion** to cause something to be unrealistically proportioned relative to something else. (The *all* can be left out.) □ *The press has blown this issue out of all proportion.* □ *Let's be reasonable. Don't blow this thing out of proportion.*

out of circulation   **1.** no longer available for use or lending. (Usually said of library materials.) □ *I'm sorry, but the book you want is temporarily out of circulation.* □ *How long will it be out of circulation?* **2.** not interacting socially with other people. □ *I don't know what's happening because I've been out of circulation for a while.* □ *My cold has kept me out of circulation for a few weeks.*

out of commission   **1.** [for a ship] to be not currently in use or under command. □ *This vessel will remain out of commission for another month.* □ *The ship has been out of commission since repairs began.* **2.** broken, unserviceable, or inoperable. □ *My watch is out of commission and is running slowly.* □ *I can't run in the marathon because my knees are out of commission.*

out of gas   **1.** having no more gasoline (in a car, truck, etc.). □ *We can't go any farther. We're out of gas.* □ *This car will be completely out of gas in a few more miles.* **2.** tired; exhausted; worn out. □ *What a day! I've been working since morning, and I'm really out of gas.* □ *This electric clock is out of gas. I'll have to get a new one.* ALSO: **run out of gas** to use up all the gasoline available. □ *I hope we don't run out of gas.*

out of hand   immediately and without consulting anyone; without delay. □ *I can't answer that out of hand. I'll check with the manager and call you back.* □ *The offer was so good that I accepted it out of hand.*

out of luck without good luck; having bad fortune. □ *If you wanted some ice cream, you're out of luck.* □ *I was out of luck. I got there too late to get a seat.*

out of one's element not in a natural or comfortable situation. □ *When it comes to computers, I'm out of my element.* □ *Sally's out of her element in math.*

out of one's head See the following entry.

out of one's mind AND **out of one's head; out of one's senses** silly and senseless; crazy; irrational. □ *Why did you do that? You must be out of your mind!* □ *Good grief, Tom! You have to be out of your head!* □ *She's acting as if she were out of her senses.*

out of one's senses See the previous entry.

out of order **1.** not in the correct order. □ *This book is out of order. Please put it in the right place on the shelf.* □ *You're out of order, John. Please get in line after Jane.* **2.** not following correct parliamentary procedure. □ *I was declared out of order by the president.* □ *Ann inquired, "Isn't a motion to table the question out of order at this time?"*

out of practice performing poorly due to a lack of practice. □ *I used to be able to play the piano extremely well, but now I'm out of practice.* □ *The baseball players lost the game because they were out of practice.*

out of print [for a book] to be no longer available for sale. (Compare to *in print.*) □ *The book you want is out of print, but perhaps I can find a used copy for you.* □ *It was published nearly ten years ago, so it's probably out of print.*

out of season **1.** not now available for sale. □ *Sorry, oysters are out of season. We don't have any.* □ *Watermelon is out of season in the winter.* **2.** not now legally able to be hunted or caught. □ *Are salmon out of season?* □ *I caught a trout out of season and had to pay a fine.*

out of service inoperable; not now operating. □ *Both elevators are out of service, so I had to use the stairs.* □ *The washroom is temporarily out of service.*

Out of sight, out of mind. a proverb meaning that if you do not see something, you will not think about it. □ *When I go home, I put my schoolbooks away so I won't worry about doing my homework. After all, out of sight, out of mind.* □ *Jane dented the fender on her car. It's on the right side, so she doesn't have to look at it. Like they say, out of sight, out of mind.*

out of sorts not feeling well; grumpy and irritable. □ *I've been out of sorts for a day or two. I think I'm coming down with something.* □ *The baby is out of sorts. Maybe she's getting a tooth.*

out of the blue See under *out of a clear blue sky.*

out of the corner of one's eye [seeing something] at a glance; glimpsing (something). □ *I saw someone do it out of the corner of my eye. It might have been Jane who did it.* □ *I only saw the accident out of the corner of my eye. I don't know who is at fault.*

out of the frying pan into the fire from a bad situation to a worse situation. (A cliché. If it was hot in the pan, it is hotter in the fire.) □ *When I tried to argue about my fine for a traffic violation, the judge charged me with contempt of court. I really went out of the frying pan into the fire.* □ *I got deeply in debt. Then I really got out of the frying pan into the fire when I was fired from my job.*

out of the hole out of debt. (Also used literally.) □ *I get paid next week, and then I can get out of the hole.* □ *I can't seem to get out of the hole. I keep spending more money than I earn.*

out of the question not possible; not permitted. □ *I'm sorry, but it's out of the question.* □ *You can't go to Florida this spring. We can't afford it. It's out of the question.*

out of the red out of debt. □ *This year our firm is likely to get out of the red before fall.* □ *If we can cut down on expenses, we can get out of the red fairly soon.*

out of the running no longer being considered; eliminated from a contest. □ *After the first part of the diving meet, three members of our team were out of the running.* □ *After the scandal was made public, I was no longer in the running. I pulled out of the election.*

out of the woods past a critical phase; out of the unknown. □ *When the patient got out of the woods, everyone relaxed.* □ *I can give you a better prediction for your future health when you are out of the woods.*

out of thin air out of nowhere; out of nothing. □ *Suddenly—out of thin air—the messenger appeared.* □ *You just made that up out of thin air.*

out of this world wonderful; extraordinary. (A cliché. Also used literally.) □ *This pie is just out of this world.* □ *Look at you! How lovely you look—simply out of this world.*

out of tune (with someone or something) 1. in musical harmony with someone or something. □ *The oboe is out of tune with the flute.* □ *The flute is out of tune with John.* □ *They are all out of tune.* 2. not in (figurative) harmony or agreement. □ *Your proposal is out of tune with my ideas of what we should be doing.* □ *Let's get all our efforts in tune.*

out of turn not at the proper time; not in the proper order. □ *We were permitted to be served out of turn, because we had to leave early.* □ *Bill tried to register out of turn and was sent away.*

out on a limb in a dangerous position; taking a chance. □ *I don't want to go out on a limb, but I think I'd agree to your request.* □ *She really went out on a limb when she agreed.*

out on the town celebrating at one or more places in a town. □ *I'm really tired. I was out on the town until dawn.* □ *We went out on the town to celebrate our wedding anniversary.*

outside, at the See *at the outside.*

out to lunch eating lunch away from one's place of work. □ *I'm sorry, but Sally Jones is out to lunch. May I take a message?* □ *She's been out to lunch for nearly two hours. When will she be back?*

overboard, go See *go overboard.*

over the hill overage; too old to do something. □ *Now that Mary's forty, she thinks she's over the hill.* □ *My grandfather was over eighty before he felt as if he was over the hill.*

over the hump over the difficult part. □ *This is a difficult project, but we're over the hump now.* □ *I'm halfway through—over the hump—and it looks as if I may get finished after all.*

over the long haul for a relatively long period of time. □ *Over the long haul, it might be better to invest in stocks.* □ *Over the long haul, everything will turn out all right.*

over the short haul for the immediate future. □ *Over the short haul, you'd be better off to put your money in the bank.* □ *Over the short haul, you may wish you had done something different. But things will work out all right.*

over the top having gained more than one's goal. □ *Our fund-raising campaign went over the top by $3,000.* □ *We didn't go over the top. We didn't even get half of what we set out to collect.*

P

packed (in) like sardines packed very tightly. (A cliché. Many variations are possible, as in the examples.) □ *It was terribly crowded there. We were packed in like sardines.* □ *The bus was full. The passengers were packed like sardines.* □ *They packed us in like sardines.*

paddle one's own canoe to do (something) by oneself; to be alone. (A cliché. Could also be used literally.) □ *I've been left to paddle my own canoe too many times.* □ *Sally isn't with us. She's off paddling her own canoe.*

pad the bill to put unnecessary items on a bill to make the total cost higher. □ *The plumber had padded the bill with things we didn't need.* □ *I was falsely accused of padding the bill.*

paint the town red to have a wild celebration during a night on the town. (Not literal.) □ *Let's all go out and paint the town red!* □ *Oh, do I feel terrible. I was out all last night, painting the town red.*

pale, beyond the See *beyond the pale.*

part and parcel See under *bag and baggage.*

part someone's hair to come very close to someone. (Usually an exaggeration. Also used literally.) □ *That plane flew so low that it nearly parted my hair.* □ *He punched at me and missed. He only parted my hair.*

par, up to See *up to par.*

pass the buck to pass the blame (to someone else); to give the responsibility (to someone else). □ *Don't try to pass the buck! It's your fault, and everybody knows it.* □ *Some people try to pass the buck whenever they can.*

pass the hat to attempt to collect money for some (charitable) project. □ *Bob is passing the hat to collect money to buy flowers for Ann.* □ *He's always passing the hat for something.*

pay an arm and a leg (for something) AND **pay through the nose (for something)** to pay too much money for something. □ *I hate to have to pay an arm and a leg for a tank of gas.* □ *If you shop around, you won't have to pay an arm and a leg.* □ *Why should you pay through the nose?* ALSO: **cost an arm and a leg** to cost too much. □ *It cost an arm and a leg, so I didn't buy it.*

pay one's debt (to society) to serve a sentence for a crime, usually in prison. □ *The judge said that Mr. Simpson had to pay his debt to society.* □ *Mr. Brown paid his debt in state prison.*

pay one's dues **1.** to pay the fees required to belong to an organization. □ *If you haven't paid your dues, you can't come to the club picnic.* □ *How many people have paid their dues?* **2.** to have earned one's right to something through hard work or suffering. □ *He worked hard to get to where he is today. He paid his dues and did what he was told.* □ *I have every right to be here. I paid my dues!*

pay the piper to face the results of one's actions; to receive punishment for something. (A cliché.) □ *You can put off paying your debts only so long. Eventually you'll have to pay the piper.* □ *You can't get away with that forever. You'll have to pay the piper someday.*

pay through the nose (for something) See under *pay an arm and a leg (for something)*.

penny saved is a penny earned, A. See *A penny saved is a penny earned.*

penny-wise and pound-foolish   a proverb meaning that it is foolish to lose a lot of money to save a little money. (A cliché.) □ *Sally shops very carefully to save a few cents on food, then charges the food to a charge card that costs a lot in annual interest. That's being penny-wise and pound-foolish.* □ *John drives thirty miles to buy gas for three cents a gallon less than it costs here. He's really penny-wise and pound-foolish.*

Perish the thought.   Do not even consider thinking of something. (Literary.) □ *If you should become ill—perish the thought —I'd take care of you.* □ *I'm afraid that we need a new car. Perish the thought.*

pick up the tab   to pay the bill. (To pick up the bill and pay it.) □ *Whenever we go out, my father picks up the tab.* □ *Order whatever you want. The company is picking up the tab.*

pie in the sky   a future reward, especially after death. (A cliché. From a longer phrase, "pie in the sky by and by when you die.") □ *Are you nice to people just because of pie in the sky, or do you really like them?* □ *Don't hold out for a big reward, you know— pie in the sky.*

pillar to post, from   See *from pillar to post.*

pink (of condition), in the   See *in the pink (of condition).*

pins and needles, on   See *on pins and needles.*

pitch in (and help)   to get busy and help (with something). □ *Pick up a paintbrush and pitch in and help.* □ *Why don't some of you pitch in? We need all the help we can get.*

pitch someone a curve (ball)   to surprise someone with an unexpected act or event. (Also used literally referring to a curve ball in baseball.) □ *You really pitched me a curve ball when you said I had done a poor job. I did my best.* □ *You asked Tom a hard question. You certainly pitched him a curve.*

plain as day, as   See *as plain as day.*

plain as the nose on one's face, as   See *as plain as the nose on one's face.*

play ball (with someone)   **1.** to play a ball game with someone. (Note the special baseball use in the second example.) □ *When will our team play ball with yours?* □ *Suddenly, the umpire shouted, "Play ball!" and the game began.* **2.** to cooperate with someone. □ *Look, friend, if you play ball with me, everything will work out all right.* □ *Things would go better for you if you'd learn to play ball.*

play both ends (against the middle)   [for one] to scheme in a way that pits two sides against each other (for one's own gain). □ *I told my brother that Mary doesn't like him. Then I told Mary that my brother doesn't like her. They broke up, so now I can have the car this weekend. I succeeded in playing both ends against the middle.* □ *If you try to play both ends, you're likely to get in trouble with both sides.*

play by ear   See under *play something by ear.*

play cat and mouse (with someone)   to (literally or figuratively) capture and release someone over and over. (A cliché.) □ *The police played cat and mouse with the suspect until they had sufficient evidence to make an arrest.* □ *Tom had been playing cat and mouse with Ann. Finally she got tired of it and broke up with him.*

play fast and loose (with someone or something)   to act carelessly, thoughtlessly, and irresponsibly. □ *I'm tired of your playing fast and loose with me. Leave me alone.* □ *Bob got fired for playing fast and loose with the company's money.* □ *If you play fast and loose like that, you can get into a lot of trouble.*

play it safe   to be or act safe; to do something safely. □ *You should play it safe and take your umbrella.* □ *If you have a cold or the flu, play it safe and go to bed.*

play one's cards close to one's vest   See the following entry.

play one's cards close to the chest AND **play one's cards close to one's vest**   [for someone] to work or negotiate in a careful and private manner. (Refers to holding one's playing cards close so that no one can possibly see what one is holding.) □ *It's hard to figure out what John is up to because he plays his cards close to his chest.* □ *Don't let them know what you're up to. Play your cards close to your vest.*

play second fiddle (to someone)   to be in a subordinate position to someone. □ *I'm tired of playing second fiddle to John.* □ *I'm better trained than he, and I have more experience. I shouldn't play second fiddle.*

play something by ear   **1.** to be able to play a piece of music after just listening to it a few times, without looking at the notes. □ *I can play "Stardust" by ear.* □ *Some people can play Chopin's music by ear.* **2.** AND **play by ear** to play a musical instrument well, without formal training. □ *John can play the piano by ear.* □ *If I could play by ear, I wouldn't have to take lessons—or practice!*

play the field   to date many different people rather than going steady. □ *When Tom told Ann good-bye, he said he wanted to play the field.* □ *He said he wanted to play the field while he was still young.*

play to the gallery   to perform in a manner that will get the strong approval of the audience; to perform in a manner that will get the approval of the lower elements in the audience. □ *John is a very competent actor, but he has a tendency to play to the gallery.* □ *When he made the rude remark, he was just playing to the gallery.*

play with fire   to take a big risk. (Also used literally.) □ *If you accuse her of stealing, you'll be playing with fire.* □ *I wouldn't try that if I were you—unless you like playing with fire.*

pocket, have someone in one's   See *have someone in one's pocket.*

poke fun (at someone)   to make fun of someone; to ridicule someone. □ *Stop poking fun at me! It's not nice.* □ *Bob is always poking fun.*

poke one's nose in(to something) AND **stick one's nose in(to something)**   to interfere with something; to be nosy about something. (Not literal.) □ *I wish you'd stop poking your nose into my business.* □ *She was too upset for me to stick my nose in and ask what was wrong.*

poles apart, be   See *be poles apart.*

poor as a church mouse, as   See *as poor as a church mouse.*

poor taste, in   See *in poor taste.*

pop the question   to ask someone to marry you. □ *I was surprised when he popped the question.* □ *I've been waiting for years for someone to pop the question.*

pot calling the kettle black, the   See *the pot calling the kettle black.*

pot, go to   See *go to pot.*

pound a beat   to walk a route. (Usually said of a police patrol officer.) □ *The patrolman pounded the same beat for years and years.* □ *Pounding a beat will wreck your feet.*

pound the pavement to walk through the streets looking for a job. □ *I spent two months pounding the pavement after the factory I worked for closed.* □ *Hey, Bob. You'd better get busy pounding those nails unless you want to be out pounding the pavement.*

pour cold water on something AND **dash cold water on something; throw cold water on something** to discourage doing something; to reduce enthusiasm for something. (Not literal in this sense.) □ *When my father said I couldn't have the car, he poured cold water on my plans.* □ *John threw cold water on the whole project by refusing to participate.*

pour it on thick See under *lay it on thick.*

pour money down the drain to waste money; to throw money away. □ *What a waste! You're just pouring money down the drain.* □ *Don't buy any more of that low-quality merchandise. That's just throwing money down the drain.*

pour oil on troubled water to calm things down. (A cliché. If oil is poured onto rough seas during a storm, the water will become more calm.) □ *That was a good thing to say to John. It helped pour oil on troubled water. Now he looks happy.* □ *Bob is the kind of person who pours oil on troubled water.*

practice, out of See *out of practice.*

practice what you preach to do what you advise other people to do. (A cliché.) □ *If you'd practice what you preach, you'd be better off.* □ *You give good advice. Why not practice what you preach?*

premium, at a See *at a premium.*

press one's luck See under *push one's luck.*

press someone to the wall See under *push someone to the wall.*

pretty as a picture, as See *as pretty as a picture.*

Pretty is as pretty does. you should do pleasant things if you wish to be considered pleasant. (A cliché.) □ *Now, Sally. Let's be nice. Pretty is as pretty does.* □ *My great-aunt always used to say "pretty is as pretty does" to my sister.*

price on one's head, have a See *have a price on one's head.*

prick up one's ears to listen more closely. □ *At the sound of my voice, my dog pricked up her ears.* □ *I pricked up my ears when I heard my name mentioned.*

prime, in one's or its See *in one's or its prime.*

prime of life, in the See *in the prime of life.*

print, in See *in print.*

print, out of See *out of print.*

promise the moon (to someone) AND **promise someone the moon** to make extravagant promises to someone. □ *Bill will promise you the moon, but he won't live up to his promises.* □ *My boss promised the moon, but only paid the minimum wage.*

proportion, out of all See *out of all proportion.*

proud as a peacock, as See *as proud as a peacock.*

public eye, in the See *in the public eye.*

pull oneself up (by one's own bootstraps) to achieve (something) through one's own efforts. (A cliché.) □ *They simply don't have the resources to pull themselves up by their own bootstraps.* □ *If I could have pulled myself up, I'd have done it by now.*

pull someone's leg to kid, fool, or trick someone. □ *You don't mean that. You're just pulling my leg.* □ *Don't believe him. He's just pulling your leg.*

pull someone's or something's teeth to reduce the power of someone or something. (Also used literally.) □ *The mayor tried to pull the teeth of the new law.* □ *The city council pulled the teeth of the new mayor.*

pull something out of a hat AND **pull something out of thin air** to produce something as if by magic. □ *This is a serious problem, and we just can't pull a solution out of a hat.* □ *I'm sorry, but I don't have a pen. What do you want me to do, pull one out of thin air?*

pull something out of thin air See the previous entry.

pull the rug out (from under someone) to make someone ineffective. □ *The treasurer pulled the rug out from under the mayor.* □ *Things were going along fine until the treasurer pulled the rug out.*

pull the wool over someone's eyes to deceive someone. (A cliché.) □ *You can't pull the wool over my eyes. I know what's going on.* □ *Don't try to pull the wool over her eyes. She's too smart.*

pull up stakes to move to another place. (As if one were pulling up tent stakes.) □ *I've been here long enough. It's time to pull up stakes.* □ *I hate the thought of having to pull up stakes.*

push one's luck AND **press one's luck** to expect continued good fortune; to expect to continue to escape bad luck. □ *You're okay so far, but don't push your luck.* □ *Bob pressed his luck too much and got into a lot of trouble.*

push someone to the wall AND **press someone to the wall** to force someone into a position where there is only one choice to make; to put someone in a defensive position. (Also used literally.) □ *There was little else I could do. They pushed me to the wall.* □ *When we pressed him to the wall, he told us where the cookies were hidden.*

put a bee in someone's bonnet   See under *have a bee in one's bonnet.*

put all one's eggs in one basket   to risk everything at once. (A cliché. Often negative. If the basket is dropped, all the eggs are lost.) □ *Don't put all your eggs in one basket. Then everything won't be lost if there is a catastrophe.* □ *John only applied to the one college he wanted to go to. He put all his eggs in one basket.*

put in a good word (for someone)   to say something (to someone) in support of someone. □ *I hope you get the job. I'll put in a good word for you.* □ *Yes, I want the job. If you see the boss, please put in a good word.*

put in one's two cents (worth)   to add one's comments (to something). (Implies that one's comments may not be of great value, but need to be stated anyway.) □ *Can I put in my two cents worth?* □ *Sure, go ahead—put your two cents in.*

put on airs   to act superior. □ *Stop putting on airs. You're just human like the rest of us.* □ *Ann is always putting on airs. You'd think she was a queen.*

put one's best foot forward   to act or appear at one's best; to try to make a good impression. (A cliché.) □ *When you apply for a job, you should always put your best foot forward.* □ *I try to put my best foot forward whenever I meet someone for the first time.*

put one's cards on the table AND **lay one's cards on the table**   to reveal everything; to be open and honest with someone. (As one might do at certain points in a number of different card games to make an accounting of the cards one has been holding.) □ *Come on, John, lay your cards on the table. Tell me what you really think.* □ *Why don't we both put our cards on the table?*

put one's dibs on something   See under *have dibs on something.*

put one's foot in it   See the following entry.

put one's foot in one's mouth AND **put one's foot in it; stick one's foot in one's mouth**   to say something that you regret; to say something stupid, insulting, or hurtful. □ *When I told Ann that her hair was more beautiful than I had ever seen it, I really put my foot in my mouth. It was a wig.* □ *I put my foot in it by telling John's secret.*

put one's hand to the plow   to begin to do a big and important task; to undertake a major effort. (A cliché. Rarely literal.) □ *If John would only put his hand to the plow, he could do an excellent job.* □ *You'll never accomplish anything if you don't put your hand to the plow.*

put one's nose to the grindstone   to keep busy doing one's work. (Never literal. Also with *have* and *get,* as in the examples.) □ *The boss told me to put my nose to the grindstone.* □ *I've had my nose to the grindstone ever since I started working here.* □ *If the other people in this office would get their noses to the grindstone, more work would get done.* ALSO: **keep one's nose to the grindstone** to keep busy continuously over a period of time. □ *The manager told me to keep my nose to the grindstone or be fired.*

put one's oar in AND **put in one's oar**   to give help; to interfere by giving advice; to add one's assistance to the general effort. □ *You don't need to put your oar in. I don't need your advice.* □ *I'm sorry. I shouldn't have put in my oar.*

put one's shoulder to the wheel   to get busy. (Not literal.) □ *You won't accomplish anything unless you put your shoulder to the wheel.* □ *I put my shoulder to the wheel and finished the job quickly.*

put one through one's paces   to make one demonstrate what one can do; to make one do one's job thoroughly. □ *The boss really put me through my paces today. I'm tired.* □ *I tried out for a part in the play, and the director really put me through my paces.*

put on one's thinking cap to start thinking in a serious manner. (A cliché. Not literal. Usually used with children.) □ *All right now, let's put on our thinking caps and do some arithmetic.* □ *It's time to put on our thinking caps, children.*

put someone or something out to pasture to retire someone or something. (Originally said of a horse that was too old to work.) □ *Please don't put me out to pasture. I have lots of good years left.* □ *This car has reached the end of the line. It's time to put it out to pasture.*

put someone or something to bed **1.** [with *someone*] to help someone—usually a child—get into a bed. □ *Come on, Billy, it's time for me to put you to bed.* □ *I want Grandpa to put me to bed.* **2.** [with *something*] to complete work on something and send it on to the next step in production, especially in publishing. □ *This edition is finished. Let's put it to bed.* □ *Finish the editing of this book and put it to bed.*

put someone or something to sleep **1.** to kill someone or something. (Euphemistic.) □ *We had to put our dog to sleep.* □ *The robber said he'd put us to sleep forever if we didn't cooperate.* **2.** to cause someone or something to sleep, perhaps through drugs or anesthesia. □ *The doctor put the patient to sleep before the operation.* □ *I put the cat to sleep by stroking its tummy.* **3.** [with *someone*] to bore someone. (Literal.) □ *That dull lecture put me to sleep.* □ *Her long story almost put me to sleep.*

put someone's nose out of joint to offend someone; to cause someone to feel slighted or insulted. (Not literal.) □ *I'm afraid I put his nose out of joint by not inviting him to the picnic.* □ *There is no reason to put your nose out of joint. I meant no harm.*

put someone through the wringer to give someone a difficult time. (As one squeezes water from clothing in an old-fashioned wringer washing machine.) □ *They are really putting me through the wringer at school.* □ *The boss put Bob through the wringer over this contract.*

put someone to shame to show someone up; to embarrass someone; to make someone ashamed. □ *Your excellent efforts put us all to shame.* □ *I put him to shame by telling everyone about his bad behavior.*

put someone to the test to test someone; to see what someone can achieve. □ *I think I can jump that far, but no one has ever put me to the test.* □ *I'm going to put you to the test right now!*

put something on ice AND **put something on the back burner** to delay or postpone something; to put something on hold. (Neither phrase is literal in these senses.) □ *I'm afraid that we'll have to put your project on ice for a while.* □ *Just put your idea on ice and keep it there till we get some money.*

put something on paper to write something down; to write or type an agreement on paper. □ *You have a great idea for a novel. Now put it on paper.* □ *I'm sorry, I can't discuss your offer until I see something in writing. Put it on paper, and then we'll talk.*

put something on the back burner See under *put something on ice.*

put something on the cuff to buy something on credit; to add to one's credit balance. (As if one were making a note of the purchase on one's shirt cuff.) □ *I'll take two of those, and please put them on the cuff.* □ *I'm sorry, Tom. We can't put anything more on the cuff.*

put something on the line AND **lay something on the line** to speak very firmly and directly about something. (Perhaps this refers to a battle line.) □ *She was very mad. She put it on the line, and we have no doubt about what she meant.* □ *All right, you kids! I'm going to lay it on the line. Don't ever do that again if you know what's good for you.*

put something through its paces to demonstrate how well something operates; to demonstrate all the things something can do. □ *I was down by the barn, watching Sally put her horse* *through its paces.* □ *This is an excellent can opener. Watch me put it through its paces.*

put the cart before the horse   to have things in the wrong order; to have things confused and mixed up. (Refers to an imaginary hitching up of a horse cart in a way that it would move in front of the horse rather than being pulled behind. A cliché. Also with have.) □ *You're eating your dessert! You've put the cart before the horse.* □ *Slow down and get organized. Don't put the cart before the horse!* □ *John has the cart before the horse in most of his projects.*

put two and two together   to figure something out from the information available. (A cliché.) □ *Well, I put two and two together and came up with an idea of who did it.* □ *Don't worry. John won't figure it out. He can't put two and two together.*

put up a (brave) front   to appear to be brave (even if one is not). □ *Mary is frightened, but she's putting up a brave front.* □ *If she weren't putting up a front, I'd be more frightened than I am.*

put words into someone's mouth   to speak for another person without permission. □ *Stop putting words into my mouth. I can speak for myself.* □ *The lawyer was scolded for putting words into the witness's mouth.*

Put your money where your mouth is!   a command to stop talking big and make a bet. (A cliché. Not literal.) □ *I'm tired of your bragging about your skill at betting. Put your money where your mouth is!* □ *You talk about betting, but you don't bet. Put your money where your mouth is!*

Q

QT, on the   See *on the QT.*

quake in one's boots   See under *shake in one's boots.*

question, out of the   See *out of the question.*

quick as a wink, as   See *as quick as a wink.*

quick on the draw   See the following entry.

quick on the trigger AND **quick on the draw**   **1.** quick to draw a gun and shoot. □ *Some of the old cowboys were known to be quick on the trigger.* □ *Wyatt Earp was particularly quick on the draw.* **2.** quick to respond to anything. □ *John gets the right answer before anyone else. He's really quick on the trigger.* □ *Sally will probably win the quiz game. She's really quick on the draw.*

quick on the uptake   quick to understand (something). □ *Just because I'm not quick on the uptake, it doesn't mean I'm stupid.* □ *Mary understands jokes before anyone else because she's so quick on the uptake.*

quiet as a mouse, as   See *as quiet as a mouse.*

R

rack and ruin, go to   See *go to rack and ruin.*

rack one's brain(s)   to try very hard to think of something. □ *I racked my brains all afternoon, but couldn't remember where I put the book.* □ *Don't waste any more time racking your brain. Go borrow the book from the library.*

rags, in   See *in rags.*

rags to riches, from   See *from rags to riches.*

rain cats and dogs   to rain very hard. (A cliché. Not literal, of course.) □ *It's raining cats and dogs. Look at it pour!* □ *I'm not going out in that storm. It's raining cats and dogs.*

rain or shine   no matter whether it rains or the sun shines. (A cliché.) □ *Don't worry. I'll be there rain or shine.* □ *We'll hold the picnic—rain or shine.*

rains but it pours, It never.   See *It never rains but it pours.*

raise one's sights   to set higher goals for oneself. □ *When you're young, you tend to raise your sights too high.* □ *On the other hand, some people need to raise their sights.*

raise some eyebrows to shock or surprise people mildly (by doing or saying something). (*Some* can be replaced with *a few, someone's, a lot of,* etc.) □ *What you just said may raise some eyebrows, but it shouldn't make anyone really angry.* □ *John's sudden marriage to Ann raised a few eyebrows.*

rake someone over the coals AND **haul someone over the coals** to give someone a severe scolding. □ *My mother hauled me over the coals for coming in late last night.* □ *The manager raked me over the coals for being late again.*

reach first base (with someone or something) See under *get to first base (with someone or something).*

read between the lines to infer something (from something); to try to understand what is meant by something that is not written clearly or openly. (Usually figurative. Does not necessarily refer to written or printed information.) □ *After listening to what she said, if you read between the lines, you can begin to see what she really means.* □ *Don't believe everything you hear. Learn to read between the lines.*

read someone like a book to understand someone very well. □ *I've got John figured out. I can read him like a book.* □ *Of course I understand you. I read you like a book.*

read someone the riot act to give someone a severe scolding. □ *The manager read me the riot act for coming in late.* □ *The teacher read the students the riot act for their failure to do their assignments.*

record, for the See *for the record.*

record, off the See *off the record.*

red, in the See *in the red.*

red, out of the See *out of the red.*

regular as clockwork, as See *as regular as clockwork.*

return mail, by See *by return mail.*

ride, go along for the See *go along for the ride.*

ride roughshod over someone or something to treat someone or something with disdain or scorn. □ *Tom seems to ride roughshod over his friends.* □ *You shouldn't have come into our town to ride roughshod over our laws and our traditions.*

ride the gravy train to live in luxury. □ *If I had a million dollars, I sure could ride the gravy train.* □ *I wouldn't like loafing. I don't want to ride the gravy train.*

riding for a fall risking failure or an accident, usually due to overconfidence. □ *Tom drives too fast, and he seems too sure of himself. He's riding for a fall.* □ *Bill needs to eat better and get more sleep. He's riding for a fall.*

right, in the See *in the right.*

right mind, in one's See *in one's right mind.*

right off the bat immediately; first thing. (Seems to refer to a ball leaving the baseball bat, but probably referred to a cricket bat originally.) □ *When he was learning to ride a bicycle, he fell on his head right off the bat.* □ *The new manager demanded new office furniture right off the bat.*

right-of-way, have the See *have the right-of-way.*

ring in the new year to celebrate the beginning of the new year at midnight on December 31. (As if ringing church bells to celebrate the new year.) □ *We are planning a big party to ring in the new year.* □ *How did you ring in the new year?*

risk one's neck (to do something) to risk physical harm in order to accomplish something. □ *Look at that traffic! I refuse to risk my neck just to cross the street to buy a paper.* □ *I refuse to risk my neck at all.*

rob Peter to pay Paul to take from one in order to give to another. (A cliché.) □ *Why borrow money to pay your bills? That's just robbing Peter to pay Paul.* □ *There's no point in robbing Peter to pay Paul. You still will be in debt.*

rob the cradle to marry or date someone who is much younger than you are. (As if one were consorting with an infant.) □ *I hear that Bill is dating Ann. Isn't that sort of robbing the cradle? She's much younger than he is.* □ *Uncle Bill—who is nearly eighty—just married a thirty-year-old woman. That is really robbing the cradle.*

rock and a hard place, between a See *between a rock and a hard place.*

rock the boat to cause trouble where none is welcome; to disturb a situation that is otherwise stable and satisfactory. (Often negative.) □ *Look, Tom, everything is going fine here. Don't rock the boat!* □ *You can depend on Tom to mess things up by rocking the boat.*

rolling stone gathers no moss, A. See *A rolling stone gathers no moss.*

roll out the red carpet for someone See under *get the red-carpet treatment.*

Rome wasn't built in a day. important things don't happen overnight. (A cliché.) □ *Don't expect a lot to happen right away. Rome wasn't built in a day, you know.* □ *Don't be anxious about how fast you are growing. Rome wasn't built in a day.*

roof, go through the See *go through the roof.*

round figures, in See *in round figures.*

round numbers, in See *in round numbers.*

rub elbows with someone AND **rub shoulders with someone** to associate with someone; to work closely with someone.

□ *I don't care to rub elbows with someone who acts like that!* □ *I rub shoulders with John at work. We are good friends.*

rub shoulders with someone   See the previous entry.

rub someone's fur the wrong way AND **rub someone the wrong way**   to irritate someone. (As if one were stroking an animal's fur, such as that of a pet cat, in the wrong direction, thus irritating the animal. The second entry form is derived from the first.) □ *I'm sorry I rubbed your fur the wrong way. I didn't mean to upset you.* □ *Don't rub her the wrong way!*

rub someone the wrong way   See the previous entry.

rule the roost   to be the boss or manager, especially at home. □ *Who rules the roost at your house?* □ *Our new office manager really rules the roost.*

run a fever AND **run a temperature**   to have a body temperature higher than normal; to have a fever. □ *I ran a fever when I had the flu.* □ *The baby is running a temperature and is grouchy.*

run (around) in circles   See the following entry.

run around like a chicken with its head cut off AND **run (around) in circles**   to run around frantically and aimlessly; to be in a state of chaos. (A cliché.) □ *I spent all afternoon running around like a chicken with its head cut off.* □ *If you run around in circles, you'll never get anything done.* □ *Get organized and stop running in circles.*

run a taut ship   See under *run a tight ship.*

run a temperature   See under *run a fever.*

run a tight ship AND **run a taut ship**   to run a ship or an organization in an orderly and disciplined manner. (*Taut* and *tight* mean the same thing. *Taut* is correct nautical use.) □ *The new office manager really runs a tight ship.* □ *Captain Jones is known for running a taut ship.*

run for one's life to run away to save one's life. □ *The dam has burst! Run for your life!* □ *The captain told us all to run for our lives.*

run in the family [for a characteristic] to appear in all (or most) members of a family. □ *My grandparents lived well into their nineties, and it runs in the family.* □ *My brothers and I have red hair. It runs in the family.*

run into a stone wall to come to a barrier against further progress. (Also used literally.) □ *We've run into a stone wall in our investigation.* □ *Algebra was hard for Tom, but he really ran into a stone wall with geometry.*

running, out of the See *out of the running.*

running start, off to a See *off to a running start.*

run out of gas See under *out of gas.*

run someone ragged to run someone hard and fast; to keep someone or something very busy. □ *This busy season is running us all ragged at the store.* □ *What a busy day. I really ran myself ragged.*

run to seed AND **go to seed** to become worn-out and uncared for. (Said especially of a lawn that needs care.) □ *Look at that lawn. The whole thing has run to seed.* □ *Pick things up around here. This place is going to seed. What a mess!*

S

safe and sound safe and whole or healthy. (A cliché.) □ *It was a rough trip, but we got there safe and sound.* □ *I'm glad to see you here safe and sound.*

same boat, in the See *in the same boat.*

same breath, in the See *in the same breath.*

same token, by the See *by the same token.*

save something for a rainy day to reserve something—usually money—for some future need. (A cliché. Also used literally. *Save something* can be replaced with *put something aside, hold something back, keep something,* etc.) □ *I've saved a little money for a rainy day.* □ *Keep some extra candy for a rainy day.*

save the day to produce a good result when a bad result was expected. □ *The team was expected to lose, but Sally made many points and saved the day.* □ *Your excellent speech saved the day.*

say Jack Robinson, before you can See *before you can say Jack Robinson.*

say-so, on someone's See *on someone's say-so.*

scarce as hens' teeth, as See *as scarce as hens' teeth.*

scarcer than hens' teeth See under *as scarce as hens' teeth.*

scot-free, go See *go scot-free.*

scrape the bottom of the barrel to select from among the worst; to choose from what is left over. (As if one were down to the very last and worst choices.) □ *You've bought a bad-looking car. You really scraped the bottom of the barrel to get that one.* □ *The worker you sent over was the worst I've ever seen. Send me another—and don't scrape the bottom of the barrel.*

scrape (with someone or something), have a See *have a scrape (with someone or something).*

scratch, not up to See *not up to scratch.*

scratch the surface to just begin to find out about something; to examine only the superficial aspects of something. □ *The investigation of the governor's staff revealed some suspicious dealing. It is thought that the investigators have just scratched the surface.* □ *We don't know how bad the problem is. We've only scratched the surface.*

scream bloody murder See under *cry bloody murder.*

screw up one's courage to build up one's courage. □ *I guess I have to screw up my courage and go to the dentist.* □ *I spent all morning screwing up my courage to take my driver's test.*

sea (about something), at See *at sea (about something).*

search something with a fine-tooth comb See under *go over something with a fine-tooth comb.*

season, in See *in season.*

season, out of See *out of season.*

seat of one's pants, by the See *by the seat of one's pants.*

second childhood, in one's See *in one's second childhood.*

second nature to someone easy and natural for someone. □ *Swimming is second nature to Jane.* □ *Driving is no problem for Bob. It's second nature to him.*

second thought, on See *on second thought.*

seed, go to See *go to seed.*

see eye to eye (about something) AND **see eye to eye on something** to view something in the same way (as someone else). □ *John and Ann see eye to eye about the new law. Neither of them likes it.* □ *That's interesting because they rarely see eye to eye.*

see eye to eye on something See the previous entry.

see the forest for the trees, not able to See *not able to see the forest for the trees.*

see the (hand)writing on the wall to know that something is certain to happen. (A cliché.) □ *If you don't improve your performance, they'll fire you. Can't you see the writing on the wall?* □ *I know I'll get fired. I can see the handwriting on the wall.*

see the light (at the end of the tunnel) to foresee an end to one's problems after a long period of time. □ *I had been horribly ill for two months before I began to see the light at the end of the tunnel.* □ *I began to see the light one day in early spring. At that moment, I knew I'd get well.*

see the light, begin to See *begin to see the light.*

see the light (of day) to come to the end of a very busy time. □ *Finally, when the holiday season was over, we could see the light of day. We had been so busy!* □ *When business lets up for a while, we'll be able to see the light.*

sell like hotcakes [for something] to be sold very fast. □ *The delicious candy sold like hotcakes.* □ *The fancy new cars were selling like hotcakes.*

sell someone a bill of goods to get someone to believe something that isn't true; to deceive someone. □ *Don't pay any attention to what John says. He's just trying to sell you a bill of goods.* □ *I'm not selling you a bill of goods. What I say is true.*

sell someone or something short to underestimate someone or something; to fail to see the good qualities of someone or something. □ *This is a very good restaurant. Don't sell it short.* □ *When you say that John isn't interested in music, you're selling him short. Did you know he plays the violin quite well?*

send one about one's business to send someone away, usually in an unfriendly way. □ *Is that annoying man on the telephone again? Please send him about his business.* □ *Ann, I can't clean up the house with you running around. I'm going to have to send you about your business.*

send someone packing to send someone away; to dismiss someone, possibly rudely. □ *I couldn't stand him anymore, so I sent him packing.* □ *The maid proved to be so incompetent that I had to send her packing.*

send someone to the showers to send a player out of the game and off the field, court, etc. (From sports.) □ *John played so badly that the coach sent him to the showers after the third quarter.* □ *After the fistfight, the coaches sent both players to the showers.*

senses, out of one's See *out of one's senses.*

separate the men from the boys to separate the competent from those who are less competent. □ *This is the kind of task that separates the men from the boys.* □ *This project requires a lot of thinking. It'll separate the men from the boys.*

separate the sheep from the goats to divide people into two groups. □ *Working in a place like this really separates the sheep from the goats.* □ *We can't go on with the game until we separate the sheep from the goats. Let's see who can jump the farthest.*

serve as a guinea pig [for someone] to be experimented on; to allow some sort of test to be performed on someone. (A cliché.) □ *Try it on someone else! I don't want to serve as a guinea pig!* □ *Jane agreed to serve as a guinea pig. She'll be the one to try out the new flavor of ice cream.*

serve someone right [for an act or event] to punish someone fairly (for doing something). □ *John copied off my test paper. It would serve him right if he fails the test.* □ *It'd serve John right if he got arrested.*

service, out of See *out of service.*

set foot somewhere to go or enter somewhere. (Often in the negative.) □ *If I were you, I wouldn't set foot in that town.* □ *I wouldn't set foot in her house! Not after the way she spoke to me.*

set foot somewhere, not See *not set foot somewhere.*

set great store by someone or something to have positive expectations for someone or something; to have high hopes for someone or something. □ *I set great store by my computer and its ability to help me in my work.* □ *We set great store by John because of his quick mind.*

set one back on one's heels to surprise, shock, or overwhelm someone. □ *Her sudden announcement set us all back on our heels.* □ *The manager scolded me, and that really set me back on my heels.*

set one's heart on something See under *have one's heart set on something.*

set one's sights on something to select something as one's goal. □ *I set my sights on a master's degree from the state university.* □ *Don't set your sights on something you cannot possibly do.*

set someone's teeth on edge **1.** [for a sour or bitter taste] to irritate one's mouth and make it feel funny. □ *Have you ever eaten* *a lemon? It'll set your teeth on edge.* □ *I can't stand food that sets my teeth on edge.* **2.** [for a person or a noise] to be irritating or get on one's nerves. □ *Please don't scrape your fingernails on the blackboard! It sets my teeth on edge!* □ *Here comes Bob. He's so annoying. He really sets my teeth on edge.*

set the world on fire to do exciting things that bring fame and glory. (Not literal. Frequently negative.) □ *I'm not very ambitious. I don't want to set the world on fire.* □ *You don't have to set the world on fire. Just do a good job.*

seventh heaven, in See *in seventh heaven.*

shake in one's boots AND **quake in one's boots** to be afraid; to shake from fear. □ *I was shaking in my boots because I had to go see the manager.* □ *Stop quaking in your boots, Bob. I'm not going to fire you.*

Shape up or ship out. to either improve one's performance (or behavior) or leave or quit. (A cliché.) □ *Okay, Tom. That's the end. Shape up or ship out!* □ *John was late again, so I told him to shape up or ship out.*

shed crocodile tears to shed false tears; to pretend that one is weeping. □ *The child wasn't hurt, but she shed crocodile tears anyway.* □ *He thought he could get his way if he shed crocodile tears.*

shoe fits, wear it, If the. See *If the shoe fits, wear it.*

shoe is on the other foot, The. See *The shoe is on the other foot.*

shoe on the other foot, have the See *have the shoe on the other foot.*

shoot from the hip **1.** to fire a gun that is held at one's side, against one's hip. (This increases one's speed in firing a gun.) □ *When I lived at home on the farm, my father taught me to shoot from the hip.* □ *I quickly shot the snake before it bit my horse.*

I'm glad I learned to shoot from the hip. **2.** to speak directly and frankly. □ *John has a tendency to shoot from the hip, but he generally speaks the truth.* □ *Don't pay any attention to John. He means no harm. It's just his nature to shoot from the hip.*

short haul, over the See *over the short haul.*

short order, in See *in short order.*

short supply, in See *in short supply.*

shot in the arm a boost; something that gives someone energy. □ *Thank you for cheering me up. It was a real shot in the arm.* □ *Your friendly greeting card was just what I needed—a real shot in the arm.*

shoulders, on someone's See *on someone's shoulders.*

should have stood in bed should have stayed in bed. (Has nothing to do with standing up.) □ *What a horrible day! I should have stood in bed.* □ *The minute I got up and heard the news this morning, I knew I should have stood in bed.*

show one's face, not See *not show one's face.*

show one's (true) colors to show what one is really like or what one is really thinking. □ *Whose side are you on, John? Come on. Show your colors.* □ *It's hard to tell what Mary is thinking. She never shows her true colors.*

show someone the ropes See under *know the ropes.*

sick as a dog, as See *as sick as a dog.*

sight, out of mind, Out of. See *Out of sight, out of mind.*

signed, sealed, and delivered formally and officially signed; [for a formal document to be] executed. (A cliché.) □ *Here is the deed to the property—signed, sealed, and delivered.* □ *I can't* *begin work on this project until I have the contract signed, sealed, and delivered.*

sign one's own death warrant　to (figuratively) sign a paper that calls for one's death. (A cliché.) □ *I wouldn't ever gamble a large sum of money. That would be signing my own death warrant.* □ *The killer signed his own death warrant when he walked into the police station and gave himself up.*

sign on the dotted line　to place one's signature on a contract or other important paper. (A cliché.) □ *This agreement isn't properly concluded until we both sign on the dotted line.* □ *Here are the papers for the purchase of your car. As soon as you sign on the dotted line, that beautiful, shiny automobile will be all yours!*

sink one's teeth into something　(A cliché.) **1.** to take a bite of some kind of food, usually a special kind of food. □ *I can't wait to sink my teeth into a nice juicy steak.* □ *Look at that chocolate cake! Don't you want to sink your teeth into that?* **2.** to get a chance to do, learn, or control something. □ *That appears to be a very challenging assignment. I can't wait to sink my teeth into it.* □ *Being the manager of this department is a big task. I'm very eager to sink my teeth into it.*

sink or swim　fail or succeed. (A cliché.) □ *After I've studied and learned all I can, I have to take the test and sink or swim.* □ *It's too late to help John now. It's sink or swim for him.*

sit on one's hands　to do nothing; to fail to help. (Not literal.) □ *When we needed help from Mary, she just sat on her hands.* □ *We need the cooperation of everyone. You can't sit on your hands!* ALSO: **sit on its hands** [for an audience] to refuse to applaud. (Not literal.) □ *We saw a very poor performance of the play. The audience sat on its hands for the entire play.*

sit tight　to wait; to wait patiently. (Does not necessarily refer to sitting.) □ *Just relax and sit tight. I'll be right with you.* □ *We were waiting in line for the gates to open when someone came out and told us to sit tight because it wouldn't be much longer before we could go in.*

sitting duck, like a See *like a sitting duck.*

sitting on a powder keg in a risky or explosive situation; in a situation where something serious or dangerous may happen at any time. (Not literal. A powder keg is a keg of gunpowder.) □ *Things are very tense at work. The whole office is sitting on a powder keg.* □ *The fire at the oil field seems to be under control for now, but all the workers there are sitting on a powder keg.*

sit up and take notice to become alert and pay attention. □ *A loud noise from the front of the room caused everyone to sit up and take notice.* □ *The company wouldn't pay any attention to my complaints. When I had my lawyer write them a letter, they sat up and took notice.*

sixes and sevens, at See *at sixes and sevens.*

six of one and half a dozen of the other about the same one way or another. (A cliché.) □ *It doesn't matter to me which way you do it. It's six of one and half a dozen of the other.* □ *What difference does it make? They're both the same—six of one and half a dozen of the other.*

skate on thin ice See under *on thin ice.*

skeleton in the closet a hidden and shocking secret; a secret fact about oneself. (Often in the plural. As if one had hidden the grisly results of murder in the closet.) □ *You can ask anyone about how reliable I am. I don't mind. I don't have any skeletons in the closet.* □ *My uncle was in jail for a day once. That's our family's skeleton in the closet.*

skin off someone's nose, no See *no skin off someone's nose.*

skin off someone's teeth, no See *no skin off someone's teeth.*

skin of one's teeth, by the See *by the skin of one's teeth.*

sleep a wink, not See *not sleep a wink.*

sleep like a log to sleep very soundly. (A cliché. Not literal, of course.) ☐ *Nothing can wake me up. I usually sleep like a log.* ☐ *Everyone in our family sleeps like a log, so no one heard the fire engines in the middle of the night.*

sleep on something to think about something overnight; to weigh a decision overnight. ☐ *I don't know whether I agree to do it. Let me sleep on it.* ☐ *I slept on it, and I've decided to accept your offer.*

slip of the tongue an error in speaking where a word is pronounced incorrectly, or where something that the speaker did not mean to say is said. (As if one's tongue had made a misstep.) ☐ *I didn't mean to tell her that. It was a slip of the tongue.* ☐ *I failed to understand the instructions because the speaker made a slip of the tongue at an important point.*

slip one's mind [for something that was to be remembered] to be forgotten. (As if a thought had slipped out of one's brain.) ☐ *I meant to go to the grocery store on the way home, but it slipped my mind.* ☐ *My birthday slipped my mind. I guess I wanted to forget it.*

slippery as an eel, as See *as slippery as an eel.*

slip through someone's fingers to get away from someone; for someone to lose track (of something or someone). ☐ *I had a copy of the book you want, but somehow it slipped through my fingers.* ☐ *There was a detective following me, but I managed to slip through his fingers.*

Slow and steady wins the race. a proverb meaning that deliberateness and determination will lead to success, or (literally) a reasonable pace will win a race. ☐ *I worked my way through college in six years. Now I know what they mean when they say, "Slow and steady wins the race."* ☐ *Ann won the race because she started off slowly and established a good pace. The other runners tried to sprint the whole distance, and they tired out before the final lap. Ann's trainer said, "You see! I told you! Slow and steady wins the race."*

smack-dab in the middle right in the middle. □ *I want a big helping of mashed potatoes with a glob of butter smack-dab in the middle.* □ *Tom and Sally were having a terrible argument, and I was trapped—smack-dab in the middle.*

smart as a fox, as See *as smart as a fox.*

smoke, go up in See *go up in smoke.*

snail's pace, at a See *at a snail's pace.*

snuff, not up to See *not up to snuff.*

snug as a bug in a rug, as See *as snug as a bug in a rug.*

sober as a judge, as See *as sober as a judge.*

soft as a baby's bottom, as See *as soft as a baby's bottom.*

soft spot in one's heart for someone or something, have a See *have a soft spot in one's heart for someone or something.*

soil one's hands See under *get one's hands dirty.*

soon as possible, as See *as soon as possible.*

so quiet you could hear a pin drop See *so still you could hear a pin drop.*

sorts, out of See *out of sorts.*

so still you could hear a pin drop AND **so quiet you could hear a pin drop** very quiet. (A cliché. Also with *can.*) □ *When I came into the room, it was so still you could hear a pin drop. Then everyone shouted, "Happy birthday!"* □ *Please be quiet. Be so quiet you can hear a pin drop.*

sow one's wild oats to do wild and foolish things in one's youth. (Often assumed to have some sort of sexual meaning, with wild oats referring to a young man's semen.) □ *Dale was out sowing his wild oats last night, and he's in jail this morning.* □ *Mrs. Smith told Mr. Smith that he was too old to be sowing his wild oats.*

spare, have something to See *have something to spare.*

spare time, in one's See *in one's spare time.*

speak of the devil said when someone whose name has just been mentioned appears or is heard from. (A cliché.) □ *Well, speak of the devil! Hello, Tom. We were just talking about you.* □ *I had just mentioned Sally when—speak of the devil—she walked in the door.*

spill the beans See under *let the cat out of the bag.*

spit and image of someone, be the See *be the spit and image of someone.*

spitting image of someone, be the See *be the spit and image of someone.*

split the difference to divide the difference (with someone else). □ *You want to sell for $120, and I want to buy for $100. Let's split the difference and close the deal at $110.* □ *I don't want to split the difference. I want $120.*

spot, in a (tight) See *in a (tight) spot.*

spotlight, in the See *in the spotlight.*

spot, on the See *on the spot.*

spread it on thick See under *lay it on thick.*

spread like wildfire to spread rapidly and without control. (A cliché.) □ *The epidemic is spreading like wildfire. Everyone is getting sick.* □ *John told a joke that was so funny it spread like wildfire.*

spread oneself too thin to do so many things that you can do none of them well; to spread one's efforts or attention too widely. □ *It's a good idea to get involved in a lot of activities, but don't spread yourself too thin.* □ *I'm too busy these days. I'm afraid I've spread myself too thin.*

spring chicken, no See *no spring chicken.*

spur of the moment, on the See *on the spur of the moment.*

square peg in a round hole a misfit. (A cliché.) □ *John can't seem to get along with the people he works with. He's just a square peg in a round hole.* □ *I'm not a square peg in a round hole. It's just that no one understands me.*

squeak by (someone or something) to just get by someone or something. □ *The guard was almost asleep, so I squeaked by him.* □ *I wasn't very well prepared for the test, and I just squeaked by.*

stab someone in the back to betray someone. (Also used literally.) □ *I thought we were friends! Why did you stab me in the back?* □ *You don't expect a person whom you trust to stab you in the back.*

stage (of the game), at this See *at this stage (of the game).*

stag, go See *go stag.*

stand one's ground AND **hold one's ground** to stand up for one's rights; to resist an attack. □ *The lawyer tried to confuse me when I was giving testimony, but I managed to stand my ground.* □ *Some people were trying to crowd us off the beach, but we held our ground.*

stand on one's own two feet to be independent and self-sufficient, rather than being supported by someone else. □ *I'll be glad when I have a good job and can stand on my own two feet.* □ *When Jane gets out of debt, she'll be able to stand on her own two feet again.*

stand up and be counted to state one's support (for someone or something); to come out for someone or something. □ *If you believe in more government help for farmers, write your representative—stand up and be counted.* □ *I'm generally in favor of what you propose, but not enough to stand up and be counted.*

start from scratch to start from the beginning; to start from nothing. □ *Whenever I bake a cake, I start from scratch. I never use a cake mix in a box.* □ *I built every bit of my own house. I started from scratch and did everything with my own hands.*

start (off) with a clean slate to start out again afresh; to ignore the past and start over again. □ *I plowed under all last year's flowers so I could start with a clean slate next spring.* □ *If I start off with a clean slate, then I'll know exactly what each plant is.*

start to finish, from See *from start to finish.*

steal a base to sneak from one base to another in baseball. □ *The runner stole second base, but he nearly got put out on the way.* □ *Tom runs so slowly that he never tries to steal a base.*

steal a march (on someone) to get some sort of an advantage over someone without being noticed. □ *I got the contract because I was able to steal a march on my competitor.* □ *You have to be clever and fast—not dishonest—to steal a march.*

steal someone's thunder to lessen someone's force or authority. (Not literal.) □ *What do you mean by coming in here and stealing my thunder? I'm in charge here!* □ *Someone stole my thunder by leaking my announcement to the press.*

steal the show See the following entry.

steal the spotlight AND **steal the show** to give the best performance in a show, play, or some other event; to get attention for oneself. □ *The lead in the play was very good, but the butler stole the show.* □ *Ann always tries to steal the spotlight when she and I make a presentation.*

steam, under one's own   See *under one's own steam.*

stem to stern, from   See *from stem to stern.*

step on it   See under *step on the gas.*

step on someone's toes AND **tread on someone's toes**   to interfere with or offend someone. (Also used literally. Note examples with *anyone.*) □ *When you're in public office, you have to avoid stepping on anyone's toes.* □ *Ann trod on someone's toes during the last campaign and lost the election.*

step on the gas AND **step on it**   hurry up. □ *I'm in a hurry, driver. Step on it!* □ *I can't step on the gas, mister. There's too much traffic.*

step out of line   **1.** to move briefly out of a line where one was standing. (Literal.) □ *I stepped out of line for a minute and lost my place.* □ *It's better not to step out of line if you aren't sure you can get back in again.* **2.** to misbehave; to do something offensive. □ *I'm terribly sorry. I hope I didn't step out of line.* □ *John is a lot of fun to go out with, but he has a tendency to step out of line.*

stew in one's own juice   to be left alone to suffer one's anger or disappointment. □ *John has such a terrible temper. When he got mad at us, we just let him go away and stew in his own juice.* □ *After John stewed in his own juice for a while, he decided to come back and apologize to us.*

stick one's foot in one's mouth   See under *put one's foot in one's mouth.*

stick one's neck out   to take a risk. □ *Why should I stick my neck out to do something for her? What's she ever done for me?* □ *He made a risky investment. He stuck his neck out because he thought he could make some money.*

stick one's nose in(to something)   See under *poke one's nose in(to something).*

stick together   **1.** to stay close together in a group. □ *It's crowded here. Let's stick together so we won't get lost.* □ *Tell the children to stick together at the picnic. I don't want to leave anyone behind.*   **2.** [for a group] to remain united on some principle or purpose. □ *We can win the election if we just stick together.* □ *Stop arguing, you two! If we all stick together, we can beat this menace!*

stick to one's guns   to remain firm in one's convictions; to stand up for one's rights. □ *I'll stick to my guns on this matter. I'm sure I'm right.* □ *Bob can be persuaded to do it our way. He probably won't stick to his guns on this point.*

Still waters run deep.   a proverb meaning that a quiet person is probably thinking deep or important thoughts. □ *Jane is so quiet. She's probably thinking. Still waters run deep, you know.* □ *It's true that still waters run deep, but I think that Jane is really half asleep.*

stir up a hornet's nest   to create trouble or difficulties. □ *What a mess you have made of things. You've really stirred up a hornet's nest.* □ *Bill stirred up a hornet's nest when he discovered the theft.*

stock, have something in   See *have something in stock.*

stock, in   See *in stock.*

stone's throw away, a   See *a stone's throw away.*

straight from the horse's mouth   from an authoritative or dependable source. (A cliché. Not literal.) □ *I know it's true! I heard it straight from the horse's mouth!* □ *This comes straight from the horse's mouth, so it has to be believed.*

straight from the shoulder   sincerely; frankly; holding nothing back. (A cliché.) □ *Sally always speaks straight from the shoulder. You never have to guess what she really means.* □ *Bill gave a good presentation—straight from the shoulder and brief.*

strike a happy medium AND **hit a happy medium**   to find a compromise position; to arrive at a position halfway between two unacceptable extremes. □ *Ann likes very spicy food, but Bob doesn't care for spicy food at all. We are trying to find a restaurant that strikes a happy medium.* □ *Tom is either very happy or very sad. He can't seem to hit a happy medium.*

strike a match   to light a match. □ *Mary struck a match and lit a candle.* □ *When Sally struck a match to light a cigarette, Jane said quickly, "No smoking, please."*

strike a sour note AND **hit a sour note**   to signify something unpleasant. □ *Jane's sad announcement struck a sour note at the annual banquet.* □ *News of the crime hit a sour note in our holiday celebration.*

strike, go (out) on   See *go (out) on strike.*

strike it rich   to acquire wealth suddenly. □ *If I could strike it rich, I wouldn't have to work anymore.* □ *Sally ordered a dozen oysters and found a huge pearl in one of them. She struck it rich!*

strike someone funny   to seem funny to someone. □ *Sally has a great sense of humor. Everything she says strikes me funny.* □ *Why are you laughing? Did something I said strike you funny?*

strike someone's fancy   to appeal to someone. □ *I'll have some ice cream, please. Chocolate strikes my fancy right now.* □ *Why don't you go to the store and buy a record album that strikes your fancy?*

strike up a friendship   to become friends (with someone). □ *I struck up a friendship with John while we were on a business trip together.* □ *If you're lonely, you should go out and try to strike up a friendship with someone you like.*

strike while the iron is hot   to do something at the best possible time; to do something when the time is ripe. (A cliché.) □ *He was in a good mood, so I asked for a loan of $200. I thought I'd better strike while the iron was hot.* □ *Please go to the bank and settle* *this matter now! They are willing to be reasonable. You've got to strike while the iron is hot.*

strings attached, with no   See *with no strings attached.*

strings attached, without any   See *without any strings attached.*

strong as an ox, as   See *as strong as an ox.*

stubborn as a mule, as   See *as stubborn as a mule.*

stuff and nonsense   nonsense. □ *Come on! Don't give me all that stuff and nonsense!* □ *I don't understand this book. It's all stuff and nonsense as far as I am concerned.*

stuff the ballot box   to put fraudulent ballots into a ballot box; to cheat in counting the votes in an election. □ *The election judge was caught stuffing the ballot box in the election yesterday.* □ *Election officials are supposed to guard against stuffing the ballot box.*

suit someone to a T AND **fit someone to a T**   to be very appropriate for someone. □ *This kind of job suits me to a T.* □ *This is Sally's kind of house. It fits her to a T.*

sweat of one's brow, by the   See *by the sweat of one's brow.*

sweet tooth, have a   See *have a sweet tooth.*

swim against the current   See the following entry.

swim against the tide AND **swim against the current**   to do the opposite of everyone else; to go against the trend. □ *Bob tends to do what everybody else does. He isn't likely to swim against the tide.* □ *Mary always swims against the current. She's a very contrary person.*

T

table, under the See *under the table*.

tail between one's legs, have one's See *have one's tail between one's legs*.

tailspin, go into a See *go into a tailspin*.

tail wagging the dog a situation where a small part is controlling the whole thing. □ *John was just hired yesterday, and today he's bossing everyone around. It's a case of the tail wagging the dog.* □ *Why is this small matter so important? Now the tail is wagging the dog!*

take a backseat (to someone) to defer to someone; to give control to someone. □ *I decided to take a backseat to Mary and let her manage the project.* □ *I had done the best I could, but it was time to take a backseat and let someone else run things.*

take a leaf out of someone's book to behave or to do something in the way that someone else would. (A leaf is a page.) □ *When you act like that, you're taking a leaf out of your sister's book, and I don't like it!* □ *You had better do it your way. Don't take a leaf out of my book. I don't do it well.*

take a load off one's feet See under *get a load off one's feet*.

take a nosedive See under *go into a nosedive*.

take cold See under *catch cold*.

take forty winks   to take a nap; to go to sleep. □ *I think I'll go to bed and take forty winks. See you in the morning.* □ *Why don't you go take forty winks and call me in about an hour?*

take it or leave it   to accept it (the way it is) or forget it. □ *This is my last offer. Take it or leave it.* □ *It's not much, but it's the only food we have. You can take it or leave it.*

take liberties with someone or something AND **make free with someone or something**   to use or abuse someone or something. □ *You are overly familiar with me, Mr. Jones. One might think you were taking liberties with me.* □ *I don't like it when you make free with my lawn mower. You should at least ask when you want to borrow it.*

take one's death of cold   See under *catch one's death (of cold).*

take one's medicine   to accept the punishment or the bad fortune that one deserves. (Also used literally.) □ *I know I did wrong, and I know I have to take my medicine.* □ *Billy knew he was going to get spanked, and he didn't want to take his medicine.*

take someone or something by storm   to overwhelm someone or something; to attract a great deal of attention from someone or something. (A cliché.) □ *Jane is madly in love with Tom. He took her by storm at the office party, and they've been together ever since.* □ *The singer took the world of opera by storm with her performance in* La Boheme.

take someone or something for granted   to accept someone or something—without gratitude—as a matter of course. □ *We tend to take a lot of things for granted.* □ *Mrs. Franklin complained that Mr. Franklin takes her for granted.*

take someone's breath away   **1.** to cause someone to be out of breath due to a shock or hard exercise. □ *Walking this fast takes my breath away.* □ *Mary frightened me and took my breath away.* **2.** to overwhelm someone with beauty or grandeur. □ *The* *magnificent painting took my breath away.* □ *Ann looked so beautiful that she took my breath away.*

take someone under one's wing(s) to take over and care for a person. □ *John wasn't doing well in geometry until the teacher took him under her wing.* □ *I took the new workers under my wings, and they learned the job in no time.*

take something at face value to accept something just as it is presented. □ *John said he wanted to come to the party, and I took that at face value. I'm sure he'll arrive soon.* □ *He made us a promise, and we took his word at face value.*

take something in stride to accept something as natural or expected. □ *The argument surprised him, but he took it in stride.* □ *It was a very rude remark, but Mary took it in stride.*

take something lying down to endure something unpleasant without fighting back. □ *He insulted me publicly. You don't expect me to take that lying down, do you?* □ *I'm not the kind of person who'll take something like that lying down.*

take something on faith to accept or believe something on the basis of little or no evidence. □ *Please try to believe what I'm telling you. Just take it on faith.* □ *Surely you can't expect me to take a story like that on faith.*

take something on the chin to experience and endure a direct (figurative or literal) blow or assault. □ *The bad news was a real shock, and John took it on the chin.* □ *The worst luck comes my way, and I always end up taking it on the chin.*

take something with a pinch of salt AND **take something with a grain of salt** to listen to a story or an explanation with considerable doubt. □ *You must take anything she says with a grain of salt. She doesn't always tell the truth.* □ *They took my explanation with a pinch of salt. I was sure they didn't believe me.*

take the bitter with the sweet to accept the bad things along with the good things. (A cliché.) □ *We all have disappointments.*

You have to learn to take the bitter with the sweet. □ *There are good days and bad days, but every day you take the bitter with the sweet. That's life.*

take the bull by the horns to meet a challenge directly. (A cliché.) □ *If we are going to solve this problem, someone is going to have to take the bull by the horns.* □ *This threat isn't going to go away by itself. We are going to take the bull by the horns and settle this matter once and for all.*

take the law into one's own hands to attempt to administer the law; to act as a judge and jury for someone who has done something wrong. □ *Citizens don't have the right to take the law into their own hands.* □ *The shopkeeper took the law into his own hands when he tried to arrest the thief.*

take the stand to go to and sit in the witness chair on the witness stand in a courtroom. □ *I was in court all day, waiting to take the stand.* □ *The lawyer asked the witness to take the stand.*

take the words out of one's mouth [for someone else] to say what you were going to say. (Also with *right,* as in the example below.) □ *John said exactly what I was going to say. He took the words out of my mouth.* □ *I agree with you, and I wanted to say the same thing. You took the words right out of my mouth.*

take to one's heels to run away. □ *The little boy said hello and then took to his heels.* □ *The man took to his heels to try to get to the bus stop before the bus left.*

take up one's abode somewhere to settle down and live somewhere. (Literary.) □ *I took up my abode downtown near my office.* □ *We decided to take up our abode in a warmer climate.*

talk a blue streak to say very much and talk very rapidly. □ *Billy didn't talk until he was six, and then he started talking a blue streak.* □ *I can't understand anything Bob says. He talks a blue streak, and I can't follow his thinking.*

talk in circles   to talk in a confusing or roundabout manner. □ *I couldn't understand a thing he said. All he did was talk in circles.* □ *We argued for a long time and finally decided that we were talking in circles.*

talk shop   to talk about business matters at a social event (where business talk is out of place). □ *All right, everyone, we're not here to talk shop. Let's have a good time.* □ *Mary and Jane stood by the punch bowl, talking shop.*

talk through one's hat   to talk nonsense; to brag and boast. □ *John isn't really as good as he says. He's just talking through his hat.* □ *Stop talking through your hat and start being sincere!*

talk until one is blue in the face   to talk until one is exhausted. □ *I talked until I was blue in the face, but I couldn't change her mind.* □ *She had to talk until she was blue in the face in order to convince him.*

target, on   See *on target.*

teacher's pet, be the   See *be the teacher's pet.*

tear one's hair   to be anxious, frustrated, or angry. (Not literal.) □ *I was so nervous, I was about to tear my hair.* □ *I had better get home. My parents will be tearing their hair.*

tell one to one's face   to tell (something) to someone directly. □ *I'm sorry that Sally feels that way about me. I wish she had told me to my face.* □ *I won't tell Tom that you're mad at him. You should tell him to his face.*

tell tales out of school   to tell secrets or spread rumors. □ *I wish that John would keep quiet. He's telling tales out of school again.* □ *If you tell tales out of school a lot, people won't know when to believe you.*

tempest in a teapot   an uproar about practically nothing. (A cliché.) □ *This isn't a serious problem—just a tempest in a teapot.* □ *Even a tempest in a teapot can take a lot of time to get settled.*

thank one's lucky stars   to be thankful for one's luck. (A cliché.) □ *You can thank your lucky stars that I was there to help you.* □ *I thank my lucky stars that I studied the right things for the test.*

That's the last straw. AND **That's the straw that broke the camel's back.**   That is the final thing. (A cliché.) □ *Now it's raining! That's the last straw. The picnic is canceled!* □ *When Sally came down sick, that was the straw that broke the camel's back.*

That's the straw that broke the camel's back.   See the previous entry.

That's the ticket.   That is exactly what is needed. (A cliché.) □ *That's the ticket, John. You're doing it just the way it should be done.* □ *That's the ticket! I knew you could do it.*

That takes care of that.   That is settled. (A cliché.) □ *That takes care of that, and I'm glad it's over.* □ *I spent all morning dealing with this matter, and that takes care of that.*

The coast is clear.   There is no visible danger. □ *I'm going to stay hidden here until the coast is clear.* □ *You can come out of your hiding place now. The coast is clear.*

The early bird gets the worm.   a proverb meaning that the early person will get the reward. □ *Don't be late again! Don't you know that the early bird gets the worm?* □ *I'll be there before the sun is up. After all, the early bird gets the worm.*

The fat is in the fire.   a proverb meaning that serious trouble has broken out. □ *Now that Mary is leaving, the fat is in the fire. How can we get along without her?* □ *The fat's in the fire! There's $3,000 missing from the office safe.*

The honeymoon is over.   The early pleasant beginning has ended. (A cliché.) □ *Okay, the honeymoon is over. It's time to settle down and do some hard work.* □ *I knew the honeymoon was over when they started yelling at me to work faster.*

the pot calling the kettle black an instance of someone with a fault accusing someone else of having the same fault. (A cliché.) □ *Ann is always late, but she was rude enough to tell everyone when I was late. Now that's the pot calling the kettle black!* □ *You're calling me thoughtless? That's really a case of the pot calling the kettle black.*

There are plenty of other fish in the sea. There are other choices. (A cliché. Used to refer to persons.) □ *When John broke up with Ann, I told her not to worry. There are plenty of other fish in the sea.* □ *It's too bad that your secretary quit, but there are plenty of other fish in the sea.*

There's more than one way to skin a cat. a proverb meaning that there is more than one way to do something. □ *If that way won't work, try another way. There's more than one way to skin a cat.* □ *Don't worry, I'll figure out a way to get it done. There's more than one way to skin a cat.*

There's no accounting for taste. a proverb meaning that there is no explanation for people's preferences. □ *Look at that purple and orange car! There's no accounting for taste.* □ *Some people seemed to like the music, although I thought it was worse than noise. There's no accounting for taste.*

There will be the devil to pay. There will be lots of trouble. □ *If you damage my car, there will be the devil to pay.* □ *Bill broke a window, and now there will be the devil to pay.*

The shoe is on the other foot. a proverb meaning that one is experiencing the same things that one caused another person to experience. (Note the variations in the examples.) □ *The teacher is taking a course in summer school and is finding out what it's like when the shoe is on the other foot.* □ *When the policeman was arrested, he learned what it was like to have the shoe on the other foot.*

thick and thin, through See *through thick and thin*.

thick as pea soup, as See *as thick as pea soup*.

thick as thieves, as See *as thick as thieves.*

thin air, out of See *out of thin air.*

thin ice, on See *on thin ice.*

think on one's feet to think while one is talking. □ *If you want to be a successful teacher, you must be able to think on your feet.* □ *I have to write out everything I'm going to say, because I can't think on my feet too well.*

thorn in someone's side, be a See *be a thorn in someone's side.*

three-ring circus, like a See *like a three-ring circus.*

through thick and thin through good times and bad times. (A cliché.) □ *We've been together through thick and thin and we won't desert each other now.* □ *Over the years, we went through thick and thin and enjoyed every minute of it.*

throw a monkey wrench in the works to cause problems for someone's plans. □ *I don't want to throw a monkey wrench in the works, but have you checked your plans with a lawyer?* □ *When John refused to help us, he really threw a monkey wrench in the works.*

throw caution to the wind to become very careless. (A cliché.) □ *Jane, who is usually cautious, threw caution to the wind and went windsurfing.* □ *I don't mind taking a little chance now and then, but I'm not the type of person who throws caution to the wind.*

throw cold water on something See under *pour cold water on something.*

throw down the gauntlet to challenge (someone) to an argument or (figurative) combat. □ *When Bob challenged my conclusions, he threw down the gauntlet. I was ready for an* *argument.* □ *Frowning at Bob is the same as throwing down the gauntlet. He loves to get into a fight about something.*

throw good money after bad   to waste additional money after wasting money once. (A cliché.) □ *I bought a used car and then had to spend $300 on repairs. That was throwing good money after bad.* □ *The Browns are always throwing good money after bad. They bought an acre of land that turned out to be swamp, and then had to pay to have it filled in.*

throw in the sponge   See the following entry.

throw in the towel AND **throw in the sponge**   to quit (doing something). □ *When John could stand no more of Mary's bad temper, he threw in the towel and left.* □ *Don't give up now! It's too soon to throw in the sponge.*

throw oneself at someone's feet   to bow down humbly at someone's feet. (Used both figuratively and literally). □ *Do I have to throw myself at your feet in order to convince you that I'm sorry?* □ *I love you sincerely, Jane. I'll throw myself at your feet and await your command. I'm your slave!*

throw oneself on the mercy of the court AND **throw oneself at the mercy of the court**   to plead for mercy from a judge in a courtroom. □ *Your honor, please believe me, I didn't do it on purpose. I throw myself on the mercy of the court and beg for a light sentence.* □ *Jane threw herself at the mercy of the court and hoped for the best.*

throw someone a curve   **1.** to pitch a curve ball to someone in baseball. □ *The pitcher threw John a curve, and John swung wildly against thin air.* □ *During that game, the pitcher threw everyone a curve at least once.* **2.** to confuse someone by doing something unexpected. □ *When you said* house *you threw me a curve. The password was supposed to be* home. □ *John threw me a curve when we were making our presentation, and I forgot my speech.*

throw someone for a loop AND **knock someone for a loop**   to confuse or shock someone. □ *When Bill heard the news, it threw him for a loop.* □ *The manager knocked Bob for a loop by firing him on the spot.*

throw someone to the wolves   to (figuratively) sacrifice someone. (A cliché. Not literal.) □ *The press was demanding an explanation, so the mayor blamed the mess on John and threw him to the wolves.* □ *I wouldn't let them throw me to the wolves! I did nothing wrong, and I won't take the blame for their errors.*

throw something into the bargain   to include something in a deal. □ *To encourage me to buy a new car, the car dealer threw a free radio into the bargain.* □ *If you purchase three pounds of chocolates, I'll throw one pound of salted nuts into the bargain.*

thumb a ride AND **hitch a ride**   to get a ride from a passing motorist; to make a sign with one's thumb that indicates to passing drivers that one is begging for a ride. □ *My car broke down on the highway, and I had to thumb a ride to get back to town.* □ *Sometimes it's dangerous to hitch a ride with a stranger.*

thumb one's nose at someone or something   to (figuratively or literally) make a rude gesture of disgust with one's thumb and nose at someone or something. □ *The tramp thumbed his nose at the lady and walked away.* □ *You can't just thumb your nose at people who give you trouble. You've got to learn to get along.*

tickle someone's fancy   to interest someone; to make someone curious. □ *I have an interesting problem here that I think will tickle your fancy.* □ *This doesn't tickle my fancy at all. This is dull and boring.*

tied to one's mother's apron strings   dominated by one's mother; dependent on one's mother. □ *Tom is still tied to his mother's apron strings.* □ *Isn't he a little old to be tied to his mother's apron strings?*

tie someone in knots to become anxious or upset. □ *John tied himself in knots worrying about his wife during the operation.* □ *This waiting and worrying really ties me in knots.*

tie someone's hands to prevent someone from doing something. (Also used literally.) □ *I'd like to help you, but my boss has tied my hands.* □ *Please don't tie my hands with unnecessary restrictions. I'd like the freedom to do whatever is necessary.*

tie the knot to get married. □ *Well, I hear that you and John are going to tie the knot.* □ *My parents tied the knot almost forty years ago.*

tight as a tick, as See *as tight as a tick.*

tight as Dick's hatband, as See *as tight as Dick's hatband.*

tighten one's belt to manage to spend less money. □ *Things are beginning to cost more and more. It looks like we'll all have to tighten our belts.* □ *Times are hard, and prices are high. I can tighten my belt for only so long.*

tilt at windmills to fight battles with imaginary enemies; to fight against unimportant enemies or issues. (As with the fictional character, Don Quixote, who attacked windmills.) □ *Aren't you too smart to go around tilting at windmills?* □ *I'm not going to fight this issue. I've wasted too much of my life tilting at windmills.*

Time hangs heavy on someone's hands. Time seems to go slowly when one has nothing to do. (Not literal. Note the variations in the examples.) □ *I don't like it when time hangs so heavily on my hands.* □ *John looks so bored. Time hangs heavy on his hands.*

Time is money. [My] time is valuable, so don't waste it. □ *I can't afford to spend a lot of time standing here talking. Time is money, you know!* □ *People who keep saying time is money may be working too hard.*

time of one's life, have the See *have the time of one's life.*

tip of one's tongue, on the See *on the tip of one's tongue.*

tip the scales at something to weigh some amount. □ *Tom tips the scales at nearly 200 pounds.* □ *I'll be glad when I tip the scales at a few pounds less.*

tiptoe, on See *on tiptoe.*

toes, on one's See *on one's toes.*

toe the line See the following entry.

toe the mark AND **toe the line** to do what one is expected to do; to follow the rules. □ *You'll get ahead, Sally. Don't worry. Just toe the mark, and everything will be okay.* □ *John finally got fired. He just couldn't learn to toe the line.*

tongue-in-cheek insincere; joking. □ *Ann made a tongue-in-cheek remark to John, and he got mad because he thought she was serious.* □ *The play seemed very serious at first, but then everyone saw that it was tongue-in-cheek, and they began laughing.*

too good to be true almost unbelievable; so good as to be unbelievable. (A cliché.) □ *The news was too good to be true.* □ *When I finally got a big raise, it was too good to be true.*

Too many cooks spoil the broth. See the following entry.

Too many cooks spoil the stew. AND **Too many cooks spoil the broth.** a proverb meaning that too many people trying to manage something simply spoil it. □ *Let's decide who is in charge around here. Too many cooks spoil the stew.* □ *Everyone is giving orders, but no one is following them! Too many cooks spoil the broth.*

too many irons in the fire, have See *have too many irons in the fire.*

to one's heart's content as much as one wants. ☐ *John wanted a week's vacation so he could go to the lake and fish to his heart's content.* ☐ *I just sat there, eating chocolate to my heart's content.*

toot one's own horn AND **blow one's own horn** to boast or praise oneself. ☐ *Tom is always tooting his own horn. Is he really as good as he says he is?* ☐ *I find it hard to blow my own horn, but I manage.*

top of one's head, off the See *off the top of one's head.*

top of one's lungs, at the See *at the top of one's lungs.*

top of one's voice, at the See *at the top of one's voice.*

top of the world, on See *on top of the world.*

top, on See *on top.*

top, over the See *over the top.*

top to bottom, from See *from top to bottom.*

toss one's hat into the ring to state that one is running for an elective office. ☐ *Jane wanted to run for treasurer, so she tossed her hat into the ring.* ☐ *The mayor never tossed his hat into the ring. Instead he announced his retirement.*

to the ends of the earth to the remotest and most inaccessible points on the earth. ☐ *I'll pursue him to the ends of the earth.* ☐ *We've almost explored the whole world. We've traveled to the ends of the earth trying to learn about our world.*

To the victors belong the spoils. a proverb meaning that the winners achieve power over people and property. ☐ *The mayor took office and immediately fired many workers and hired new ones. Everyone said, "To the victors belong the spoils."* ☐ *The office of president includes the right to live in the White House and at Camp David. To the victors belong the spoils.*

tough act to follow a difficult presentation or performance to follow with one's own performance. (A cliché.) □ *Bill's speech was excellent. It was a tough act to follow, but my speech was good also.* □ *In spite of the fact that I had a tough act to follow, I did my best.*

tough row to hoe a difficult task to undertake. (A cliché.) □ *It was a tough row to hoe, but I finally got a college degree.* □ *Getting the contract signed is going to be a tough row to hoe, but I'm sure I can do it.*

town, go to See *go to town.*

town, out on the See *out on the town.*

tread on someone's toes See under *step on someone's toes.*

trial, on See *on trial.*

true to one's word keeping one's promise. □ *True to his word, Tom showed up at exactly eight o'clock.* □ *We'll soon know if Jane is true to her word. We'll see if she does what she promised.*

try one's wings (out) AND **try out one's wings** to try to do something one has recently become qualified to do. (Like a young bird uses its wings to try to fly.) □ *John just got his driver's license and wants to borrow the car to try out his wings.* □ *I learned to skin-dive, and I want to go to the seaside to try out my wings.* □ *You've read about it enough. It's time to try your wings.*

try someone's patience to do something annoying that may cause someone to lose patience; to cause someone to be annoyed. □ *Stop whistling. You're trying my patience. Very soon I'm going to lose my temper.* □ *Some students think it's fun to try the teacher's patience.*

tune (with someone or something), out of See *out of tune (with someone or something).*

turn a blind eye to someone or something to ignore something and pretend you do not see it. □ *The usher turned a blind eye to the little boy who sneaked into the theater.* □ *How can you turn a blind eye to all those starving children?*

turn a deaf ear (to something) to ignore what someone says; to ignore a cry for help. □ *How can you just turn a deaf ear to their cries for food and shelter?* □ *The government has turned a deaf ear to the homeless.*

turn on a dime to turn in a very tight turn. □ *This car handles very well. It can turn on a dime.* □ *The speeding car turned on a dime and headed in the other direction.*

turn one's nose up at someone or something AND **turn up one's nose at someone or something** to sneer at someone or something; to reject someone or something. □ *John turned his nose up at Ann, and that hurt her feelings.* □ *I never turn up my nose at dessert, no matter what it is.*

turn, out of See *out of turn.*

turn over a new leaf to start again with the intention of doing better; to begin again, ignoring past errors. (A cliché.) □ *Tom promised to turn over a new leaf and do better from now on.* □ *After a minor accident, Sally decided to turn over a new leaf and drive more carefully.*

turn over in one's grave [for a dead person] to be shocked or horrified. (A cliché. Not used literally, of course.) □ *If Beethoven heard Mary play one of his sonatas, he'd turn over in his grave.* □ *If Aunt Jane knew what you were doing with her favorite chair, she would turn over in her grave.*

turn someone's stomach to make someone (figuratively or literally) ill. □ *This milk is spoiled. The smell of it turns my stomach.* □ *The play was so bad that it turned my stomach.*

turn something to one's advantage to make an advantage for oneself out of something (that might otherwise be a disadvantage). □ *Sally found a way to turn the problem to her advantage.* □ *The ice-cream store manager was able to turn the hot weather to her advantage.*

turn the other cheek   to ignore abuse or an insult. (Biblical.) □ *When Bob got mad at Mary and yelled at her, she just turned the other cheek.* □ *Usually I turn the other cheek when someone is rude to me.*

turn the tide   to cause a reversal in the direction of events; to cause a reversal in public opinion. □ *It looked as if the team was going to lose, but near the end of the game, our star player turned the tide.* □ *At first, people were opposed to our plan. After a lot of discussion, we were able to turn the tide.*

twiddle one's thumbs   to fill up time by playing with one's fingers. □ *What am I supposed to do while waiting for you? Sit here and twiddle my thumbs?* □ *Don't sit around twiddling your thumbs. Get busy!*

twinkling of an eye, in the   See *in the twinkling of an eye.*

twist someone around one's little finger   to manipulate and control someone. (A cliché.) □ *Bob really fell for Jane. She can twist him around her little finger.* □ *Billy's mother has twisted him around her little finger. He's very dependent on her.*

twist someone's arm   to force or persuade someone. □ *At first she refused, but after I twisted her arm a little, she agreed to help.* □ *I didn't want to run for mayor, but everyone twisted my arm.*

two shakes of a lamb's tail, in   See *in two shakes of a lamb's tail.*

U

under a cloud (of suspicion) to be suspected of (doing) something. □ *Someone stole some money at work, and now everyone is under a cloud of suspicion.* □ *Even the manager is under a cloud.*

under construction being built or repaired. □ *We cannot travel on this road because it's under construction.* □ *Our new home has been under construction all summer. We hope to move in next month.*

under fire during an attack. □ *There was a scandal in city hall, and the mayor was forced to resign under fire.* □ *John is a good lawyer because he can think under fire.*

under one's own steam by one's own power or effort. □ *I missed my ride to class, so I had to get there under my own steam.* □ *John will need some help with this project. He can't do it under his own steam.*

under the counter [for something to be bought or sold] in secret or illegally. (Also used literally.) □ *The drugstore owner was arrested for selling liquor under the counter.* □ *This owner was also selling dirty books under the counter.*

under the table in secret, as with the giving of a bribe. (Also used literally.) □ *The mayor had been paying money to the construction company under the table.* □ *Tom transferred the deed to the property to his wife under the table.*

under the weather   ill. □ *I'm a bit under the weather today, so I can't go to the office.* □ *My head is aching, and I feel a little under the weather.*

under the wire   just barely in time or on time. □ *I turned in my report just under the wire.* □ *Bill was the last person to get in the door. He got in under the wire.*

up a blind alley   at a dead end; on a route that leads nowhere. □ *I have been trying to find out something about my ancestors, but I'm up a blind alley. I can't find anything.* □ *The police are up a blind alley in their investigation of the crime.*

up in arms   rising up in anger; (figuratively or literally) armed with weapons. □ *My father was really up in arms when he got his tax bill this year.* □ *The citizens were up in arms, pounding on the gates of the palace, demanding justice.*

up in the air   undecided; uncertain. (Also used literally.) □ *I don't know what Sally plans to do. Things were sort of up in the air the last time we talked.* □ *Let's leave this question up in the air until next week.*

upset the apple cart   to mess up or ruin something. □ *Tom really upset the apple cart by telling Mary the truth about Jane.* □ *I always knew he'd upset the apple cart.*

up to one's ears (in something)   See the following entry.

up to one's neck (in something) AND **up to one's ears (in something)**   very much involved in something. □ *I can't come to the meeting. I'm up to my neck in these reports.* □ *Mary is up to her ears in her work.*

up to par   as good as the standard or average; up to standard. □ *I'm just not feeling up to par today. I must be coming down with something.* □ *The manager said that the report was not up to par and gave it back to Mary to do over again.*

use every trick in the book to use every method possible. □ *I used every trick in the book, but I still couldn't manage to get a ticket to the game Saturday.* □ *Bob tried to use every trick in the book, but he still failed.*

utter a word, not See *not utter a word.*

V

vacation, on   See *on vacation.*

vanish into thin air   to disappear without leaving a trace. □ *My money gets spent so fast. It seems to vanish into thin air.* □ *When I came back, my car was gone. I had locked it, and it couldn't have vanished into thin air!*

Variety is the spice of life.   a proverb meaning that differences and changes make life interesting. □ *Mary reads all kinds of books. She says variety is the spice of life.* □ *The Franklins travel all over the world so they can learn how different people live. After all, variety is the spice of life.*

vicious circle, in a   See *in a vicious circle.*

victors belong the spoils, To the.   See *To the victors belong the spoils.*

virtue of something, by   See *by virtue of something.*

vote a straight ticket   to cast a ballot with all the votes for members of the same political party. □ *I'm not a member of any political party, so I never vote a straight ticket.* □ *I usually vote a straight ticket because I believe in the principles of one party and not in the other's.*

W

wagon, on the See *on the wagon*.

wait-and-see attitude a skeptical attitude; an uncertain attitude where someone will just wait and see what happens. □ *John thought that Mary couldn't do it, but he took a wait-and-see attitude.* □ *His wait-and-see attitude didn't influence me at all.*

waiting list, on a See *on a waiting list*.

wait on someone hand and foot to serve someone very well, attending to all personal needs. □ *I don't mind bringing you your coffee, but I don't intend to wait on you hand and foot.* □ *I don't want anyone to wait on me hand and foot. I can take care of myself.*

walk a tightrope to be in a situation where one must be very cautious. (Also used literally.) □ *I've been walking a tightrope all day. I need to relax.* □ *Our business is about to fail. We've been walking a tightrope for three months.*

walk on air to be very happy; to be euphoric. (Never used literally.) □ *Ann was walking on air when she got the job.* □ *On the last day of school, all the children are walking on air.*

walk on eggs to be very cautious. (Never used literally.) □ *The manager is very hard to deal with. You really have to walk on eggs.* □ *I've been walking on eggs ever since I started working here.*

walk the floor to pace nervously while waiting. □ *While Bill waited for news of the operation, he walked the floor for hours on end.* □ *Walking the floor won't help. You might as well sit down and relax.*

wall, go to the See *go to the wall.*

walls have ears we may be overheard. (A cliché.) □ *Let's not discuss this matter here. Walls have ears, you know.* □ *Shhh. Walls have ears. Someone may be listening.*

warm the bench [for a player] to remain out of play during a game—seated on a bench. □ *John spent the whole game warming the bench.* □ *Mary never warms the bench. She plays from the beginning to the end.*

warm the cockles of someone's heart to make someone warm and happy. (A cliché.) □ *It warms the cockles of my heart to hear you say that.* □ *Hearing that old song again warmed the cockles of her heart.*

wash one's hands of someone or something to end one's association with someone or something. □ *I washed my hands of Tom. I wanted no more to do with him.* □ *That car was a real headache. I washed my hands of it long ago.*

waste one's breath to waste one's time talking; to talk in vain. □ *Don't waste your breath talking to her. She won't listen.* □ *You can't persuade me. You're just wasting your breath.*

watched pot never boils, A. See *A watched pot never boils.*

water off a duck's back, like See *like water off a duck's back.*

water under the bridge past and forgotten. (A cliché.) □ *Please don't worry about it anymore. It's all water under the bridge.* □ *I can't change the past. It's water under the bridge.*

weak as a kitten, as See *as weak as a kitten.*

weakness for someone or something, have a   See *have a weakness for someone or something.*

wear more than one hat   to have more than one set of responsibilities; to hold more than one office. □ *The mayor is also the police chief. She wears more than one hat.* □ *I have too much to do to wear more than one hat.*

wear out one's welcome   to stay too long (at an event to which one has been invited); to visit somewhere too often. (A cliché.) □ *Tom visited the Smiths so often that he wore out his welcome.* □ *At about midnight, I decided that I had worn out my welcome, so I went home.*

weather, under the   See *under the weather.*

well-fixed   See the following entry.

well-heeled AND **well-fixed; well-off**   wealthy; with sufficient money. □ *My uncle can afford a new car. He's well-heeled.* □ *Everyone in his family is well-off.*

well-off   See the previous entry.

well-to-do   wealthy and of good social position. (Often with *quite,* as in the examples.) □ *The Jones family is quite well-to-do.* □ *There is a gentleman waiting for you at the door. He appears quite well-to-do.*

were, as it   See *as it were.*

wet behind the ears   young and inexperienced. □ *John's too young to take on a job like this! He's still wet behind the ears!* □ *He may be wet behind the ears, but he's well trained and totally competent.*

What is sauce for the goose is sauce for the gander.   a proverb meaning that what is appropriate for one is appropriate for the other. □ *If John gets a new coat, I should get one, too. After all, what is sauce for the goose is sauce for the gander.* □ *If I get* *punished for breaking the window, so should Mary. What is sauce for the goose is sauce for the gander.*

what makes someone tick what motivates someone; what makes someone behave in a certain way. □ *William is sort of strange. I don't know what makes him tick.* □ *When you get to know people, you find out what makes them tick.*

When in Rome, do as the Romans do. a proverb meaning that one should behave in the same way that the local people behave. □ *I don't usually eat lamb, but I did when I went to Australia. When in Rome, do as the Romans do.* □ *I always carry an umbrella when I visit London. When in Rome, do as the Romans do.*

When the cat's away the mice will play. Some people will get into mischief when they are not being watched. (A cliché.) □ *The students behaved very badly for the substitute teacher. When the cat's away the mice will play.* □ *John had a wild party at his house when his parents were out of town. When the cat's away the mice will play.*

when the time is ripe at exactly the right time. □ *I'll tell her the good news when the time is ripe.* □ *When the time is ripe, I'll bring up the subject again.*

Where there's a will there's a way. a proverb meaning that one can do something if one really wants to. □ *Don't give up, Ann. You can do it. Where there's a will there's a way.* □ *They told John he'd never walk again after his accident. He worked at it, and he was able to walk again! Where there's a will there's a way.*

Where there's smoke there's fire. a proverb meaning that some evidence of a problem probably indicates that there really is a problem. □ *There is a lot of noise coming from the classroom. There is probably something wrong. Where there's smoke there's fire.* □ *I think there is something wrong at the house on the corner. The police are there again. Where there's smoke there's fire.*

whisker, by a See *by a whisker.*

white as the driven snow, as   See *as white as the driven snow.*

wide of the mark   **1.** far from the target. □ *Tom's shot was wide of the mark.* □ *The pitch was quite fast, but wide of the mark.* **2.** inadequate; far from what is required or expected. □ *Jane's efforts were sincere, but wide of the mark.* □ *He failed the course because everything he did was wide of the mark.*

wild-goose chase   a worthless hunt or chase; a futile pursuit. □ *I wasted all afternoon on a wild-goose chase.* □ *John was angry because he was sent out on a wild-goose chase.*

win by a nose   to win by the slightest amount of difference. (As in a horse race where one horse wins with only its nose ahead of the horse that comes in second.) □ *I ran the fastest race I could, but I only won by a nose.* □ *Sally won the race, but she only won by a nose.*

wind, in the   See *in the wind.*

wire, down to the   See *down to the wire.*

wire, under the   See *under the wire.*

wise as an owl, as   See *as wise as an owl.*

with all one's heart and soul   very sincerely. (A cliché.) □ *Oh, Bill, I love you with all my heart and soul, and I always will!* □ *She thanked us with all her heart and soul for the gift.*

with both hands tied behind one's back   See under *with one hand tied behind one's back.*

wither on the vine AND **die on the vine**   [for something] to decline or fade away at an early stage of development. (Also used literally in reference to grapes or other fruit.) □ *You have a great plan, Tom. Let's keep it alive. Don't let it wither on the vine.* □ *The whole project died on the vine when the contract was canceled.*

with every (other) breath [saying something] repeatedly or continually. □ *Bob was out in the yard, raking leaves and cursing with every other breath.* □ *The child was so grateful that she was thanking me with every breath.*

with flying colors easily and excellently. □ *John passed his geometry test with flying colors.* □ *Sally qualified for the race with flying colors.*

within an inch of one's life very close to taking one's life; almost to death. (A cliché.) □ *The accident frightened me within an inch of my life.* □ *When Mary was seriously ill in the hospital, she came within an inch of her life.*

with no strings attached AND **without any strings attached** unconditionally; with no obligations attached. □ *My parents gave me a computer without any strings attached.* □ *I want this only if there are no strings attached.*

with one hand tied behind one's back AND **with both hands tied behind one's back** under a handicap; easily. (A cliché.) □ *I could put an end to this argument with one hand tied behind my back.* □ *John could do this job with both hands tied behind his back.*

without any strings attached See under *with no strings attached.*

without batting an eye without showing alarm or response; without blinking an eye. (A cliché.) □ *I knew I had insulted her, but she turned to me and asked me to leave without batting an eye.* □ *Right in the middle of the speech—without batting an eye—the speaker walked off the stage.*

without further ado without further talk. (A cliché. An overworked phrase usually heard in public announcements.) □ *And without further ado, I would like to introduce Mr. Bill Franklin!* □ *The time has come to leave, so without further ado, good evening and good-bye.*

wit's end, at one's See *at one's wit's end.*

wolf in sheep's clothing something threatening disguised as something kind. (A cliché.) □ *Beware of the police chief. He seems polite, but he's a wolf in sheep's clothing.* □ *This proposal seems harmless enough, but I think it's a wolf in sheep's clothing.*

woods, out of the See *out of the woods.*

word, go back on one's See *go back on one's word.*

word go, from the See *from the word go.*

word of mouth, by See *by word of mouth.*

words stick in one's throat, have one's See *have one's words stick in one's throat.*

work like a horse to work very hard. (A cliché.) □ *I've been working like a horse all day, and I'm tired.* □ *I'm too old to work like a horse. I'd prefer to relax more.*

work one's fingers to the bone to work very hard. (A cliché.) □ *I worked my fingers to the bone so you children could have everything you needed. Now look at the way you treat me!* □ *I spent the day working my fingers to the bone, and now I want to relax.*

work out for the best to end up in the best possible way. □ *Don't worry. Things will work out for the best.* □ *It seems bad now, but it'll work out for the best.*

world, in the See *in the world.*

world of one's own, in a See *in a world of one's own.*

world, out of this See *out of this world.*

worst comes to worst, if See *if worst comes to worst.*

worth its weight in gold   very valuable. (A cliché.) □ *This book is worth its weight in gold.* □ *Oh, Bill. You're wonderful. You're worth your weight in gold.*

worth one's salt   worth one's salary. (A cliché.) □ *Tom doesn't work very hard, and he's just barely worth his salt, but he's very easy to get along with.* □ *I think he's more than worth his salt. He's a good worker.*

wrack and ruin, go to   See *go to wrack and ruin.*

wrong, in the   See *in the wrong.*

wrong track, on the   See *on the wrong track.*

X

X marks the spot   this is the exact spot. (A cliché. Can be used literally when someone draws an *X* to mark an exact spot.) □ *This is where the rock struck my car—X marks the spot.* □ *Now, please move that table over here. Yes, right here—X marks the spot.*

Y

year in, year out   year after year, all year long. □ *I seem to have hay fever year in, year out. I never get over it.* □ *John wears the same old suit, year in, year out.*

You can say that again! AND **You said it!**   That is true.; You are correct. (The word *that* is emphasized.) □ MARY: *It sure is hot today.* JANE: *You can say that again!* □ BILL: *This cake is yummy!* BOB: *You said it!*

You can't take it with you.   You should enjoy your money now, because it is no good when you're dead. (A cliché.) □ *My uncle is a wealthy miser. I keep telling him, "You can't take it with you."* □ *If you have money, you should make out a will. You can't take it with you, you know!*

You can't teach an old dog new tricks.   a proverb meaning that old people cannot learn anything new. (Also used literally of dogs.) □ *"Of course I can learn," bellowed Uncle John. "Who says you can't teach an old dog new tricks?"* □ *I'm sorry. I can't seem to learn to do it right. Oh, well. You can't teach an old dog new tricks.*

Your guess is as good as mine.   Your answer is likely to be as correct as mine. □ *I don't know where the scissors are. Your guess is as good as mine.* □ *Your guess is as good as mine as to when the train will arrive.*

You said it!   See under *You can say that again!*

246

Z

zero in on something to aim or focus directly on something. □ *"Now," said Mr. Smith, "I would like to zero in on another important point."* □ *Mary is very good about zeroing in on the most important and helpful ideas.*